FOREWORD BY JONATHAN HOLMES IV
PREFACE VII

1
INNOCENT BYSTANDER 1

2
'THE BIG LEAGUE' 13

3
'THE MOONLIGHT STATE' 43

4
'FRENCH CONNECTIONS' 84

5
'BRANDED' 110

6
'BANNED AID' 143

7
'THE DEAD HEART' 176

8
'TWO CONFESSIONS' 209

9
DIRTY SECRETS 239

APPENDIX I
CHRIS MASTERS: A TELEVISION CAREER 244

FOREWORD

At the beginning of Chapter 2 of *Inside Story*, Chris Masters recalls our first meeting. I don't remember it as clearly as he. I do remember the first time I saw him.

It was towards the end of 1982, and I had been executive producer of *Four Corners* for about six months. I was engaged on that perennial pursuit of executive producers, the hunt for good reporters. Mike Berry, my deputy, came in to my office with a VHS tape. 'You said you wanted a real Australian,' he said. 'Have a look at this bloke.'

It was a short, ten-minute report for *Countrywide*. It was about the disgraceful living conditions of the Aboriginal population of a small NSW country town. Past their dilapidated shacks, an awkward, bespectacled, earnest figure strode toward the camera, beating out the rhythm of his words with sharp, downward gestures. He was not a natural television performer. He was neither glamorously good-looking nor especially fluent. But he was undeniably, inimitably Australian. And there was something more. You believed at once that **he** believed in the importance of what he was saying. He had about him an aura of angry honesty.

It was that tape which led to the telephone call which led to Chris Masters joining *Four Corners*. None of us, including Chris, had any idea that he would turn into the most formidable investigative journalist in Australian television history. But as you read his own account of his work, the qualities that made him so come shining through. The ability to see the simple essentials through the fog of circumstance; the awesome capacity for hard work; the meticulous attention to detail; the determination to expose the system and not just the immediate villain; the ability to persuade frightened people to trust him.

They trust him because they sense his honesty. And those who hoped that if they kept their heads down he would go away, reckoned without his anger. It is slow-burning, and obstinate. He

CHRIS MASTERS
INSIDE STORY

Dear Peter,
Hope you enjoy this the author works for "4 Corners" an investigative program on the ABC. Russ is enjoying his work on channel 2. "730 Report"

Love Mother.

Angus&Robertson
An imprint of HarperCollins*Publishers*

For Alice

AN ANGUS & ROBERTSON BOOK
An imprint of HarperCollinsPublishers

First published in 1992 by
CollinsAngus&Robertson Publishers Pty Limited (ACN 009 913 517)
A division of HarperCollinsPublishers (Australia) Pty Limited
25–31 Ryde Road, Pymble NSW 2073, Australia

HarperCollinsPublishers (New Zealand) Limited
31 View Road, Glenfield, Auckland 10, New Zealand

HarperCollinsPublishers Limited
77– 85 Fulham Palace Road, London W6 8JB, United Kingdom

Copyright © Chris Masters 1992

This book is copyright.
Apart from any fair dealing for the purposes of private study,
research, criticism or review, as permitted under the Copyright Act,
no part may be reproduced by any process without written
permission. Inquiries should be addressed to the publishers.

National Library of Australia
Cataloguing-in-Publication data:

Masters, Chris.

  Chris Masters, inside story.
  ISBN 0 207 16176 3.
  1. Masters, Chris. 2. Television journalists —
  Australia — Biography. I. Title

070.92

Cover photograph courtesy of the ABC
Printed in Australia by Griffin Press

5 4 3 2 1
95 94 93 92

refuses to accept, as so many of us do, that the world is as it is, and the best thing is to mind our own business. It is wrong that working girls should be enslaved by heroin-dealing pimps who buy protection from the system; that two young boys should die unregarded in the desert; that a doctor should scar his patients and overcharge the state for doing it; that a European power should bring terror and death to our corner of the world. It is not only wrong; it makes him angry.

All this may make Chris Masters sound a solemn and wowserish character. He is anything but. Those who have only seen him on the screen are often astonished, when they meet him, to discover a man with an impish sense of mischief, and somewhat disconcerted by his schoolboy love of scatological jokes. That too comes through in *Inside Story*. The tale of the 'Terror from the Skies' in Eritrea is lavatory humour at it finest.

But this is not just a memoir. It is also a manual, by one of its greatest practitioners, on the art of television journalism. One of the few things which Chris and I have in common is that neither of us has spent a day in a newspaper, or had any formal journalistic training. Perhaps that is why Chris takes his trade so much more seriously than many of his colleagues. The cynicism so often bred in the newsrooms of the great daily newspapers is entirely absent from his make-up. Journalism is a profession much despised by ordinary Australians. And Chris, who is an ordinary Australian, despises sloppy or sensational or dishonest journalism more than most. It is, for him, quite simply a betrayal of public trust.

As for television, it is a medium often looked down upon by journalists in other media — and often, with good reason. It is even easier to be glib, and superficial, and sensational on television than it is in print. And for those whose job puts them in front of the camera, there is the ever-present lure of cheap celebrity.

But for those who come to love it, television is an unrivalled medium for the telling of true stories. When the facts, and the emotions, and the words, and the sounds, and the pictures come together right, a few minutes of television have an impact which acres of newsprint cannot match. To achieve that happy concatenation is infuriatingly difficult. It requires the skilled efforts not of one person, but of many. If it happens for Chris far more often than for most of us, it is because he knows how to draw out the best in those around him.

If the real hero of this book is its author, it has a heroine too. She is large, and bumbling, and occasionally blowsy. She has shed much of her fat in recent years; she has been forced to start visiting the pawnshop to pop a bit of independence here and morsel of integrity there, to raise the ready to keep going from day to day. If she is not very careful, she will end up selling her soul. But it is she, more than anyone, who has made Chris Masters's career possible, even if for half of it she barely knew he existed. She is, of course, Australia's Auntie, the ABC.

We live in the age of Economic Rationalism. In the Federal Treasury, the young men with their econometric models are sharpening their axes in the hope, perhaps, of soon being allowed to cut still deeper into the much-hacked body of the Public Sector. There are precious few politicians left, in any party, who believe that public money can and should be spent for the public good. But what Chris Masters has done for this country he could not have done had he worked for companies whose ultimate motive was profit.

It would be nice to think that young men and women could read this book — perhaps between stints at the microphone in some country radio station — and aspire to a career in the ABC which will take them to the heights of investigative journalism. This book is packed full of invaluable advice for those who want to follow in Chris's footsteps. I only wish I could be certain that in twenty years — or ten — the ABC will still have the money, the freedom, and the guts, to let them do it.

JONATHAN HOLMES
19 November 1991

PREFACE

There is little time to look over the shoulder at *Four Corners*. Before one report is broadcast we are already turning our attention to the next. The strain of looking in front can bring about a conditioned oblivion to the rising cloud of dust behind.

The experience of being forced to look back in order to write this book has been awkward. It was written on the run and inevitably came second to the project at hand. The words appeared and disappeared from the screen of my laptop computer beside plastic containers of Chinese food in a motel room in Mt Isa. They were scribbled on a notepad while cramped between camera boxes in the back of a van during teeming rain on a hillside in Northern Greece. They came to life while my son stood at my elbow proffering his latest feat of Lego engineering on a rare free weekend. It has taken a while and I must apologise to the long line of people who have been standing, waiting.

The idea for the book belongs to Nick Brash of Bow Press, who sold the idea to Collins/Angus and Robertson and myself in 1988. He suggested that I should try to explain the craft of television journalism through the retelling of some of my reports. He said I should just 'write it down' and it would work. It was good, simple advice, which only fell down because I didn't respond with anything resembling speed.

My first excuse was that I was flat out trying to understand the job I had just begun at Channel 10. When the job failed I was flat out trying to find another excuse. In the end there did not seem to be much choice but to start writing it down.

I returned to a permanent job at the ABC at the end of 1989. More excuses interrupted progress, but by then the book was well and truly alive and tugging at my elbow. It crawled for the next two years, never getting the free run of time that good writing deserves.

The crawl also provoked the odd exasperated phone call from publisher Lisa Highton. I thank them all at Collins/Angus and Robertson for their patience. I am very sorry that Nick Brash succumbed to cancer before the book was finished. It was a good idea, Nick.

My family is owed apologies and gratitude. I would never have been able to make those programmes, let alone write this book, if there were strenuous complaints. Although complaints would have been reasonable, they were rarely heard.

My office mate at *Four Corners*, Mark Colvin, is also to be thanked. Our office is so tiny that completed chapters kept falling on his desk. So Mark became something of a de facto, unpaid editor. He would ultimately have a significant influence on the manuscript.

Elsewhere in this book I have said I am a journalist and not a missionary — but while there is no mission in this work, I did come across an objective somewhere along the way. If the book does stimulate a sense of professionalism among my peers then it does us all a service.

Our awards system not only frequently rewards the story and not the storytelling, but sometimes gives prizes to reports that were known to have breached ethical standards.

The debate about standards in our profession is frequently hijacked by politicians, lawyers and the like. The debate about what constitutes good and fair journalism is rarely led by journalists. It is not hard to see why. I was lecturing a class of television researchers recently, expounding on the merits of the worthy story over the sexy story. One of the researchers raised her hand and asked plaintively, 'what if the boss does not want a worthy story?'. I realised then that I did not have much of an answer.

With a bit of luck some of the bosses who do read might look through this book and begin to think about commissioning the odd worthy story. There is a great deal of honesty, dedication, talent and toil in our business that deserves reward . . . and you never know, if quality journalism was encouraged, the public might even like it.

CHRIS MASTERS

1

INNOCENT BYSTANDER

I can recall reading a story in my more impressionable days about North American Indians attacking wagon trains in the era of the wild west. The Indians had not initially meant to harm the invading settlers. They were perplexed by the unremitting monotony of the slow moving trains. So they swooped down, waving their spears and yelling fiercely, to alarm the plodding animals and jolt the creaking covered wagons into unaccustomed action. But naturally enough, the terrified occupants of the wagons did not see it this way. They fired on the Indians and mayhem swept across the prairies.

The story made an impression in my later life as I have sometimes felt a bit like one of the Indians as they fidgeted and stared impatiently from the hill. I have frequently set out to rattle Australians from their apathy and have just as frequently been startled by a fusillade of return fire.

I am unusually fond of Australians, new settlers and old settlers alike, and have never thought it unpatriotic to disturb the status quo. In this respect journalism has proved a suitable profession. But I can't pretend I saw it as a life's mission. Even after I passed into adulthood, I had little idea what I wanted to be.

I think I was 24 years old when I discovered I had been short-sighted for my entire life. My first set of spectacles at that age revealed the previously undiscovered texture and detail of my surroundings.

At around the same time, a sound I had grown up with but never particularly noticed began to take on meaning. The sound was the chatter of my mother's typewriter. She was a journalist through all those years so my first apprenticeship had been with her, but had passed without my noticing.

My next apprenticeship was to the Australian Broadcasting Commission, as it was then known. My educational qualifications were unspectacular, which in that hallowed era of high employment, seemed to guarantee a job in the Public Service.

I joined the ABC on the tenth of March 1966. They gave me a mailbag and with it I wandered into the desert of ABC bureaucracy. I soon abandoned the mailbag but held on to a range of simple duties which were performed with eagerness. Although the work required no great creativity and intelligence, I learned it can be satisfying to do even simple work with thoroughness and efficiency. There would be times later when I would think wistfully of those days.

I was called a 'Transcriptions Assistant'. I did not announce this loudly beyond the precincts of the ABC because I had no reason to expect people to understand what it meant and worse still, it did not sound like a profession.

In those days, there was very little 'live radio' beyond the reading of the news and sporting coverage. The great bulk of the programmes were carefully, and often ponderously, prescripted and pre-recorded. My main job was to ensure the many hundreds of tapes carrying the daily programmes were correctly labelled and assembled in the three main studios from which were broadcast the First, Second and Third network programmes.

One of my listless predecessors had not bothered to update the tapes for the long-running radio soap, *Blue Hills*. The Third Network broadcast programmes to country listeners — and was somewhat like the Third World — under resourced, out of sight and out of mind. The country folk waited politely, but after three or four days of listening to the same episode they began to complain.

When it was my turn to service the studios I determined to take good care of the Third Network. I had grown up in the bush and was quietly hopeful I might return one day.

I was an assiduous tape filer, ever determined to please my superiors but after a while began to wonder whether my superiors took much notice. One of my bosses in the early years had taken to the bottle. Late one afternoon I turned a corner to find him peeing against an office partition.

Perhaps the pursuit of excellence did not have much to do with punctilious tape filing after all. My greatest achievement at that time probably had more to do with paper planes.

One of the distractions of office staff on the seventh floor of the Forbes Street studios was to stand at the window, creasing and folding paper in all sorts of elegant configurations. We would toss our small planes into the wind to see who could achieve the greatest distance. On one occasion the wind lifted my small craft and carried it high into the air above Woolloomooloo. It sailed serenely for hundreds of metres across busy William Street to settle finally somewhere in the dockland far below. It was certainly my greatest moment so far.

But meanwhile there was much to be observed by this wide-eyed if still myopic country boy. The ABC studio building straddled one of the foothills of Australia's most decadent stretch of real estate, Kings Cross. There was probably something ironic about starting my career in this heartland of Australian organised corruption and disorganised sleaze.

Once as I arrived at work I noticed a distraught woman who had sought refuge in the ABC being comforted by the commissionaire, a beefy ex-detective. The woman was escaping a flasher who had exposed himself somewhere nearby. Just as she was explaining what had happened, she turned and shrieked. The flasher was walking through the door. It was not his lucky day. The flasher turned out to be a fellow worker at the ABC. He had taken the opportunity for a morning matinee performance on his way to work and was now giving the commissionaire a chance to make a final arrest.

I survived all this until 1972, the year I collected a cherished job in the bush and my first set of glasses.

The glasses came about because of the distance in the Newcastle studio between the microphone and the clock on the wall. One of my tasks was to read short 'Regional News Bulletins' which required a precision cross back to the network programmes. When I kept missing the cross some sensible person suggested I have my eyes checked, and soon after a new world crept into focus.

My first permanent regional post was to the ABC office in Albury. The job was a bit more like a profession and thankfully, a bit easier to explain. I was now a 'Talks Officer Grade 1, (Assistant to the Regional Manager)'.

My new manager was another former broadcaster who was now close to retirement. I don't know whether he was out of favour with the ABC General Manager of the day, Talbot Duckmanton. It may have been the case, as my new boss had a pet duck which he deftly named, 'Manton'.

An early introduction to the diversity of the work in the bush came from listening to our own bulletin, and a stringer newsreader, Cleaver Bunton, who was also Australia's longest-serving Mayor. It began like this: 'Here is the News for the Riverina and North Eastern Victoria prepared by Cleaver Bunton and read by Cleaver Bunton. Today the Mayor of Albury, Cleaver Bunton said . . . '

Cleaver became a national story in 1975 when Prime Minister Whitlam was struggling to hold on to his government. Our stringer newsreader was appointed by NSW

Premier, Tom Lewis, to fill a Senate vacancy. Along with the Queensland appointment, Albert Field, for a short time our stringer newsreader held the reins of the balance of power in the Federal Parliament. The national press advanced on Albury and the Cleaver Bunton story led news bulletins all across the land.

We in the bush spent a lot of time waiting for big stories to break but when they did the locals were swept aside like an earth wall in a country flood. This was the first but not the last time I was to realise that being a local reporter had its disadvantages.

But I liked Albury. I could ride my bike to work. I could take my canoe for a paddle on the Murray River after work. I could drive to the snow in winter. I could sample the produce from the Rutherglen vineyards and make friends I would keep for life. It was also a great place to raise a family.

I might have stayed in Albury, I might be there still — but after 10 years I was restless. In 1975 our first daughter, Clare, was born, and when just six months old, Clare, my wife Tanya, and myself, embarked on a brave trek around the world. When we returned in the following year the restlessness was rediscovered undisturbed among the unpacked souvenirs.

We moved on to Tamworth where a second daughter, Alice, was born. I was the 'Acting Manager' of the ABC regional station, a job I was to occupy for only six months as the incumbent was engaged in his own bout of sabbatical world travel.

Tamworth was a cool place. I think because it was known we would not stay long people were cautious about becoming friendly, pretty much in the same way a farmer is careful not to become fond of a working dog.

While I was there a job came up at the Rockhampton regional office. It was for a 'Talks Officer Grade 2'. I won the appointment and now was required to make a fool of myself in front of the camera as well as the microphone. Rockhampton had a small television studio. The year was 1977, and although colour television had been introduced across the nation, Rockhampton's small studio was still an outpost, lost in the dark ages of black and white.

But those same dark ages in the Queensland regional offices had nurtured a long line of ABC luminaries like Jim Downes, Andrew Olle, Richard Carleton, Allan Hogan and Tony Joyce. The old regional service was a bit of an elephant's graveyard for those approaching retirement or disgrace but it was also an excellent training ground for the debut performers.

If there was anything at all that bothered me it was the faint notion that television was probably a bit less respectable than radio.

But to my surprise and delight I found that while I had stumbled and bumbled on radio, the natural ability I so missed in radio found me in my television work. It seemed easier and I suspect, despite my earlier prejudice, more honest.

Rockhampton was not an easy place to make a home. The city was dominated by transient workers so there was no great eagerness to plant trees and nourish community pride. It was also very hot, as the Berserker Ranges guarded the city against any relief from the sea breeze.

It was a strange place to build a city. The British author, Trollope, who visited Rockhampton a century ago, called it the city of 'sin, sweat and sorrow'. He said it was so hot that when the locals died and went to hell they had to take their blankets with them.

We found a house on the coast about 30 kilometres away. We lived above the beach, with a flame-red Poinciana tree spread out before a tropical slide show. There was nothing but a strip of sand and the Barrier Reef beyond. It was paradise, but I have to say paradise can be a pain in the bum.

I could never settle in, but at least the work was absorbing.

I would rush between Rockhampton and Longreach (equivalent in distance to rushing from Paris to Rome) in an old Ford Falcon, with a cameraman who told marvellous lies about sexual conquests and stared strangely at the emus.

Sometimes, we would do five or six stories a day, each shot on one ten minute roll of film. We would return, edit, narrate, promote and present all by ourselves. The joke was that it was only a matter of time before they stuck a broomstick up your bum so you could sweep the floor and read the news at the same time.

Interviewing mavericks like the Mayor of Rockhampton, Rex Pilbeam (Australia's second-longest serving mayor) and the Minister for Everything, Russ Hinze, had its value. It was a bit like swinging at an ironbark with a tomahawk. Many reporters developed their interviewing biceps this way, and if we owe these characters nothing else, we can at least say thanks for the education.

Rockhampton was a crash course in journalism. But it also set a long fuse of anger and gave me a valuable insight into the way Queensland was run; an insight which would later serve me well.

I remember arriving at the fringes of the mining towns and whiffing the notion of Bjelke-Petersen free enterprise. It smelled the same as the bullshit I had passed further back. Cartels and monopolies abounded. Anyone who hoped to provide some healthy competition would be instantly run out of town by a press gang of Country Party cronies. I don't think I developed an acute 'political conscience' then and I don't have one now. It just made me angry.

I reported on the monopolies. On our tiny local television programme I waved papers in front of the camera and bellowed at some of the injustices, and was astonished when there was no reaction.

In 1979 my daughter Alice, just 18 months old, began to sleep badly. Some of her first words were used to explain her problem. 'Mine eye', she would say, 'it hurts'. The local doctor thought the problem was not too serious, but my wife Tanya had a fierce maternal conviction that bad news was waiting.

She carried little Alice into Rockhampton where an English eye specialist was visiting. He diagnosed that Alice was sufferering Retinablastoma, a rare cancer which attacked the eye.

Twelve hours later, Alice and Tanya were in Sydney at the Eye Hospital, and Alice's right eye was removed. Alice was fitted with a false eye and my little girl and my wife flew back to Rockhampton. Clare and I met them at the airport. Alice had learned to walk in hospital.

The first steps I saw her take were towards me across the tarmac. I gathered her up and hugged my little girl. Her arms clamped tight around my neck. I can feel them still.

Our daughter's illness required regular treatment which could only be properly provided in the capital cities. I was desperate to move, but unknown reporters from the bush were in no great demand in the big city.

I won a chance of a job at least, with a trial period reporting for the new *Nationwide* programme due to begin the following year. So, for the first weeks of 1979 I laboured hard at the ABC Brisbane office, anxious to impress my new bosses, only to discover the job had already been promised to someone else.

Making the return trip to Rockhampton was not easy. I felt I had let my family down, most particularly my little girl. Despite the lack of a job, I made up my mind to make the move anyway . . . to Sydney, where the best care was on offer.

And then came a telephone call, if not from heaven, from somewhere nearby. Ian McGarrity, an executive in the ABC Rural Department, was working in Brisbane when my *Nationwide* reports went to air, and was interested enough to offer me some temporary work with the *A Big Country* unit.

A Big Country operated under the auspices of the Rural Department. They were a curious bunch. Their wardrobe was straight out of Wilcannia while their vocabulary loitered somewhere near Paddington. But they were good at what they did.

The basic unstated editorial objective of *A Big Country* was to discover what was good about Australia. We were given a camera crew and a fortnight in the bush, and we had to tell our stories with pictures — something not often taught in News and Current Affairs, where words are king. I was an eager student. Film-making is an exciting business.

The Rural Department then commissioned a series of history programmes with Professor Geoffrey Blainey. It is odd and unfair that Blainey is now possibly best known for his views on immigration. As he has said, he has had no control over the shaping of his own reputation. The immigration fracas managed to obscure the great breadth and depth of his work.

Blainey and I traversed 50 000 years in 18 months. Having one of Australia's great minds as a companion for the journey, was a privilege not to be forgotten.

It had sometimes seemed during my apprenticeship with the ABC that a prime qualification for management was to be psychotic, alcoholic, a closet queen or all of the above. I am not sure why I fell from favour. Perhaps I should have let myself be kissed in the firestairs.

This had to be the bleakest period of my life. Alice's cancer returned. She died on New Year's Eve, as the sun set for the last time on the decade. Alice was three and a half years old.

I was so unhappy when I later returned to work, at times I felt a plague on my company. One boss in particular appeared to find my misery a dead weight in the office and he seemed to be moving to get rid of me. We fell into dispute.

Anyway, after a few weeks of sulky looks, I was shunted to

the *Countrywide* programme. It felt like being dropped to reserve grade. I kept up a constant whinge for the next couple of months — until I noticed that I was actually enjoying the work.

I had actually been done a favour. *Countrywide* required me to pick up a microphone again and report. Instead of pretending to be a film director, I now had to pretend to be a journalist. I had not been thrilled about journalism the first time around, but this time it was easier.

In simple truth, I had grown up. Television's worship of youth means that we often allow children to tell us what is going on in the world. I was no better at it when I was 25 than the current battery of Grant Kenny lookalikes. But now I was 35, and the difference was significant. In the intervening years I had learned a few things — notably a degree of scepticism.

I made half a dozen programmes for *Countrywide*, before there was a phone call inviting me to join *Four Corners*.

I loved *Four Corners*. I still do. The best thing about the place is that your colleagues want you to do well. This strikes me as a touch unusual — elsewhere they seem to want you to fall flat on your face.

In my second year at *Four Corners* I won a Walkley Award, Australia's premier prize for journalism. I was travelling to Canberra to collect the award from our Prime Minister, Bob Hawke, when for the first time I met the investigative journalist, Wendy Bacon. Wendy had also won a Walkley, and she talked about how nervous she felt about entering the company of the esteemed bunch of journalists who would be attending the ceremony.

I told her I felt exactly the same way. Wendy had trained as a barrister. I was more likely to think of myself as a film-maker — and yet we were heading off to collect the top awards for journalism.

From that moment, I determined to call myself a journalist.

My profession had at last discovered me, rather than the other way around.

The course to this discovery had been an unusual one, weaving and twisting all the way. At varying intervals I sat through practical seminars in storytelling, film-making, journalism and on Australian history. I also learned my basic survival skills from the ABC. It is a large, clumsy organisation but if you are allowed to forage you will discover quiet corners of excellence.

On ABC regional radio stations I made appalling, embarrassing blunders in the comparative obscurity of the bush, but the country audiences were long suffering and tolerant. I remain guilty and grateful to this day.

Being stranded in Queensland during the moral famine of the Bjelke-Petersen years also taught me a kind of battlefield journalism. If there was a state in Australia where you had to fight to tell people what was going on, the fight was more conspicuous in Queensland. And if you look at the pedigree of many of Australia's more notable journalists, it is interesting how often Queensland and those years feature in their careers.

Best of all I learned some story-telling skills. There are not too many Jumbo jet crashes and terrorist attacks in places like Albury, Tamworth and Rockhampton. So I had the lesson forced on me that news is not something that always happens in front of you — sometimes it has to be discovered.

Fortunately, I had been largely spared the cynicism of the nicotine-stained sub-editors who convince too many young journalists it is quicker, slicker, sharper and smarter to cheat the public and hold them in contempt.

Perhaps that explains my own naive, lunatic behaviour in the following years, when I stood like Leunig's innocent bystander, apparently oblivious to the fury I inspired among governments, criminals, tyrants and my wife, Tanya.

I don't expect many aspiring television journalists to

follow an identical course — but it would have been worthwhile for me to have known some of these things before I started out. I should have had a clear objective, rather than discovering my metier by simple good fortune — but it was a marvellous apprenticeship.

2

'THE BIG LEAGUE'

I can clearly remember the first time I walked into *Four Corners*. Jonathan Holmes, the programme's executive producer, was standing near the doorway talking to one of the film editors. The film editor introduced us; 'This is Jonathan,' he said. 'Hello John,' I replied; and a flicker of irritation from the Cambridge-educated pom was enough to ensure I had called him 'John' for the first and last time.

As executive producer, Jonathan was the boss. Beyond the line up of researchers and reporters and office staff there was a small team of producers.

Although producers are a now common feature of news and current affairs this was not so much the case back in 1983. We could not expect to be assigned a producer for every story, but for the first report, for the reporter's initiation, it was considered important.

The producer's role is not so easily explained and the Hollywood definition is only a distant relation. Essentially the producer was expected to take overall responsibility for the organisation, the budget and the direction of the film crew. The reporter took charge of the editorial content, the script, narration and on-camera appearances. I have never been quite sure but I think the producer is boss.

But in reality the demarcation lines blur delightfully. Some of the work can't be swapped around but mostly it is shared. The producer and reporter are two journalists collecting and sharing the information they discover.

The journalist I would share the next three months with was *Four Corners'* most senior producer, Peter Manning. If I am to credit anyone with teaching me how to be an 'investigative' reporter it must be Peter, or rather 'Manno'. Peter is a large, friendly bear of a man. His carefree manner conceals intellectual energy and persistence that has made him a powerful figure in Australian journalism for the best part of two decades.

We got on well. After a time he called me 'Blotto'. This reflected no capacity of mine to soak up alcohol but rather some energy for absorbing detail. It was a rare and happy circumstance that a fast friendship also formed with our boss, the executive producer, who remained 'Jonathan'. I had learned by now that nothing about Jonathan lent itself to the diminutive.

Television is one of the few media that requires corporate creativity. The importance of everyone getting on well, though obvious enough, is sometimes overlooked. People who despise one another will cut and run at the first opportunity.

The business is not a personality contest and we are supposed to be professional enough to overcome personality differences. The reality, however, is that it helps to like someone you will probably end up seeing more of than your own spouse.

I walked through that door with no perceptible reputation. *Four Corners* had very definitely taken a punt with the unknown from the bush. But luckily for me I wandered onto the current affairs centre stage at a time when they were searching for reporters who looked and sounded Australian. Jonathan, I discovered, was irritated by what he saw as upper-class British artifice throughout the ABC. Oddly enough it had taken a pommy to begin an important and overdue depomification programme.

Four Corners was known within the ABC as 'The House of Lords'. It had a reputation for tackling elitist subjects, the sort of things that were talked about at North Shore dinner parties. This was also something Jonathan and Peter wanted to change.

They were revolutionaries, keen to put a bomb under a programme that had a proud history but had become weary and complacent. And here again I was fortunate.

Among the meagre baggage I carried through the door was an idea that we might do something of interest to the more ordinary Australian, something perhaps about sport. Peter and I, as commoners, were keen to head, if not to the gutters, then at least for the back alleys of Australian urban life.

We began working on a programme about corruption in sport — or corruption of sport. We were not sure which. There were stories going around about rigged cricket and basketball matches. There were suspicions about the financial management of the NSW Rugby League. A few people in the boxing profession were also grizzling about alleged crooked behaviour. So we started what is known as a 'dig'. It would become what is known as a 'big dig' but we didn't know that at the time.

Despite the considerable resources of the media, the big dig happens all too infrequently. A big dig can improve public perceptions about an important issue virtually overnight. A big dig will wake us all up, give the public a much needed jolt and probably add some gloss to the tarnished reputation of the mass media.

But because of proprietorial pressure, short-sighted competitiveness, self-censorship and a general lack of self-respect, the media continues to concentrate on the mass, giving more importance to the quantity of information peddled, rather than the quality of that information.

Despite the clear public benefits to everyone (except perhaps the proprietors) we remain essentially a volume industry. Reporters are rewarded more for the amount of work they plough through than the value of that work.

Most reporters are stuck with a career that will rarely carry them beyond the routine of court and social rounds. It was more plain luck than careful planning that had brought me to one of the few areas in the media where I would be given more than a few hours to chase a story.

As it turned out this first story would end up taking an unprecedented three months to complete, at some pain to my new colleagues and more particularly my boss.

The *Four Corners* schedule required a programme to air every week, so the rations being stuffed into my saddlebags had to be taken from the baggage of my workmates.

Whenever you begin something like this, it is important you have a fallback position, a reliable 'Plan B'. There is always the chance, a very good chance, that even after three months, and all the effort in the world, you might not uncover the important reef of information that will make the story.

In this case 'Plan B' was a story about corruption of the sporting ethic. We knew if we could not stand up the corruption investigation we would still have to meet the demands of the schedule. The safe option, conforming to more established *Four Corners* convention, would have looked at 'Pyjama cricket' and the 'Rah Rah' boys of Rugby Union.

My early notes betray enthusiasm and lack of order. I had little experience in 'investigative' journalism. This was not true of Manning. In another life he might have been a Catholic priest in an inner urban mission.

Peter has that delightful Irish gift of being open-hearted and cunning at the same time. One of his early jobs in journalism was to write the 'Dog of the Week' story for one of the Sunday papers. This was when the paper would single out and photograph one dog from a kennel of mongrels to be saved and found a home. I don't know how he coped with the responsibility.

I was lucky to have strayed beneath his protective shadow

so early in my time at *Four Corners*. There was considerable breadth to Peter's own journalistic pedigree. He had learned his important 'village voice' journalism as a former editor of the *Leichhardt Local*. As one of the charter members of the *This Day Tonight* school of troublemakers he became a powerful force in mainstream journalism, incurring the enormous wrath of the then NSW Premier, Sir Robin Askin. Peter had also worked for a term at the *Bulletin* under the tutelage of Donald Horne. For another spell he edited the radical national weekly, *Nation Review*.

Perhaps it was these experiences that contributed to the essential vision that enables a reporter to place information, to determine its prominence and perspective within the national lexicon.

He knew much about Sydney and even more about journalism, and he would share all he had to know with me. My enduring memory will always be my standing at the lift with my finger on the 'Door Open' button waiting for him to complete a phone call to one of the multitude of 'lost dogs' he continued to collect along the way.

My approach was simple enough. I would arrive early in the morning, write out a long list of who I should call, and call them all. Peter taught me the value of typing up notes of the conversations so we would be kept in touch with each other's work.

He gave my industriousness some focus. Best of all he showed me how to approach a story from the point of view of what you can tell, rather than what you cannot tell. Peter was no fan of the legion of hacks who stumble off to the pub after work and gossip about what won't be in the paper the next day.

The very early work reveals no particular direction. There are notes that reach as far as West Australia and suspicions about judging for the Sandover medal in Australian Rules Football. There are notes about rumours of scandal in South

Australian basketball. There is a reference to Brisbane Rugby Union players receiving 'bribes', and a lot of talk about kickbacks to media commentators from sporting sponsors.

After about two weeks of this the research began to concentrate on the sport of Rugby League. There may have been a certain inevitability to all this. Peter and I had both played schoolboy Rugby League and had kept up an interest in the sport.

Peter and I made an appointment to meet a former senior official of the game, a man who in his playing days inspired terror in the opposition and awe in the spectators because of his rhinoceros-like charges up the paddock. We were a little surprised when he insisted the encounter be incognito, and nominated a suburban park as the ideal meeting place. Peter and I waited for some time in the park before the fearsome footballer emerged from behind a tree. He spoke awkwardly about some problems with the League, obviously nervous at the prospect of being seen talking to *Four Corners*.

The long lists of people to telephone were kept up. They ranged from referees to sponsors, from media commentators to sports medicine specialists.

Jonathan Holmes by now assigned an on-air date and a film crew was scheduled to begin shooting. On February 10, 1983 I blocked out six sequences for the start of filming. They were as follows:

ADMINISTRATION, REFEREES, HEALTH, GAMBLING, CLUBS and MEDIA.

So the programme was going to question the quality of management, the standard of refereeing, the physical damage done to the players, legal and illegal gambling on the matches, the big money the poker machines generated in the clubs and the illicit fringe benefits some sporting commentators appeared to be collecting.

It was not a bad programme and I suppose we could have stopped there. But it was going to be of doubtful interest beyond NSW and Queensland, where the popularity of Rugby League did not travel. Peter and I began to feel that with some more work the programme would be a lot better.

We were aware by now of intense suspicion about the behaviour of one of the game's whistleblowers. The Sydney sporting community's sense of fair play had been offended by a series of controversial referee rulings.

Too many fans were convinced their favourite game was crook. And it wasn't just the fans. We filmed an interview with one respected former international referee who shared his concern and suspicion with us.

The other hot story, largely ignored by the sporting press, was about kickbacks to media commentators by sporting sponsors. There seemed to be a bit of a trade in not so 'free' plugs that would be interspersed through the commentary. It was a grubby and greedy little trade that collected, for some commentators, a piggy bank of tax-free spending money. We found and interviewed a Sydney businessman who told of paying an inducement to a well-known broadcaster.

Both the interviews were strong, but to stand them up we needed corroboration. It is surprising how often even experienced journalists fall into the trap of thinking that if they have an allegation, they have a story. As Peter taught me, if there is anything that is fundamental to 'investigative' journalism, it is the need to check and corroborate and check again.

So we continued the hunt and interviewed another retired sporting commentator who said the practice of kickbacks was rife. There is one quote I will always remember. Sporting journalists, he said, 'would be corrupted for a cup of tea'.

The observation travelled with me for many years and extended well beyond the sports arena. I am often surprised at how cheaply we will sell out and I have wondered at times not just whether we are a nation of crooks, but, worse still, whether we are a nation of cheap crooks.

We took our cameras to the edge of the playing field to film the game in action. For me, this was the best part of the assignment. I could draw on my own film-making background and the breadth of the more healthy *Four Corners* budget by getting the best possible pictures.

We hired a high-speed 'Mitchell' camera and recorded some superb slow-motion vision. A great and possibly even unique benefit of *Four Corners* is that there is mostly the time and sometimes the money to achieve production values akin (in look only) to the glossiest margarine commercial.

We also poked our noses everywhere and anywhere and before long it became clear the most conspicuous odour emanated from Rugby League Headquarters itself. We learned of all the battered former second-rowers who would turn up at the weekly meetings and consume large plates of Chinese food and jugs of free beer, in exchange for a vote that ensured the administration retained their considerable power and control.

The NSW League turned over millions of dollars but it did not allow itself to be subjected to proper company audits. Despite the popularity and wealth of the game, spectator facilities were looking threadbare.

Among all the rumours and sub-rumours, one story persisted about the NSW Rugby League Chairman, Kevin Humphreys, having a passion for gambling, and having beaten a fraud charge some years earlier under suspicious circumstances.

The on-air date loomed closer and it became less and less likely that we would meet it. Normally a schedule allowed two weeks research, two weeks filming and two weeks editing.

We had now spent most of the six weeks on research. Jonathan became anxious about the lack of footage shot so far.

He was, I am sure, far less anxious than me. I knew that as the new boy, I would not normally be indulged with lengthy preparation time. This privilege usually takes years to earn. My old Rural colleagues began to wonder what I was doing.

I was excited by the story prospects, but I was worried too. Peter, who had already been at *Four Corners* for two years, was just excited. He told Jonathan we should be left to keep on researching. Jonathan groaned and turned to the task of turning up the heat on the other reporters.

Peter and I worked every day, day and night and in time a focus developed as one morsel of information stood out more and more sharply from the rest.

One excursion took us to a backyard garage beside a fibro home in Sydney's west. This was the office of a well-known fellow journalist, Bob Bottom. Our discussion with Bob was wide ranging.

One thing he mentioned was the story of the Kevin Humphreys' fraud charge. Bob told us that a magistrate, Wally Lewer, was believed to have been suspicious about the way Chief Stipendiary Magistrate Murray Farquhar behaved during the case. Bottom thought the Independent MP, John Hatton, might know more.

Hatton's office, in NSW Parliament House, was hardly less modest. Hatton fought a lonely struggle against public corruption at a time when the issue did not seem to count for much. His sincerity and independence acted as a lightning rod for all sorts of information. One document which found its way into his safe was an account of Lewer's concerns about the Humphreys case.

All this was tantalising but we needed more. The next step was finding Wally Lewer. There is a maxim in the research business: 'when in doubt look up the telephone book'. A former Lewer associate told us he had left NSW and retired to Queensland. We thought we might have to check every electoral roll in that state.

Then inspiration drove Peter to the Brisbane phone book and soon the number was discovered. The former NSW Deputy Chief Stipendiary Magistrate was home, and willing to talk as long as the conversation was strictly 'off the record'.

The *Four Corners* budget did not stretch to unlimited air travel, but fortunately we had other reasons to travel to Brisbane.

Brisbane was the other major centre for Rugby League. The Queensland footballers copped a hiding year after year from their big spending southern rivals. Sydney's poker machine dollars inevitably lured Brisbane's best players south. The Queensland public's sense of fair play was offended when their weakened teams were then crushed with the help of players nurtured in the north.

But unlike the south, the much less powerful and less wealthy Queensland Rugby League allowed itself to be subjected to company audit. There was a sense that Queensland was not just having its bank of talent robbed but was also not getting a fair enough share of the game's profits.

There was enmity on and off the field. Peter and I thought some of the Brisbane officials might be encouraged to shine some light on the shadowy accounting practices down south.

We were right. Some of the Brisbane officials spoke 'off the record', about their serious suspicion that profits were being 'skimmed'. They told us that the international matches, which drew huge crowds and presumably attracted huge receipts, did not attract much scrutiny from the League accountants.

But the important meeting was with Lewer. In a sense we now had two stories. One was about sport. One was about justice. They probably did not have much to do with each other but we continued to treat them as one story.

We met Wally Lewer in the ABC staff canteen in Brisbane. The former NSW Deputy Chief Stipendiary Magistrate proclaimed himself something of a moral refugee. Wally was clearly a principled man, and for his principles he had taken a battering. He had escaped the sin city of the south and was now in retirement. His choice of a place to take refuge may not have stood the test of time but there is much about Wally that has endured.

He was, in absentia, to have a profound effect on his home state. Wally had the courage to tell us his story. The tea leaves floated undisturbed at the rim of my cup. The polystyrene sandwich went untouched. I was too busy scribbling notes. Peter asked most of the questions. Lewer's account began to make the picture clear.

In 1976 a $52 519 shortfall was discovered after a series of routine audits at the Balmain Leagues Club. Kevin Humphreys was then the Balmain Club Secretary/Manager. By the time the case appeared before the NSW courts he had been appointed to the powerful post of President of the NSW Rugby League.

Lewer's story began with an account of what happened on the morning of August 11, 1977, the day Humphreys' committal hearing was to begin. What he said suggested that the then Chief Stipendiary Magistrate, Murray Farquhar, used the name of Premier Neville Wran to attempt to influence the outcome of the case.

Lewer's story included the now famous words, 'The Premier is on the phone.' Farquhar's secretary, Vin D'Agostino, had spoken them to Farquhar in the presence of other magistrates on that morning.

Farquhar appeared to then manoeuver the process of selecting a magistrate to hear the case. When Kevin Jones was chosen, Farquhar was alleged to have called Jones in and applied some pressure. The magistrate Jones (now deceased) was said to be honest, mild mannered and competent, but 'no match for a bully like Farquhar'. Lewer said Jones later spoke to another magistrate, Kevin Waller, saying that Farquhar had instructed him not to commit Humphreys for trial. Farquhar had given the clear impression that the direction came from Premier Neville Wran himself.

The committal hearing lasted two days and as it transpired, Humphreys was not committed for trial. Jones, we were told, had been urged not to take notice of Farquhar, and to follow his own conscience.

We can never know if he did respond to influence, but there was a confusing contradiction in his summing up. A magistrate is obliged by law to commit a defendant for trial before a judge and jury if a prima facie case is established. Jones appeared to find that such a case was established, stating that he was satisfied Humphreys took the money for his own benefit, and that a jury might accept the evidence supporting the allegation.

Neverthless Jones dismissed the charge and Humphreys walked out of the court, a free man.

It was an important story. Lewer was an unusually credible and reputable witness but he was speaking with us 'off the record'. There is frequent confusion and misunderstanding about what 'off the record' means — even among journalists themselves. So spelling it out is often worthwhile. 'Off the record' certainly means the source must remain secret and unattributable. Whether it means the information can or cannot be broadcast is something that has to be determined by the parties involved.

I find it a very useful tool, a quick way of discovering a purer truth so that the bulk of the available time can be given over to independently proving or disproving the information. It is tempting to take the step of offering a secrecy contract in return for valuable information but it is not a step to be taken without hesitation. If we promise a conversation is 'off the record' and we will go to gaol rather than reveal a source, then we must be prepared to mean it.

By taking the step we are not only seeking the trust of the witness, but exercising considerable trust ourselves. I have no wish to go to gaol because, ever eager for information, I have thrown my trust at a cheat and a liar.

But in this case the witness was of unusually high character. Here was 'off the record' information of rare, premium quality. If Lewer could be persuaded to tell the story 'on the record' it would help us enormously.

The quietly spoken former magistrate agreed the story should be told but could not be budged or bullied towards a recorded interview. He argued politely and sensibly, that to stand alone as a witness in such a serious matter would be suicidal.

I have to confess I was prepared to leave it at that but Peter was not. He persisted with a fiercer politeness. Manning is an occasional cricketer, a Saturday afternoon fast bowler. I began to feel sorry for the diminutive Lewer who stood before a determined barrage of deliveries, all aimed squarely at his conscience.

'The story is too important to be left untold,' Peter said. 'You must give us an interview, or at the very least a statutory declaration, outlining your evidence.'

In the end I think we were beaten by the light. Lewer had to leave. We were due back in Sydney. Peter had not given up, and I was learning something about not taking no for an answer.

The next step was to find other witnesses. We had spoken to some people in politics and the judiciary who confirmed what they knew of the story. But some were not central to the events; others were too timid to take the risk of going public.

After a time, however, Kevin Waller agreed to see us. Waller's evidence was crucial because he was one of the few people present on the morning of the Humphreys case and, we understood, the sole witness to Kevin Jones' account of his conversation with Farquhar, immediately after Jones was selected to hear the case.

We told him what we knew. Unlike Lewer, Waller was not

in retirement and as a working magistrate, was still a NSW public servant. The career consequences of him cooperating with a couple of renegades from the badlands of the media were obvious. We left him to think about it.

Farquhar's clerk, Cam Aboud was next. Aboud had left the magistracy and was now conveniently located in new premises within walking distance of the ABC. We pestered him for weeks. He sat in his new office and told us what he knew with a weary eye trained on the consequences.

I began to learn another lesson which became quickly set in concrete. People do not tell all on the first visit. It stands to reason they need to develop some degree of trust before they part with important information. There is a necessary process of getting to know one another. It is time-consuming, too much so for most media deadlines. It might take five visits or fifteen. It often does. This is probably the hardest work of all. People are not likely to trust you unless they sense you have a sincere interest in them, as well as their story.

There is no point in feigning an interest. The worst 'investigative' reporters are the ones who come on like wall-cladding salesmen. I have watched them work and listened later to them puzzling over why they get little cooperation. I have sat in silent sympathy with the unknown witness and understood why the public esteem of journalists ranks down there with the hucksters of this world.

We returned to see Kevin Waller. He would not be interviewed. He would not give us a written statement but all was not lost. Waller did allow us to question him about the event, and then agreed to 'verbally adopt' a statement we read to him.

What this meant was that we would state in his presence our account of what had happened. He would verify the account as fair and accurate and agree to stand by the story should he be required to give evidence in court.

The prospect of becoming a high-profile witness in such a

controversial matter attracted no enthusiasm from Waller. The NSW Coroner had the look of a man who was a witness at his own inquest. He had my respect.

We returned to Queensland and repeated our torment of Wally Lewer. I seem to recall it was a Sunday night. We were downstairs in his study. Lewer was worried, weary and more than a little irritated by our persistence.

But he finally agreed to pen his initials to the bottom of a statement we had prepared. He must have known that Sunday night would be the first of a succession of sleepless nights. The admirable Mr Lewer deserved a more peaceful retirement.

We returned to our motel in the Brisbane Valley at about 11 p.m. I don't know why I remember this, but there were two 'working girls' plying their trade from neighbouring rooms. The image sticks in my mind like a ghostly signpost to a future scandal.

Peter and I sought the simpler pleasure of food and wine. There was a Chinese restaurant still open. There usually is. I enjoyed that meal very much, and hope we toasted the Wallers and the Lewers of this world. They are hard to find.

People often ask about the risks of investigative journalism. There are risks but they are usually overstated; and they are nothing compared to the risks we ask our witnesses to take. For us there was the celebratory pleasure of a late night supper. For Lewer and Waller there was indigestion and insomnia.

Peter and I returned to Sydney. The hard part was yet to come. The programme still had to be squeezed through the legal filter.

I began working on the script. There was still more filming to do and as far as Peter was concerned, the research was far from complete. I was later to see how he would research right up until the last possible moment. Research, he told me, was the heartbeat of a good story.

A rough draft was prepared of the programme. We called it

'The Big League'. Lawyers like to see the programme or at least a draft of the script, before they can offer any advice.

Jonathan Holmes, Peter and I caught a taxi to Phillip Street. This is the street of lawyers (sometimes known as the Street of Tongues), which stands parallel to Macquarie Street and NSW Parliament House.

I can remember them asking me how much of all this I thought we should broadcast. I said 100 per cent. My innocent belief was that we were public servants and the public should be served with 100 per cent of our labours.

But that is not the way the system works. The Queen's Counsel assigned to vet the programme was a large, jovial man, John Traill. His junior counsel was Terry Tobin, a terrier-like former journalist.

Some recollections of the meeting remain. I can still see the ample figure of Traill on his hands and knees checking the details of our account of the various meetings over a hand-drawn map of the magistrate's rooms.

I can remember someone bringing sandwiches and wondering who was going to pay. I recall the flush of recognition that this was serious, and the distinct realisation that what we had uncovered might not be broadcast.

When I reach now for my notes of that meeting, the book opens magically at the right page and the words stare up at me, 'TELL CHIEF JUSTICE'.

This was the contingency plan. Our knowledge of an alleged serious conspiracy to pervert the course of justice made us 'accessories after the fact'. If we could not satisfy the ABC that the story could be defended in court, then we were to take the story to the Chief Justice. The Chief Justice as it happens was Sir Laurence Street.

But our job is to broadcast. Another note says: 'if we believe the story is fair we have an obligation to tell it'. Somewhere I have also scribbled these words, 'other side will stop at nothing to crush us'.

Peter and I needed to strengthen the evidence. The lawyers would not tell us what to do. They would only advise us of the weaknesses. Although this might seem a bit frustrating there is good sense in the formula. I am a firm believer in journalists being journalists and lawyers being lawyers. A journalist should not allow a lawyer to take editorial charge of a story.

Equally, a journalist should be careful not to try to act too much like a lawyer, in the preparation of the work. I suspect a more serious impediment to an informed public than the iniquities of the defamation laws is self-censorship within the media.

Lawyers do not drive the story. They save us from ourselves by acting as a protective barrier to stop the story careening into the innocent.

Journalists sometimes feel they need to know the law backwards before they feel competent to tackle issues that are large and litigious. This is one reason why such issues are rarely tackled, and it is not a very good reason.

If lawyers were in charge of the world's information flow I suspect our newspapers would be much thinner and even more difficult to understand.

The fundamental difference in the objectives of the journalist and the lawyer in getting a report published is this: journalists have to believe in the truth of their own story; lawyers have to believe they can defend the story in a court of law. The sure way to keep both parties happy is for the journalist to believe the story and have enough evidence to prove the truth of the story to the satisfaction of the courts.

We don't have to be lawyers to do our work well. It seems to me we do need to have important basic knowledge about the rules of contempt, defamation, injunctions and the like; but this can be acquired in days rather than years. This basic knowledge, however, is essential because when you prepare a programme like this, you are not just preparing for a broadcast, you are preparing for a potential court case.

Not all the defences are built into the programme; many may not be seen on the screen. But they must be there in the background; files and files of papers, bringing congestion to our offices and comfort to our lawyers.

So in this way our work drifted like a North Sea iceberg towards its on-air date. The great bulk of it would have to stay frozen beneath the surface.

There were more meetings, secret meetings. Some members of the Wran Government helped us. There was a little bit of help from the Opposition, but not much. We had one important meeting with a senior public servant. Another serving magistrate talked and a former senior public servant agreed to a meeting. All spoke 'off the record' but what they told us helped us, at least, to believe our own story.

The great majority of these contacts were made by Peter. His contact book, a journalist's most precious tool of trade, was choked with names and numbers. My contact book was a mere slip by comparison. But that is no longer the case. The best way to build a contact book is obvious enough. You must first make the contacts.

I remember Peter asking me to call a policeman in a suburban police station to check a detail. I was a bit anxious about a blind approach to an unknown authority figure. As it turned out the policeman was friendly and cooperative. The name was entered in my fledgling book and the lesson was learned. You never get anywhere if you don't make the phone call.

Meanwhile the story about Rugby League was ambling along at a comfortable slow jog. We had taken possession of all the League's published accounts we could find. We had made many a visit to the office of Corporate Affairs to conduct company searches. We hired an independent accountant to conduct an informal audit of the sparse amount of material that could be scraped from the public record. We also kept up our visits to referees, players, sponsors, officials and the like.

The filming was proceeding in a patchy way which is not ideal. It is best to use the same film-crew and make sure the filming is consistent. The crew is then better able to understand the story and there is less wasted time, effort and footage. But the slow drip of information in this story did not lend itself to a self-contained filming schedule.

Worse still, the story was emerging as one dominated by 'talking heads'. A programme which is little more than wall to wall interviews is not exciting television. But in this case there was the opportunity of entertaining vision through the sport of Rugby League.

We organised to film players training, filmed a parade of the Australian Rugby League team, the triumphant 'Kangaroos', who had returned from another successful tour, and we captured some more good vision of the action on the field.

One person who could help a little with organising all of this filming was a prominent Rugby League figure who was also the coach of the powerful St George Club. He had told me as much as he could about the darker side of the game but he was a bit of a late-comer, so did not have a great deal to say.

I had some serious worries about my meetings with this man, so kept them to a minimum. The St George coach was my oldest brother Roy. A failed tilt at the Rugby League administration would have crippled his sporting career. Roy did not help a great deal, but more to the point, he did not hinder.

One of Roy's rivals, however, was a huge help. The best Rugby League team in NSW at the time, Parramatta, was coached by a rock solid human embodiment of Sydney culture, Jack Gibson. Gibson is like a mobile version of the Blue Mountains. He is large and appealing and doesn't say much.

Jack might not have been a purist about the law, but he had a great sense of justice, and a charming turn of phrase. 'He's got so much shit in his boots . . . ' was one description of Humphreys. Jack did not like the way Humphreys was running the game. He did not like the way the Parramatta Club appeared to be suffering. Parramatta was not in favour with the game's administration and there were fierce complaints about the way the club was treated by one referee.

When we asked Gibson on camera about Humphreys and the fraud case he told us what he knew. It was a big step for Jack. The Sydney underworld/mateship code of behaviour demands silence and self-protection.

I suspect Jack felt Humphreys had lost the right to that protection. The game was in trouble. Jack told us how, in 1976, Humphreys had come to him in a distressed state wanting to borrow money. He had a gambling problem, and he needed to replace the money taken from the safe of the Balmain Club. Gibson lent Humphreys the money in return for a promise he would not gamble again. But according to Jack, Humpreys was back playing 'Two-Up' the very next night.

We interviewed Jack. We interviewed Humphreys. The Rugby League boss knew the interview would be unlikely to be favourable, but to his credit, he did not try to brush us off. The boss of the League was doing his duty. We brought in two cameras, as we sometimes do for the more serious interviews.

Peter had taught me how to structure the interview. The general form is the softer questions come first and the toughest ones are saved for last. There had been a lot of time to build our research on Humphreys so some of the questions struck like hammer blows.

But they had to be asked. You can sometimes measure a journalist by their willingness or unwillingness to ask the 'tough' question. The journalist does not have to be rude and offensive but they can't shirk their duty either. In answering the questions Humphreys was polite, composed and just a little bit pale.

But most participants would not be interviewed. We had collected some powerful information, but finding a satisfying means of conveying the information was becoming a dilemma.

The lawyers could not understand the problem. 'Why doesn't Chris just write it down and read it out?'

But names and places and dates can be boring enough in print let alone on television. An endless monologue of a complex series of events could easily leave the viewer bored and bewildered.

It was Jonathan who first suggested 'reconstructing' the events. It has been a device which has been used, and abused, to the point where I am reluctant to resort to it. But in those days it was an innovation in Australia.

The lawyers were horrified. The story was risky enough on its own. To invite actors to 'interpret' events which none of us had personally witnessed considerably aggravated the risk that we would not be believed by the public or the courts.

But we accepted the risk on the basis that we would be scrupulous about what was reconstructed and how it was done. Peter and I worked out the ground rules. We would reconstruct only scenes which were essential to the central allegations; only scenes which had been described to us in detail by at least one witness, who had already agreed to testify in court or to a Royal Commission. Above all we would put into the actor's mouths only those words — and there were very few of them — which had appeared in quotation marks in the statements our witnesses had adopted.

We would also clearly label each such scene as a dramatic reconstruction. With the benefit of a bit more experience it may have been more sensible not to give the actors any dialogue but rather encompass the same information within the reporter's narrative. Getting actors to deliver lines without unneccessary dramatics is not easy and it is important that the information is as clean and uncluttered, as devoid of variable interpretation as possible.

Even so the scenes worked well enough as a means of conveying this important and complex information without overly distressing our lawyers. When they saw the recordings, John Traill and Terry Tobin declared them 'defensible'.

A few days before the programme was due to go to air, Peter rang Kevin Humphreys to tell him the material we had collected, including the interview, would be broadcast.

This is one of the worst tasks we can ever perform. We cannot escape the fact our work can bring damage and ruin to people. I am not aware of an Australian Journalists Association rule insisting we make the phone call but the rule of decency is obvious enough.

Peter was shaking when he came off the phone. A television programme had appeared from nowhere and shattered a powerful man. Humphreys greeted the news with 'O.K., thanks very much. Goodbye'.

We also telephoned the office of the NSW Premier, Neville Wran. Humphreys had approached Wran back in 1977 to discuss his plight. Wran had also been named by Farquhar as the man who allegedly did not want Humphreys committed for trial. Wran's lawyers replied, stating the report was 'highly defamatory, totally indefensible and false'. He would not appear.

There was a week of work ahead of us in getting the programme to air. Alongside the high drama of working on a report that threatened the government of the day I had a few other practical problems to cope with.

Writing a script for a fifty minute documentary is not a matter of taking the effort required for a ten minute report and multiplying it by five. There are new skills that need to be developed for the structuring of longer reports. Jonathan was feared by some of the reporters for the way he dismembered ailing structures and lobotomised sloppy thinking. He was equally ruthless with me, but I was still able to appreciate the lesson of pruning and training a story so that there was a logical development.

Peter helped me to stop trying to cram so much into my sentences. He threw out all the unnecessary words and urged me to replace some of the 'smart' language with words that were more readily understood.

I think I was also helped a little in my writing by a small diary I had begun to keep at the urging of my taxation accountant. The diary was meant to record extraneous expenses but, as well, became a record of the day's thoughts and happenings.

For my writing, keeping the diary was probably the best move I ever made. Writing, like every skill, benefits from practice. My few minutes in the evening in front of the diary were similar, in a way, to the minutes my daughter would spend each morning in front of the piano.

Getting practice in front of a camera, however, was a very different matter. A lot of what was involved in the process was new to me. I was expected to go into the studio and perform, but I didn't even have any proper clothes. Jonathan sent me off to David Jones and I returned with a new grey suit.

We shot the studio segments in one trying day. For the first take I was so nervous I could barely speak. But I took a deep breath and forced myself to concentrate. There are many reporters who are lovers of the camera. I have never been one of them. For me, neither actor nor performer, it is all a bit of trial.

What I have found is that the performance will work if you have important words that you believe should be spoken. This was very definitely the case, but I was still glad when it was over.

Peter and I then moved on to the recording booth where the final narration track would be recorded. True to form, I could see him through the glass, telephoning witnesses in the hope that even in the final minutes more would be discovered.

The ABC had now been advised by the lawyers that the programme was defensible and could be screened but that was not enough. I don't know much of what went on over my head in the stratosphere of management. I was not there. I can remember Holmes picking up a videotape copy of the programme and taking it up to Broadcast House.

My new pommy boss was probably more of a loyal advocate for the report than many a home-grown executive producer. He had no certain career in Australia to protect, he had no life-long allegiances to feel sensitive about. What he had was clear sight and courage; and he used all of it to see the programme to air.

We could hardly be certain he would succeed. Although the lawyers had given the opinion the programme could be defended it was highly defamatory of at least three people, including the Premier of NSW, who was also the National President of the ALP. Wran threatened to sue the ABC as indeed he later did.

By now the ALP had won office in Canberra and the new Prime Minister, Bob Hawke, was our new paymaster. Win or lose, the ABC was likely to incur the lasting enmity of some very powerful figures in the ruling government. I have never been a political animal, or taken much interest in the intrigues of Canberra. But even I could appreciate the risks involved for my employer.

Early on the evening of Friday April 29, I returned to the *Four Corners* office to find a spontaneous gathering of staff. We had not said a great deal about the work, but the word had got around. *Four Corners* stalwarts like Peter Ross and Jim Downes were generous. They gave me helpful advice on scripting and presentation and best of all stood solidly in support of the new boy.

There was talk about what we would do if the ABC chose

not to broadcast 'The Big League'. There was talk of resignation. My *Four Corners* career threatened to be the shortest ever . . . not even one programme to air.

It was not until seven o'clock that evening that Holmes received a phone call saying we would be running the following night. The ABC Chairman at the time, Dame Leonie Kramer, had overruled another board member and supported the programme.

The secretaries, transcription typists, reporters, sound recordists and editors who had waited back, allowing their evening meals to go cold, all cheered. One more glass of wine was squeezed from the cardboard cask before they headed for the bus.

Manning, Holmes and I spent the Saturday in an editing house making final changes. I went back to the studio with Jonathan Holmes at 6 p.m. I put on my impressive grey suit and practised reading the apology we had prepared in case we received a last minute injunction preventing the programme's transmission. The injunction did not arrive, but I was not able to make it home in time to see my first *Four Corners* report go to air.

By the time I got home it was almost over. At the very end the narrative explains that the matters raised were too serious to be dealt with in any way other than by an independent, public inquiry.

Our editor, Barbara Bedford, had then cut to some slow motion Rugby League vision underlaid with some well-chosen music, which managed to convey the magnitude of the moment.

Watching it eight years later there is still an involuntary intake of breath. People have since told me that it was one of those moments that is imprinted in the memory in bold type. They can remember the meal they were eating at the time, mouth open before the television set, with the spaghetti sliding from the fork. The journalist and broadcaster, Mike Carlton, later said he had to 'pick himself up off the floor'.

The credits were rolling when the phone rang, and then rang again for the next four hours. One of the callers was my brother Roy, the football coach. With a hint of pride in his voice, he said, 'I didn't know you were going to say those things'.

Back at the ABC the phones were also ringing. It is a good idea to make sure the phones are well attended after such broadcasts. People often ring in with useful, additional information. I still have a copy of the switchboard log which records the many hundreds of calls received in the following days, and indeed some were very helpful.

The programme had a powerful impact. Kevin Humphreys resigned as Chairman of the NSW and Australian Rugby League. A new administration incorporated the League and introduced a more accountable system for watching the dollars.

The system of appointing referees also had a shrill whistle put to its ear. Few people could deny it is now a better serviced, more honest, more popular sport.

Perhaps the episode on Rugby League was a very different story to the main thrust of the report but I am glad we included it.

The programme was a watershed in the history of the Eastern state's most popular winter sport. Eight years after 'The Big League', the game has a much stronger following, now including women and families, and not just beer-swilling males. There is much more serious concern about the health of players, and although there are the inevitable squabbles about referees' decisions, I hear no complaints of cheating.

But any shy pride we could take in the work had to wait. The innocent bystander had to put his umbrella up in the few weeks following the broadcast. Sydney unleashed that fierce storm of retribution I had been warned about. They didn't know much about me so they tended to blame Peter, which was an arrangement that suited me reasonably well.

Even so the excommunication was no fun for Peter. He

was shunned by many lifelong friends. There were many arguments at dinner parties in the years to follow. I have never been a member of the ALP or any political party, but there is a frequent assumption that journalism is part of the party's cause. Time and time again I was told that people like 'us' had a duty to protect the Labor Party.

The ALP, which is not known for the scope of its mercy, banned *Four Corners* on later occasions when we sought interviews. Many in the party were convinced the programme was part of a political conspiracy to destroy Wran, and some probably still believe this.

The conspiracy theory was given extra impetus by a mischievous letter, distributed far and wide, outlining an intricate 'plot'. The letter spoke of a conspiracy between the ABC, the presiding Chief Stipendiary Magistrate Clarry Briese, and NSW Opposition Leader Nick Greiner. At the bottom was a version of my signature. NSW police investigating the matter later correctly determined that the letter was a forgery; but by then much of the damage was done. The mud had stuck.

I suppose Neville Wran could say the same thing; and in fact he did. Not long after the broadcast Peter was driving through the city and saw a newspaper poster: 'WRAN STEPS DOWN'. The government had agreed to a Royal Commission. The Chief Justice, Sir Laurence Street, would head it and we would be obliged to cooperate.

The majority of our witnesses had spoken with us 'off the record'. We telephoned each of them and asked if they would allow us to pass on their records of interview to the Commission. All but about ten of the one hundred or so witnesses agreed. Most stuck by their story, a few did not.

Peter and I were summoned separately to a meeting with the counsel assisting the Commission, Michael Grove QC. I found the questions not particularly searching.

The Street Royal Commission ran for about two months.

To many, it was Sydney's favourite soap opera. Neville Wran was infuriated by the humiliation of it all, and gave every impression that in a different age Manning and I would have been dressed in ball and chain and living on pig food.

Neville Wran was exonerated by Sir Laurence Street. I am happy to make it clear I do not quarrel with the decision.

There has been debate down the years about what the programme meant to say — and a general impression that, because the Street Royal Commission exonerated Neville Wran, in one respect at least, *Four Corners* got it horribly wrong. But in fact the Royal Commission found that in all important respects the programme was correct. Sir Laurence Street found that there had been a perversion of the course of justice, that it had been caused by the intervention of the Chief Stipendiary Magistrate, Murray Farquhar; and that Farquhar had claimed to be acting on the instructions of the Premier.

What the programme did say was that Wran's name had been used by Murray Farquhar in the context of the Humphreys case; whether Wran had in fact intervened we could not say. Our story had not accused Wran, but there is no denying the trouble it caused him.

The Commission could have extended its terms of reference and asked more questions; but I can't see the judgment on Wran would have been different.

If I could do it again, I would write it differently to emphasise more the possibility that Murray Farquhar might have been using the Premier's name without Wran's knowlege or authority.

But even with the benefit of hindsight I would still rather have named Wran than referred to him in ambiguity . . . that is, as 'a senior NSW politician'. Some backbencher in Queensland or elsewhere would have revealed his identity within a week.

We were not able to test the defence that the importance of the issue justified our naming Wran. Without any forewarning to us, and despite contrary advice from a leading QC, the

ABC settled out of court and paid Wran's legal fees. I was not happy, but I respect their right to make these judgments.

The ABC had planned in defending 'The Big League' broadcast to rely on the rarely used Section 22 of the NSW Defamation Act, which is sometimes known as the 'Qualified Privilege' defence.

We could not prove that Farquhar had received a telephone call from the Premier. We could only argue that he claimed to have received such a call. But such was the importance of the issue of an attempted perversion of the course of justice, I believe we were justified in reporting what occurred in those magistrates' rooms on August 11 and 12, 1977. The Section 22 defence meant we would be judged on whether we believed that what we stated was true, that we were acting without malice, and that publication was 'reasonable in all the circumstances'.

If we had lost the case, it would not only have cost the ABC a very large amount of money, but it would have been an even greater blow to journalism. That was a risk. But we do sometimes uncover important stories that have, contained within them, an aspect that is unprovable. The opportunity to test the right of the media to publish such stories was lost with the decision by the ABC to settle.

Thinking back I am still confident the decision to broadcast was a correct one. I can well understand that Neville Wran would not agree. He was forced to stand down from the job to which he was elected by the people of NSW. He was forced to undergo the stress and humiliation of a public inquisition and found himself the butt of rumour and innuendo long after he was formally exonerated — and all for something he played no part in.

But there is some chance that he managed to hang on to a vestige of his sense of humour. Two months after the broadcast Neville Wran and my brother Roy came face to face at an official function. There was talk of 'The Big League' programme. Wran told Roy, 'None of us should be held responsible for the sins of our fathers — or in your case, your brother'.

But there was an ethical, as opposed to a legal justification for broadcasting the report. The fact that Murray Farquhar had told a fellow magistrate that the Premier did not want Humphreys committed was an issue too important to ignore. It was clear to us that all those who knew the case — and that included much of the NSW magistracy — believed that the Premier had been involved.

The story was a cancer that had been eating away at the NSW judiciary for six years. Although the story had been around for that length of time, although it was known to the legal community and members of the government, it had never been dealt with and by our reading, was never likely to be dealt with unless we published.

The programme, like all programmes, had some flaws, but Peter and I and Jonathan and all the others who worked on it will not forget it. Humphreys was convicted of fraud, Farquhar was gaoled for conspiring to pervert the course of justice and NSW, I think, became a little less cynical about the power and inevitability of corruption.

The programme also had, I suspect, a significant influence within the Australian television news and current affairs industry. 'The Big League' saw the coming out of the 'blockbuster'. There was some recognition that one story could have a major impact, and that there was value in putting time and resources into long-term projects.

The best lesson I learned through all this was simple and enduring: aim high and tell them something they did not know yesterday.

I was anxious to try something like this again and said so to Jonathan and Peter. Jonathan said I would never make another programme like 'The Big League' in all my life. I told him I thought he was wrong.

3

'THE MOONLIGHT STATE'

There are many beginnings to Queenland's famous Fitzgerald Inquiry. There are two that concern myself and both involve plane travel. The first journey was to Canberra, midway through 1986. I was half way through a *Four Corners* report, at the stage when you began turning your mind to the next story.

The Australian Capital Territory spread out below like a crumpled army blanket. From behind one of the rough, scrubby folds of the neighbouring hills, the city raised an eyebrow at the aircraft's approach.

Our Governor-General and almost Prime Minister, Bill Hayden, once told me a problem with Canberra was that it was too ordered. The sensible design of our nation's capital was disturbing to a population conditioned to chaos. The observation made a lot of sense.

What I noticed about the place was that it was a good home for information. This is where many of the nation's secrets wash up and one that was about to be revealed to me would more than satisfy my own mild taste for chaos.

I used the occasion, as I often did, to look up a friend in the police force. By now I had accumulated many such friends. Other journalists might call them contacts. Through progressive alienation we have allowed our police forces to become secret societies, within which like-minded cells gather in silence for encouragement and self-protection. Sometimes, very rarely, outsiders gain associate membership status. Police reporters are common associate members and somehow, somewhere along the line I was so initiated.

The first rule of membership is you must not 'give up your mate'. In this case my 'mate' was an intelligence analyst with the Australian Bureau of Criminal Intelligence. I am about to give him up for two reasons. The first is that he has left the organisation, the second is that he is happy for me to do so.

Peter Vassallo is quietly spoken, bespectacled, keen on sailing model yachts and trying to look beyond the horizon. He is one of the people who encourages me to believe a police force can never be entirely corrupted. There are some people who will innately resist dishonesty.

Just as corrupt police have antennae for one another, so too do the more honest police. Among Peter's network of friends was a Queensland police officer who was in deep trouble because he had been offered and received a bribe.

There is nothing unique about police taking bribes but in this case the bribe was offered by a superior officer. The problem for the junior policeman was that it was more dangerous to reject the bribe than to accept it. The cost of being found honest it seemed, was greater than the cost of being found corrupt. So here was a smell of epidemic corruption that would be pursued at the next opportunity.

So, to the next plane ride. I remember the date well. It was September 27, 1986. Here is part of my diary entry for that day: 'Fly to Brisbane. Meet a man who looks more like a farmer than a cop'. The cop who looked more like a farmer was Jim Slade. Slade was a policeman who liked his work but could see a life beyond policing. He was undoubtably helped in this regard by his wife Christine. Chris liked her native garden, she taught Aboriginal children part-time and was full of a quiet decency that is common in Queensland.

Jim Slade told me about the bribe offer. I was struck by his dilemma. To return the money meant transportation to the Queensland equivalent of Siberia. To accept the money meant the end of his family's self-respect, because that is what happens. They are corrupted too. The Slades put the money in a plastic bag and hid it under the bed.

Jim was told the money came from Gerry Bellino, who was believed to command a small empire of brothels and illegal casinos based in Brisbane's Fortitude Valley. It appeared that Slade's superior had passed it to him to buy his silence. Some work Slade had done for the Bureau of Criminal Intelligence probed the activities of the Bellino brothers.

We sat at a laminated table in a Brisbane suburban pub. My notebook perched awkwardly, attempting a hopeless unobtrusiveness. Jim was awkward also. Talking to a journalist was close to an unnatural act. He kept apologising for betraying the superior who came so close to ruining his life. The police brotherhood has an unstated masonic rule of silence.

The crooks in the force convince the honest ones that bad publicity hurts them all. The honest cops feel bound by male mateship and a quasi-military loyalty to their partners. The secrecy deal suits the crooks perfectly and inevitably the honest police suffer.

Slade was suffering now. He and his wife had been haunted by the money for too long. They sought a compromise solution by handing the money back without causing too much mess and fuss. In consequence he was moved from the Bureau of Criminal Intelligence and was being shunned by his 'mates'. There was now the added discomfort of revealing all to one of those bastards from the media.

The bastard from the media promised the conversation was 'off the record'. I told Jim I would make use of the information and search for independent corroboration. In the meantime he would remain a secret, unattributable source until deemed otherwise (which is now, self-evidently, the case).

I could tell from the start this was a good story. The scent of institutional corruption gave it scale. The *cri de coeur* of the Slades gave it passion. I was angry at the notion that honesty could be so cunningly press-ganged into a career with the other side.

Jim and I reached an agreement across the no man's land of laminex. We shook hands and I left. Here now is the rest of my diary entry for that day. 'Fly back. Go to bed. Hear the phone. Dad tells me my mother died at 1130.'

I have never liked September much. It was the month of study and exams and bad luck. My mother, a great lover of Australia and people, died of cancer on that bleak September day.

The rest of the year ambled listlessly to a close. Television journalists, like schoolteachers and parents of school-aged children, are mostly obliged to take holidays at the end of the year. This is when our programmes go into recess and we quietly hope that current events oblige by taking a rest too.

I stuffed the camping gear in the back of the car, tried to have a holiday and then tried even harder to complete the journey back to work. I was not just depressed by my mother's death but about the miserable work I was bound to pursue at *Four Corners*. The workload is relentless and the subject matter often cheerless.

Nineteen eighty-seven was my fourth year and I was stumbling and weary, a sprinter trapped in a marathon. While the distance covered so far had delivered me a reasonable fund of experience it was also responsible for a developing emotional callus.

On January 18, 1987, I stopped at my parent's house at Austinmer on my way back from the camping holiday. 'Gloomy day. Walk about the garden. Rotting peaches on the ground. Would not be when Mum was there. A child of the depression they would have been turned into jam or a pie.'

For a long time I was nourished by a belief, I am sure I

inherited from my mother, that people are basically good. Some of my hard-bitten colleagues will cringe but it seems to me if a journalist believes in anything it should be this. We have to believe the information we peddle is of public benefit and that there is a public will to be informed. It helps to have some confidence that the public favours decent, honest administration, that they don't want the crooks in charge. This belief was about to be exposed to its most punishing test.

On my first day back at work I got down to some serious whingeing. I think the bruising was not only because of the potholes in the track behind but through anticipation of what was up ahead.

Peter Manning was now running *Four Corners*. He very considerately assigned me the most tolerant of all ABC producers, Shaun Hoyt. Shaun, like myself, had a slight strain of Queensland in her pedigree which would prove invaluable.

I was something of a mongrel son of the tropics, having grown up a centimetre or so south of the border and much later lived and worked in the deep north. In that time Shaun and I had seen many a media assault on 'Battleship Queensland'. Whereas we mostly appreciated the objective, it was possible to be offended at times by the snide tone of the reporting. A strong report which sounded like just another smart-arsed southerner having a shot at Queensland could end up as comfort for the enemy. We both saw 'Battleship Queensland' take many a direct hit over the years and marvelled at how its pace never faltered. Shaun and I ruminated over this as we tore the plastic from the cutlery on the long flight north.

Cairns was like a sauna. 'For the pleasure seekers, not the muckrakers. Sit under umbrella by pool buying drinks for very little reward. Perhaps you just don't learn anything in these places. Too hot to think.'

We talked to crooks and cops and pilots and a former SAS officer who had fought with the Montagnards in Vietnam. Previous *Four Corners* work taught us how easy it was to fly or ship drugs in through the yawning open door of northern Australia. The theory was the far north was one important centre for drug trafficking and the Queensland police were not doing all they could to combat the trade.

Before I left for the north I managed to access, without his knowledge, a copy of Jim Slade's report to the Queensland Bureau of Criminal Intelligence on drug trafficking in the north. Some of the information was sound, the rest was more in the form of crude intelligence which would have to be refined before it could be broadcast.

It was important, as ever, to have a fall-back position in case the better story should fail. There was every likelihood this would be so. Finding solid evidence on a drug trafficking ring is difficult enough for teams of police with the very best intelligence gathering equipment and the power to compel people to cooperate. Shaun and I were pathetically ill-equipped in comparison. Our fall-back story was one on the difficulties of coastal surveillance in the north.

Despite the torpor of the tropics we made some quick progress. We heard about a woman who had worked closely with some drug traffickers and was well placed to talk if she could be persuaded. I found her phone number and tried to make an appointment.

Believe it or not, this is the job at its most terrifying, when your story careers around a corner into an unwelcome dead end. There are few worse setbacks than an exclusive witness's firm refusal to talk.

I have, in my time sweated over many a telephone. There is no technique that guarantees success. If there is a skill it probably has little to do with journalism, and more to do with the mysterious and unexplainable. All I can say is it helps to be honest. When a journalist calls, people's bullshit detectors are instantly turned on. It is also worth remembering there is no long-term profit in deceiving a witness. If you do end up in court, you want them as friends, not enemies.

I find it also helps to be curious. Everybody has a story to tell and there is a frequent compulsion to tell it. Some of the best 'investigative' journalists are quite simply, good listeners. I have to admit there is an additional benefit in working in television.

When, sick with anxiety, I telephoned the person, one of the first questions asked was what to wear.

The witness had a fascinating story. There was talk about cops and crooks growing marijuana in the bush. There was further talk of a moonlight plane trip by the 'mafia' and about a stash of heroin still buried in an old World War Two bunker on the Atherton Tablelands. Much of this was direct evidence but even so it would have to be supported.

Journalists are as fond of 'direct' evidence as lawyers and police. Direct evidence means a first-hand account of something as opposed to hearsay evidence, which could be second- or third-hand information. Direct evidence has the same status as a new car warranty. To the courts at least, the rest is about as credible as the blurb in a second-hand car yard.

Shaun and I returned to Cairns where we stayed for another week. We scheduled a long list of people to see and then talked and made notes well into the night. The work seemed even harder than usual because away from the big cities people are more cautious. They come to these places to escape trouble.

I waited for the information to burst from the skies with the afternoon storms and grew impatient. The gust and swirl of information in the big cities is easier. You miss most of it but at least you keep busy.

We made plans to fly to Brisbane with one stop at Rockhampton on the way. A well-known maverick former Mareeba cop, Lindsay Ross Dickson, had broken ranks and retired not far away. He had a small fish restaurant on the coast at Yeppoon with the unforgettable name, 'Sea Food and Eat It'.

Investigative journalists are very fond of the newly retired. They are some of the few people who can speak without strong concern about the career consequences of whistle-blowing.

I was later to learn that on the day we left Cairns a senior policeman sought out the local casino proprietor for an appointment at 'Barnacle Bill's' waterfront restaurant. The cop told him *Four Corners* was in town and they would have to keep their heads down for a while. The casino proprietor replied that in consequence the $4000 weekly payments would cease until it was safe to resume.

We had no choice but to take a small Twin Otter milk-run flight down the coast. So ungracious and persistent was my whining it could be heard above the roar of the motors. Shaun and I played scrabble on the way. She shut me up by letting me win.

Ross Dickson was aproned and busy. Our conversation dived and plunged between the wrapping, the salting and the cash register. He was a great yarner. He knew the inner workings of the Queensland Police Force well and was prepared to give up some of its secrets. I might have caught Ross when retirement was getting a little boring. His anxious wife Ann looked wearily across the restaurant, probably wishing I would choke on a fish bone. Policing is a ruthless business. She knew, as Ross and I knew, that somewhere there would be a dirt file on Ross Dickson or one that could be invented. If needed, his old friends would not hesitate to use it without mercy.

The next day we were in Brisbane. Anxious about the scale of the task in front I called for reinforcements. Peter Manning sent up Debbie Whitmont, a lawyer who was working at the time as a *Four Corners* researcher.

I knew by now that it was unwise to attempt to do this work alone. The problem is not so much the risk of physical danger but the need to have a friend alongside. A witness can turn around and deny that words were spoken or worse. As I was to discover later, some of the police I was up against were prepared to arrest and charge me with a mythical offence. The fact that I was mostly accompanied by colleagues who could disprove the charge probably made it a lot more difficult for them. The most obvious benefit, however, is there is too much work to be done and more will be achieved if it is shared.

Brisbane was the home base of the institution of the Queensland police. The information we had collected so far supported the promise of Jim Slade's story. The institution was crook. Too often, police with doubtful reputations were being promoted. For the honest police within the force, the big picture was difficult to see, let alone describe. But outside, Brisbane was beginning to take on the brazenness of Kings Cross.

In Fortitude Valley, on the edge of the city, 'The World by Night' had just been reduced to ashes, along with many similar style premises. A war of the pimps was under way. The pimps were scavengers, latter-day slave traders, but such was their wealth and power, police and politicians had become passive spectators.

Young women would enter the trade in the hope of making some quick capital so they could start a hairdressing business, buy a BMW or take a European holiday. The work soon proved so difficult and degrading that they would be taking drugs in order to cope. In no time they would be working for the needle, their dreams of a business, car and world travel having totally disintegrated.

Some would attempt to go solo and work for themselves but they complained the pimps would pursue, bash and even rape them. They said they found it difficult to afford the high advertising tariffs in the Brisbane newspapers. And when they did advertise their new work location, police would selectively raid them, inevitably forcing them back into the embrace of the pimps.

Australia's sex industry is astonishingly profitable. One secret of Australian private life which was soon to be revealed to me was the surprisingly high percentage of males who are regular clients. One of the women told me of a regular visit every Sunday morning to a respectable home where she 'serviced' a man while his family attended Mass. There were many such stories.

'The World by Night' was a popular Brisbane nightclub run by Gerry Bellino and his partner Vic Conte. Although it was unlicensed, liquor was somehow available. To select police, it was available at no charge. Upstairs, by the men's toilet, there was an entrance to the uncertain charm of 'Scarlett's', a brothel. Conte and Bellino appeared to run another brothel close by, 'The House of the Rising Sun' in a similar busy street. You would have to have suffered acute glaucoma, spent your entire life in a monastery or been an elected official of the National Party to be ignorant of what was on offer. There was a bold marquee and a red light of searchlight proportions. An overweight, underdressed blonde lady sulked in the window.

An identical image peered down from a more suitable piece of real estate only metres away. This was the province of the so-called competition. Many thousands of homeward bound commuters could not miss spotting Hector Hapeta's main brothel. 'Top of the Valley' commanded a useful corner position at a major Fortitude Valley junction. It seemed to me that in the tradition of giant pineapples and giant prawns you see at coastal tourist towns, a giant penis erected nearby would not have been out of place. It would have been no less blatant.

We divided the work. There were witnesses to find and interview. There were newspaper files to search. Old film and tape had to be resurrected and viewed. Land title and company searches would help prove the ownership of the brothels and illegal casinos.

Deb Whitmont got the short straw and headed for the Titles Office and Corporate Affairs Commission. This was before the

Australian Securities Commission created its national data base. Company searches, in those days, had to be completed laboriously, state by state. This made it tough for busybodies like us, and easy for the crooks, who could hide their loot beneath mountains of documents and micro-fiche. Indefatigable Deb had to scale the mountains, checking company ownership and looking for lists of directors. Once she located a company she would see where it was registered, and then check at that office to see what other companies were registered. Then it was back to the Corporate Affairs Commission to see whether any of the people we were looking at had assets in these new companies.

Meanwhile Shaun searched the newspaper files. There were plenty of laudatory stories of Police Commissioner Terry Lewis opening shows and being nominated as Father of the Year but not much about the suspected corruption journalists were happy to gossip about in the pubs.

I headed for the ABC film library. There are many occasions when you give thanks for working at the ABC. Before the latest round of budget cuts the national broadcaster could boast an excellent library. Every time I looked into it I realised what a treasure of modern history was stored there. Hunting through the Brisbane library I found that a programme canvassing a similar theme to the one we were investigating had run four years earlier on *Nationwide*.

A frustrated policeman had been encouraged to blow the whistle on corruption in the force. It was a strong, revealing report but it changed nothing. The policeman, Bob Campbell, paid a huge price for his moment of courage and truth. We had since learned he fled the force, pursued by writs and venom, and was now in hiding.

The report was followed by footage of a press conference featuring the then Police Minister, Russ Hinze. Hinze had a remarkable charm and was actually very popular with journalists because he was always good for an easy story.

Journalists would go away sated by the first impression, not wanting to look further.

At the press conference Hinze baldly denied the existence of the illegal casinos that some assembled journalists happily frequented. He angrily railed at Campbell for daring to betray his mates and their families. There was no mercy. Astonishingly, the extensively corpulent Russ even attacked Campbell for carrying a bit too much weight. The only response I could detect was the faint scribble of biros. Hinze then turned on Allan Hall, the reporter who prepared the story. When Hall raised a voice of protest Hinze spat at him furiously, telling him he would be out of a job tomorrow. I could have been watching *Alice in Wonderland* right down to the last 'off with his head'.

In the days following the broadcast there were no stinging editorials. Another television channel broadcast a 'puff piece' on Hinze soon after and the Brisbane River continued its quiet and muddy flow.

There was a sobering lesson in all this. Not just for myself but for any potential whistleblower. In the days ahead I would telephone a succession of retired, battered policemen. I can remember well their words. 'Forget it, go away. You will only make it worse. Today's news is tomorrow's wrappings. The public don't care anyway.'

They made a lot of sense. The *Courier Mail* had, in January, published one good story by Phil Dickie on the ownership of Brisbane brothels but it also made no difference.

Shaun and Deb had spoken to Dickie. He was keen on the story but there did not appear to be much public appetite for more. To be fair, I have to admit it is much harder for local journalists to disturb what appears to be a natural order. There is an understandable reluctance to attack someone you might end up seeing on the bus every day. It is even harder to savage someone who has become a reliable source of stories. After a time, police roundsmen will commonly identify and sympathise with the people they have to deal with every day, the police themselves.

For the period of our research we remained deliberate outsiders. I did not go near the office of Police Public Relations. I saw little point. There is a time to go through the front door, and there is a time to go around the back. Lewis's minders would hardly help me dig up the dirty secrets. It is harder work, but it is better to do the digging yourself. In this kind of work, knowing your enemy can mean keeping a sensible distance. In my case it wasn't difficult working out who the enemy was. They kept following me.

There was no chance of keeping our work secret. We were approaching too many people. Someone was going to alert the opposition. Before long, it was clear they were watching us closely. We would talk with a policeman and the policeman would be immediately interviewed by superiors who wanted to know what we were up to. I got a bit nervous when I realised how closely they were watching.

I was worried enough to feel I should alert some of my friends in the police, so began to make regular calls to the south. If the Queensland police were watching me and monitoring my calls it was as well to take out some insurance. This came in the form of regular contact with a senior officer of the National Crime Authority, and my friend, Peter Vassallo in the ABCI.

There is a common paranoia about phone tapping in Australia. For the most part the fear is unfounded. There is an enormous amount of work involved in tapping telephones, whether it is done legally or illegally. The happy truth is that the great majority of us aren't nearly as worth the effort as we like to think. However, I know that on at least one occasion I have been 'legally' tapped. My friends advised this time I was being monitored the easier way, that is without the imprimatur of a warrant, so it was as well to be careful.

For many of the calls better kept private I would walk

down the road from the hotel to a small bank of public telephones. As I recall, when I entered the booth, a man in sensible shoes made his way into the adjoining booth.

Both officers, Peter in Canberra and the other in Sydney, were later questioned about my contact with them. An entry in my diary for February 23 mentions Peter Vassallo having been grilled for 3 hours. It was a stressful time for Peter, who seriously risked the loss of his career.

As it happens, on that same date there is a first mention of the *Four Corners* investigation by another compulsive diarist.

Sir Terence Lewis's growing concern about Four Corners's enquiries is reflected in a dozen separate entries in his work diary. The Lewis diary also records increasing contacts with his Assistant Commissioner and liaison officer to the National Crime Authority, Graeme Parker. The complaint from Queensland which prompted the interrogation came from Parker.

Assistant Commissioner Parker was also behind the interrogation of Jim Slade and other officers who were discovered to have had contact with *Four Corners*. There was a slight flurry of panic accompanying his pressing interest in our inquiries. The Parker panic, if anything, intensified my suspicion and later eliminated any surprise when his own high rank within Terry Lewis's unholy order of thieves was revealed.

Another important contact I made was with another man who would suffer because of my attention. John Stopford was a veteran of Brisbane's underworld. John had waded into the swamp of the prostitution and drug trade some years earlier. He had run an escort agency and formed a relationship with one of his girls. The girl was a heroin user.

As is common, John began using heroin himself. He followed another underworld convention and became a police informant. There is a tired inevitability to the story. He was bashed, thrown in gaol where he was labelled a 'dog', an informant, and bashed again.

To his considerable credit, John was now doing his best to break the pattern, to challenge the inevitable. When he left gaol, he skirted the swampland of old and made for the mangroves and sanctuary of Stradbroke Island. He had custody of a young son, Jay. John and Jay were very close.

John Stopford would not have rated a bold mention in any underworld *Who's Who*. He had never been a heavy criminal, he wasn't mean enough. But he had seen a great deal and was nagged by a need to tell his story. Earlier John had spoken at length with a Brisbane ABC reporter, Peter Cassuben. Peter taped the conversation and now, very generously, lent me the tapes.

I am not proud of what happened next. I listened to the tapes and was very impressed. I spoke to a good friend in the Australian Federal Police, Dave Moore. Dave was keen to hear the tapes and although I had no permission to do so, I passed them on. Dave was meant to listen alone and give them back to me but news of the tapes leaked out. Somewhere in the tapes was information which suggested some state police could have acted corruptly. The head of the AFP in Brisbane, stupidly, astonishingly, passed the information on to the state police. Assistant Commissioner Parker took possession of the tapes. I learned that the police Stopford named were told of the allegations.

It was clear John Stopford could help us a great deal. Moreover, he had shown a rare inclination to cooperate. Now, without even meeting him, I managed to put this valuable witness at risk. It was not a great start.

I made contact with John. It was decided it would be wiser to meet in Sydney, away from the pressing attention of the Queensland cops.

I don't think either of us will forget our first encounter. John was with his son. The meeting place was Taronga Park Zoo. Considering the fact that I had so neatly cast him into the lion's den, the choice was uncomfortably appropriate. The animals would hopefully entertain and distract Jay while John and I talked. I had no choice but to immediately reveal my own miserable indiscretion regarding the tapes. Stopford listened impassively. He had a face that was used to bad news. It was midweek. There weren't many people around. He started to look behind him as we kept on walking. I must have been somewhere near the rhinoceros enclosure when I asked John if he would give us an on camera interview. He was a little tight lipped when we left the zoo.

I also had to tell him in return we would give him our heartfelt thanks and little else. We were paying John's hotel bill and covered the cost of his air-fare but we could not pay him for his story.

Chequebook journalism is a common, unattractive feature of the profession. If you pay a witness for a story the evidence is automatically devalued, certainly in the eyes of the courts. The theory is that witnesses who work for reward might be encouraged to say anything. Even worse, they might be persuaded by a larger sum to later reverse their story. The media itself has an uneven view of the merits and demerits of chequebook journalism. There is a sensible argument that people should at least be reimbursed for their time, and there may be exceptional occasions when a larger sum is deserved.

The same game is played by police, who regularly reward informants (and sometimes keep a percentage for themselves). Some Queensland police would later insist we paid John Stopford this larger sum. They were not just hypocritical, they were wrong.

John would waver, and earnestly regret the decision many times, but at this time he agreed. We filmed the interview at Shaun's home, shooting late into the night.

Film programmes like *Four Corners* prefer natural locations, rather than the sterile doctor's waiting room-like atmosphere of the studio. We only very rarely record our interviews in the studio. To the despair of many a spouse, we are great offenders when it comes to bringing our work home. This time it was Shaun's turn to look nervously as the cameraman stretched the gluey gaffer tape across her newly painted walls, and clamped bulky camera lights to the architraves.

It was nearly midnight when the interview began. John detailed the so-called 'syndicate' which monopolised Queensland's brothel trade. He gave evidence of payments to police of what seemed at the time to be astronomical sums. The hundreds of thousands of dollars he nominated as being paid to select senior police as protection money later proved a conservative estimate.

It was a strong interview but it had to be checked, proved, supported. John Stopford appeared to me to be an honest man, but he was an honest man who had been a brothel keeper and heroin addict. The courts have little regard for such witnesses, which is often a problem. You don't find too many clergymen or justices of the peace who are expert witnesses on the brothel and drug trade.

Shaun and I returned to Brisbane. The schedule and the budget were beginning to stretch uncomfortably. Deb had to be left behind to continue work in Sydney.

The hotel staff greeted us kindly and we settled back into our familiar rooms at the Tower Mill Hotel, on a hill just above the city centre. I went a little bit mad in that hotel room. We were comfortable and well looked after but a photograph album of the family is no substitute for the real thing. The wallpaper would surround me, I would flick the television set on for company and then reach for the telephone and get back to work.

When it answered there was the invariable death rattle of many of the defeated honest cops who continued to tell me the exercise was pointless.

At a small social gathering I got into an argument with a fierce young Brisbane lawyer, Shane Herbert, who took a similarly defeatist position. I gritted my teeth and counterpunched as best I could. My argument was that you could not give in. There was a professional responsibility at least to try to expose as much of what was going on as possible. I was angry, partly because I believed what I was saying and was sick of all this clever, buttoned down cynicism. But I was also angry because I suspected Shane was at least half right. There was an excellent chance I would end up doing more harm than good.

The Brisbane papers continued to pimp themselves, carrying their expensive prostitution advertisements, along with stories about another prostitute found dead from a heroin overdose. At the same time politicians were trying to convince themselves and others there was no prostitution in the massage parlours and no drugs in the non-existent brothels.

In the corner pubs when the police gathered to gossip they would comfort one another with the fantasy that it was all right to take a little spending money from the SP bookies and the brothel keepers. You could not stamp out prostitution or gambling, they would tell each other. The best you can do is keep it under control and by having a few 'protected' operators, they were managing just that.

They would go on to insist that while prostitution and gambling were to be tolerated, under no circumstances would they condone and protect those scummy drug dealers.

But the drug and prostitution trades are inseparable ugly sisters. The brothel keepers knew what the police did not want to know. And that was once they managed to pay off the cops to be protected for minor crime, they were being handed a licence to graduate to more serious crime. Police could not arrest the criminals without arresting themselves.

The proposition that Sir Joh had stopped the devil at the border was laughable, and the self-delusion extremely wearing but it wasn't all painful. I found myself spending more and more time with the Federal Policeman, Dave Moore. Dave's wife Josie was also in the 'job', that is the Federal Police. They would cook me pasta, and let me pat their dog and trip over their young, inquisitive son. There was a quiet rule about not talking too much about work. In time you learn what constitutes help and what constitutes problems. When you recognise the latter you might ask advice but are wise to leave it there. It is unfair to trade on a friendship to a point where you ask a friend to take an unfair risk.

But even so, Dave was such a good friend and such an intensely decent man, he could not help but do just that. He and a few others began to watch out for Shaun, Debbie and me. It did not hurt for the Queensland police to know the Feds were alert to what was going on.

In time the watching game became ridiculous. On one occasion a fat man in an old brown Holden was noticed sitting outside the hotel. The licence number was traced to a 'Rent-a-Wreck' agency used by the Queensland Police Bureau of Criminal Intelligence. The whole business began seriously to get me down. I wasn't a criminal, I was a journalist — but I was being treated like a criminal, like an enemy. It is very depressing to recognise you are in enemy territory in your very own country.

What probably got me down most of all was the plight of the so-called 'working girls'. One night I found my way awkwardly into the 'Manhattan' nightclub. There was a flesh parade, and the scream of motorbikes crashing and burning on a large video monitor. There was the smell of beer and vomit and acres of males illuminated irregularly by the strobe lighting, looking alternatively shy, dangerous, lustful and drunk. The women stepped between them, near naked, holding ice buckets which the men stuffed with money. The brave among the spectators stretched and grabbed. The eyes of the women gleamed with hatred. Over the public address system an announcement was made that the lucky door prize could be redeemed in flesh at the brothel up the road.

When we filmed outside these brothels some of the young women, as thin as refugees, came outside wild-eyed and weary. They were not as angry as they were frightened we would scare off the clients and there would not be enough money to service their addiction.

The prostitutes made a great deal of money but kept less than 50 per cent. The drug dealers continued to prowl the brothel perimeters like hyenas. The few police who protected the trade were protected, in turn, by a few politicians. The public paid the policemen's wages and continued to re-elect the politicians. This was the natural order that could not be challenged.

Nigel Powell tried to challenge it when he worked as an officer of the Licensing Branch which policed the brothel and casino trade. He resigned from the force when he realised how dangerous it was to be honest.

When Police Minister Bill Gunn was quoted, early in 1987, as claiming there was no prostitution in the massage parlours, Powell was stung into action.

The former policeman wrote a letter to the *Courier Mail*, outlining his experiences in the Licensing Branch. The letter was lengthy, detailed and highly plausible. Powell not only exposed the nonsense of the no prostitution claim, he also revealed many of his concerns about police failing to touch the untouchables who controlled the prostitution industry.

Nigel was an excellent witness. He supported Stopford's story and he was credible, he would be believed. Nigel was subsisting as a university student, but he sought no compensation for his story. He just wanted it told and was disappointed the *Courier Mail* had held his letter for months, without making any apparent use of it.

Nigel was another who helped save my sanity. So too was the man who led us to him, Terry O'Gorman. Terry is a stocky, smiling, red-headed lawyer who belongs to one of Brisbane's most remarkable families. The O'Gorman brothers are well known in Brisbane. They all seem to work in the law, but in recent times something of a feud had developed between the police branch and the lawyer branch. What bound them however, was an Irish stubborness and a marvellous, uncompromising sense of Catholic justice.

Brisbane is small enough to be crowded with coincidence, and one such coincidence was that an O'Gorman had actually initiated Nigel Powell's entry to the Queensland Police Force. Years earlier, Powell came upon a man kicking a dog in the street. He intervened to help the dog, a fracas occurred and a policeman arrived. The policeman was one of the O'Gormans. Like Powell, he sided with the dog and then in later conversation suggested Powell, a former British Bobby, rejoin the force. Both men, and the incident, deserve a cherished place in Queensland history.

Shaun and Deb and I worked day and night, seven days a week for most of the three months. We spoke to hundreds of people, spreading the net wide and then sifting out the witnesses with the most useful information. I also did my best to bury myself in the history and culture of the Queensland Police Force.

We drove up to the Sunshine Coast to speak with the former Liberal Treasurer, Sir Thomas Hiley, who had uncovered the corruption of a former Police Commissioner, Frank Bischof.

When Bischof was confronted with evidence of large scale pay-offs from SP bookmakers he simply said, 'What do you want me to do?'. The government appeared non-plussed and came up with no better answer than a suggestion he resign.

It was another example of history missing an important opportunity to set a moral standard. When Bischof departed, he left the system which helped create him in good shape.

I read as much as I could about Bischof and learned as much as I could about a range of landmark cases drawn from recent Queensland history. There was the 'Whiskey Au Go Go' firebombing, the mysterious disappearance of the prostitute,

Simone Vogel, and the equally suspicious death of another prostitute, Shirley Briffman, who had tried to blow the whistle on police corruption.

But the case that captured most of my attention was the Herbert/Freir matter. Two policemen, Jack Herbert and Neal Freir, had been charged with attempting to bribe another policeman, Arthur Pitts, back in 1974. (Herbert and Freir were both later acquitted.)

The Commissioner at the time, Ray Whitrod, had soldiered hard against the crooks under his command and this was to be a make or break prosecution. There were two camps within the force engaged in bitter warfare. Whitrod and Pitts and many others, lined up against the likes of Herbert, Lewis and their so called rat-pack.

The successful prosecution of Herbert, in particular, would have been a significant victory for Whitrod. But he was defeated in a way that is telling of the treachery within police culture. The 'rat-pack' perceived a weakness — a tolerance of fabricated evidence—amongst some of the police who supported Whitrod. 'Verbals', were in all likelihood, generally acceptable to both camps, but outside the closed ranks of the police force, this was not well understood.

A secret tape recording was made of one of the police engaged in the prosecution of Herbert and Freir. The policeman was heard in the apparent process of inventing testimony. When it was produced in court the case collapsed, and so too did the Whitrod purge.

So the cops who took a quid and happily invented evidence, defeated the cops who would not take a quid but condoned the occasional 'verbal'. Whitrod resigned on November 16, 1976, soon after the completion of the case. On December 14, one of the chief rats he had struggled to hunt from the force, Terence Lewis, moved into his chair. It must have been an appalling time for the valiant Whitrod, but at the police club the rogue's gallery was jubilant.

I soaked all this in and much more. I did my best to understand Premier Sir Joh Bjelke Petersen's relationship with his new Commissioner. What was clear was Lewis, unlike Whitrod, would not be so resistant to his force becoming something of an extension of Sir Joh's National Party. There was some evidence that Terry had already answered the bidding of Joh in a way that would ensure enduring gratitude from the Premier.

All this research was obviously not going to end up on the screen. Colleagues in commercial television have criticised me for 'over researching' but it is a criticism I am happy to answer. I knew that the lawyers would be happy for the extra perspective and I also knew that I was developing an important understanding of the way the police behaved and were likely to react. This would prove crucial later when the endgame was played out.

Of the hundreds of people we spoke with, in the end, only seven were interviewed. Nigel Powell, the former Licensing Branch cop and police prosecutor, was one of the first. He told us what he knew and no more. There was also the interview with John Stopford and another with the former Mareeba detective, Ross Dickson. A young woman who worked in one of the illegal casinos and a man who worked in the male brothels appeared on camera but in silhouette. We could hear their words but not see their faces. Two more witnesses, a serving policeman and a prostitute wanted even greater anonymity. They were interviewed and then actors were recruited to repeat their words.

The practice of using actors as substitutes for actual witnesses is a last resort. I anticipated it would be seen as a weakness and attacked. I was right. 'What a lot of rubbish, more like soap opera than current affairs', was the inevitable response and I left myself wide open for it.

The rationalisation for using actors at the time was that the information was too important to abandon, simply because the medium of television made the telling of the story too difficult. Newspaper journalists make frequent use of unidentified sources without needing to apply any greater disguise than anonymity. Radio reporters can, with minimal difficulty, use sound distortion to throw a cloak over their witnesses.

We did not want to be defeated by our own lack of imagination so the technique was used, but used very carefully. A sound interview was recorded with the proper witness. A transcript of the interview was made and the tape then erased. The actors had to follow the words in the transcript with precision.

It is true the disguise meant these witnesses would not have to stand and be counted and this no doubt weakened their position. But there was every reason not to want to stand. The climate of intimidation in Queensland was cyclonic. Past whistleblowers had copped a merciless gale of abuse for their moment of public duty, so the reticence to stand and be counted was one I well understood.

Most of our witnesses, I am glad to say, had the courage to do just that. Besides, we were not relying on the seven witnesses alone. Each in turn illustrated an important feature of the corruption mosaic and each was connected to the other by a library of paper. One paper in particular was beautiful. Perfectly proportioned and so shining with facts it would draw the eye time and again. If journalists love a good sentence then investigative journalists obviously love a good document.

The document was a real estate contract showing the exchange of a property from the possession of Gerry Bellino and Vic Conte into the hands of a man known as Jack Reginald Herbert, the very same man who had defeated a corruption charge back in 1976.

Herbert, like Powell, was a former British policeman who went on to serve with the Queensland Licensing Branch, but there the similarity ended. Jack Herbert would later candidly admit he was a liar and a thief, and by all accounts well gifted in both areas. Most corrupt police appear to prefer to sell out for small sums, sometimes through lack of imagination but more often because they are nervous about accumulating too many unexplainable assets. Herbert, in contrast, was positively entrepreneurial. By his own estimate he received $1.1 million in graft payments between 1979 and 1987.

For months now his name had kept emerging in conversations with that stumbling legion of demoralised former colleagues. After the 1976 corruption trial he left the force claiming there was nothing but a meagre pension to sustain himself and his wife Peg.

A decade later, however, Herbert was known to be doing very well. We also knew that Jack and Peg Herbert were close to the Police Commissioner, Sir Terence Lewis and his wife, Hazel. We could see that the former British bobby was a likely nexus between the criminals outside the force and the criminals inside the force.

Herbert was known to be a meticulous man and the very neatly tailored style of the corruption system had a certain Herbert cut to it. Corruption in the south is very much the proverbial can of worms. It is random, disorganised and maddeningly difficult to trace. Jack Herbert's 'joke' as he called it was carefully organised so that the bulk of the graft flowed to the top. If 'the joke' was the system, then the joker in the so-called rat pack was Herbert himself. I sensed that Herbert was important and so the inquiry shifted focus in his direction.

Deb Whitmont's titles searches revealed that in the decade since he left the force Herbert had amassed more than a million dollars worth of property. That piece of paper I fell in love with linked Jack Herbert to Gerry Bellino and Vic Conte through a property purchase. Herbert bought a Bowen Hills house for a stated figure no greater than that paid by Conte and Bellino some years earlier.

It was not 'smoking gun' evidence on its own, but it did help complete the picture. And by now the business of completing the picture and getting home was a serious preoccupation. I am fond of sunny Queensland but the fondness was fading and although I wasn't fully aware of it at the time, I was beginning to swim a little too far beyond the flags.

The small band of troublemakers from *Four Corners* now threatened a multi-million dollar illicit industry and the captains of enterprise were concerned.

I have said before that the risks of investigative journalism are overstated. I have never been bashed or beaten or shot at. But there are times when you can't help but take chances in order to get a little closer to the truth. Any person who takes their work seriously is most likely prepared to take sensible, professional 'risks'. What I should also point out is the risks were not just mine to take. When the research phase wound up and the filming began cameraman Chris Doig and sound recordist Guntis Sics flew up to join Shaun, Debbie and me.

The closest any of us came to physical danger was on a weekend, midway through March 1987. My diary entry for the Saturday records a meeting in the ABC carpark with a cop. 'Good man, very bright and clever survival techniques. Self-imposed blindness.' Later, while driving with the crew, 'Spot three surveillance cars. Why don't they look for crooks?'. Then there is mention of a visit late that evening to an illegal casino above 'The Roxy', another Valley nightclub run by Tony Bellino. 'Manage to get in . . . with Nigel. Manager talks, no doubt reassured by presence of policeman (ex).'

While the gambling went on behind me, the manager chatted freely, complaining about a feud between Tony Bellino and his brother Gerry, who ran the nightclub and casino across the road.

My presence in that room presented another moral dilemma. If I was to confess my proper identity it is likely I would have been quickly shown the door. On the other hand it would have been improper and indefensible to presume a false identity. We are not characters drawn from detective thrillers, but serious journalists who can never pretend to be anything else.

When the manager did at last bother to ask me what was my profession, Nigel swiftly changed the subject and spared us all the embarrassment. The conversation continued along another tack for some minutes. The manager invited Nigel and I to stay and play but we declined. Meanwhile the film crew was shooting outside.

We had sensibly, and I think for the first time ever, hired a bodyguard. The bodyguard was instructed to prevent anyone getting hurt and to act as a shield for any violence when we filmed outside these clubs and brothels. We were glad of his presence.

About midnight Nigel and I left the casino and I returned to the hotel to sleep. The crew remained to do a little more filming while Shaun and the bodyguard stood by. As our camera recorded, Tony Bellino, irritated by our constant presence, snapped and ordered his small conga line of hoods to 'smash his camera, and his face too'. Cameraman Chris Doig and sound recordist Guntis Sics retreated while our minder moved to shield them from the advance of the toughs.

He was one and they were three. One mandrill-like minder stepped around the shield, grabbed the camera and smashed it to the street in full view of the emerging nightclub crowd.

Shaun and the crew, still shaken, appeared at my room at 2 a.m. to tell me about it. We went to the Valley police station to report the incident. The irony did not escape us.

Soon after dawn I was woken again, by a telephone call from a friendly policeman. He had someone he thought I should meet. He told me to dress quickly and run down the road to a familiar phone booth, beyond the presumed watching eyes of other police. Minutes later, out of breath, I was there. A car sped into view, a door flung open and I was away.

Conventional anti-surveillance procedures aren't as tidy as they sound. I was flung around in the back seat. My notebook is an abstract of a madly streaking pen, even more illegible than usual. It was hurled and jolted across the page as we jumped a median strip and sped across a golf course in one police car to avoid the attention of another. It was a night and day of ironies.

The most serious danger was one I knew nothing about at the time. Many months later, on the day of the Brisbane Rugby League Grand Final my brother was introduced to a Brisbane undercover detective by a former Australian Rugby League captain, Tom Raudonikas. The policeman was with my brother the entire day, at the end of which he said there was something to confess. The policeman said he had been party to a plot to set me up on a child molesting charge.

The plan was neat, simple and ruthless. I would have been telephoned and told an important witness wanted to see me at a Valley motel. There I would be arrested and 'verballed'. Police would claim I had admitted to a union with a 14-year-old male prostitute.

The prospect of me taking the risk and attending the meeting on my own was real enough. On more than one occasion I had followed up similiar opportunities but I would be much more careful in the future.

I soon realised how damaging this would have been. The stigma associated with such an offence like this could well have destroyed the credibility of our work and my own reputation. And I was saved apparently by nothing more than circumstance and good luck. The undercover cop told Roy he was called to Cairns to give evidence in a trial and by the time he came back to Brisbane I had returned to Sydney.

The undercover cop while in his confessional mood, told Roy that he mentioned this because he understood that the cops were not finished with me yet and I should be warned.

We had flown back to Sydney on Friday March 27. There was a weekend at home, a visit to see my father and then back to the office and the end of the work most often despised, the script. A colleague, Mark Colvin, has a good description of the process of starting a script. He says it is like standing on the edge of a cold swimming pool.

The typewriter glared at me, I glared back and the script began to appear. The ABC lawyers gathered around the table outside to prod and punish. Facing the child molesting charge might have been easier.

The Head of the ABC Legal Department is Bruce Donald. Bruce could make a fortune in private enterprise but has instead chosen to protect a public fortune in defamation payments. He is strict, but sensibly so.

Bruce wanted to know the basis for every assertion in the programme and he was punctilious about it. He questioned persistently, once asking me how I actually knew a certain brothel was a brothel. Had I attended it myself? I snapped at Bruce, telling him I had not taken the research that far but knew of witnesses who could speak of what went on behind the glaring red light.

As it happened it was a fair enough question, but I was in no mood to be punished even by a friend. The process was not pleasant but as ever, I have to grudgingly admit, it was worthwhile. It is better for the information to survive punishment in the privacy of the *Four Corners* office than be found wanting in a public court.

When a report is defamatory, the publisher will frequently seek independent analysis of the risks involved. So the inquisition was not to be conducted by Bruce alone. He brought in one of Sydney's sharpest defamation lawyers, Michael Sexton.

Michael is tall, slim and neat in both appearance and vocabulary. The torture was resumed with my new interrogator slipping easily into the role of devil's advocate. Every sentence of the script was subject to scrupulous punishment and as usual I became petulant and over-defensive.

There is an important lesson here too, which as usual was learnt the hard way. Michael and I travelled back up to Queensland to re-interview a key witness. He wanted to secure a signed statement. The statement would not be needed for the broadcast but was of value if we were later challenged in court.

On the plane I discovered there was more to my companion beyond the talent for ruthless cross-examination I had witnessed so far. My steely-eyed interrogator was gentle and amusing, a human being as well as a lawyer. I came to realise while sitting beside him that the harsh questioning was not personal. He was attacking the proposition and not the person. This is something every witness should know and every lawyer should make as clear as Michael managed to do.

When we returned from Queensland with the statement in hand, the programme was at last ready for transmission. It did not tell all the story just as I have not told it all now. We had uncovered a great deal of evidence about the drug trade in Queensland but there was not the time to improve the information to a point where we could get it to air. There was too much to say and too many reasons why we could not say it all. But we had managed to say enough.

However, I was far from optimistic. In my three months in Queensland I had allowed myself one well-worn joke. I had seen the crooked police chewing on the gristle of corruption in the Chinese restaurants which flanked Police Headquarters. I had seen the Australian Federal Police and the National Crime Authority look the other way or give up. My only hope was that if the AFP would not get them and the NCA could not get them, then the MSG might.

I had not counted on Tony Fitzgerald. That is another story. The ultimate reforms in Queensland can be attributed more to a rare triumph of the law than a victory for journalism.

I am grateful for the presence of the lawyers who drove that inquiry because they saw a once-only chance. Fitzgerald and Gary Crook and Ralph Devlin and Bob Mulholland also managed to drive themselves beyond the point of exhaustion. I wish I had met them earlier.

Lawyers and journalists, like Serbs and Croats, mostly act as if there is no choice but to exist as natural enemies. This time, much to my genuine surprise, the media–law alliance proved a profitable one. The main problem for me was that I was used to Sydney lawyers.

In 'Cynical City' principle often takes second place to pragmatism. I can remember a Sydney lawyer telling me before the Street Royal Commission that even though he had information helpful to our case there was no sense in him presenting it because he had a house at St Ives. The house at St Ives was partly paid for by lucrative government work so there was clearly no sense in taking a chunk out of the hand that feeds.

One reason the Government has not properly taken on the police in NSW in the way they should have decades ago, is that too many Sydney lawyers have gone along with a bit too much. Police are an integral part of the justice system and the system, despite many conspicuous blunders, is loath to admit fault.

The quiet rule is: it is better to pretend the system is pure so we can all maintain our faith. It is the same thinking that preserves the police brotherhood. It is the same nonsense that discourages serious self-examination.

On too many occasions the wisdom of the courts has proved little match for the cunning of the police. Such was the fate of the 1963 National Hotel Royal Commission in Queensland.

In the last half of this century most of our states have seen some form of judicial inquiry into allegations of public corruption. The results rarely left the public with an assurance that corruption had been torn out by the roots and left to wither.

The National Hotels Inquiry shared much of the plot of the Fitzgerald Inquiry. There were the same suspicions of bent cops, sly grog and organised prostitution. There was also the identical suspicion that the chief protector was the top cop, the later disgraced Commissioner, Frank Bischof. As it happened Bischof had a small team of loyal protégés, one of whom was Detective Senior Constable Terence Lewis.

Constable Lewis was one of the many officers to give evidence before the inquiry. The Royal Commissioner, Justice Harry Gibbs, found no evidence of organised prostitution and little fault with the police. The finding was not believed by a great many police and probably a great many members of the Queensland public.

As it turned out it was not believed by a great many Queensland lawyers either. Twenty-four years later members of the Brisbane legal community were still smarting and twitching under their white wigs at the prospect that the wool in those wigs had been pulled over their eyes. The National Hotel Inquiry was seen as a lost opportunity. The reprieve gave the crooks time to strengthen their power base and refine the systems that ensured promotion from within and profits from without. Lawyers watching from the wings began to sense they were dealing with an even more dangerous evil. If not aware of the large scale corruption payments they had some idea of the large scale practice of peddling corrupt evidence.

The lawyers were angry and I was to see just how angry when I arrived in Brisbane just after the programme was broadcast.

'The Moonlight State' went to air the day after Mother's Day, May 11, 1987. On the following day, according to my diary, I was 'woken by my own blood pressure'. That day the Queensland Government announced a thorough inquiry was to be conducted and within a week I was summoned back to Queensland.

A lawyer spotted me as I walked out of a lift in the Inns of

Court building and pushed me against a wall. He glared into my eyes and told me that if I was bullshitting about the allegations in my programme I would be run out of town — not by the cops but by the lawyers. This was the first hint that the motivation was there to get this one right.

To my pleasant surprise the lawyers were well motivated. But finding the skills to investigate the investigators was another matter. The lawyers had been offered, and accepted, a team of Queensland police to assist the inquiry. It was not a good start. It was hard not to see police investigators showing greater loyalty to their own. It was even harder to imagine witnesses with damaging evidence about police happily cooperating with other members of the brotherhood. I also pointed out that a favourite means of nobbling inquiries in the south had been through the appointment of the investigating police.

We reached a compromise. Initially at least, the witnesses I would pass on would be seen by the lawyers only. This suited the witnesses and gave the lawyers time to evaluate the merit of the assigned police.

A first meeting between two of the brothel workers and the lawyers is well remembered and I suspect, significant. The women arrived well dressed and well spoken. One was a moonlighting high school teacher. Both had worked as part-time receptionists in a massage parlour and both were the types of people lawyers love. They were presentable witnesses.

The two women explained point by point the way the industry worked and how the regular payments to police were made. They identified the present head of the Licensing Branch, Allen Bulger, as one who was receiving money. The room was very quiet as they spoke but somewhere during it all I think I heard the rustle of disappearing innocence.

Four Corners had lost its own innocence about public inquiries years earlier. Having anticipated a whitewash we made sure we arrived in Queensland equipped with a formula that would help strip the whitewash away. We learned the value of keeping some information in reserve. If the government is to claim that after exhaustive investigation it can find no evidence of public corruption it is handy to be able to produce the very information it says does not exist.

We had good information on Inspector Bulger and another Licensing Branch cop, Senior Sergeant Harry Burgess. I resisted naming them in the programme mainly because I wanted to attack the institution rather than the individuals. I believed that had we named Bulger and Burgess they might have been ritually slaughtered and the system let off the hook. The police force is often a heartless place. They talk about the sanctity of the brotherhood right up to the moment of sacrifice. It happens all the time yet astonishingly the brotherhood inevitably endures.

The information about Burgess and Bulger and a range of more senior police was a useful starting point for the Fitzgerald investigators. I think some of the best work *Four Corners* managed was after 'The Moonlight State' went to air. It is to the credit of the ABC that energy and resources were diverted to something that, although to the public benefit, was never going to be broadcast.

In the first days of the inquiry I drove between Brisbane and the Gold Coast with one of the Fitzgerald lawyers, introducing a range of witnesses, listening to their stories again and helping gain their confidence. Over the next weeks we were able to make contact with a long list of witnesses and put most of them in touch with the lawyers. We also passed on copious notes that helped explain and background the substantial allegations.

Because the ABC was given standing before the inquiry we were able to introduce witnesses and evidence that would otherwise have been unavailable. By now the ABC had won a level of trust from many of the witnesses that could not be directly deposited with Fitzgerald but could be transferred through our account.

Most of the meetings occurred 'in camera'. A great many of the witnesses feared public exposure not just for the sake of personal survival but for reasons as simple and obvious as worrying what their neighbours might think. A former sex worker who now headed the local marching girls association had an understandable reluctance to have her past put on parade.

For these reasons the early stages of these large public inquiries require a lot of good 'in camera' work. When the information bank grows there is a better chance the right witnesses will be called and even more important, the right questions will be asked.

Fitzgerald also conducted the public side of the inquiry with remarkable skill. Getting the balance right between what is discovered and what is disclosed is an impossible business. If Fitzgerald had allowed himself to be chained to the strictest interpretation of the laws of evidence, if he had not protected some of his key witnesses, I doubt very much that it would have worked nearly so well.

When the Fitzgerald Inquiry began the crooked cops were concerned, but they did not believe they were seriously threatened. They had outwitted the lawyers before and had no reason to believe they would not do it again. They told each other that as long as they all kept their mouths shut Fitzgerald would never breach the line of police brotherhood.

Fitzgerald appeared to take the view that he should listen to everything, in the way that ordinary members of the public listen to everything when they make an assessment of a situation, but give weight to the first-hand evidence. In doing so, much more evidence was brought forward, the case against the police gained strength, and the ranks of brotherhood began to crumble.

There is a risk that when an inquiry maintains a brave public face impure information and unfair allegations are likely to be aired. There were occasional blunders. I cringed at times at the thought that the whole tawdry affair was being turned into a soap opera.

But I came to see that through the tabloid press fascination with bent cops, free booze and loose women, Queensland was waking up. The other side of the gullibility that allowed Sir Joh and Sir Terence to flourish was a refreshing lack of cynicism. When the problem was identified, the Queensland public responded in a way that you might not expect in the south.

At the time of writing, four years later, the prosecutions continue, more than 120 so far. Sir Terence was sentenced to fourteen years gaol. Sir Joh was tried for perjury but the case was finally dropped after the jury failed to reach a verdict. Four other ministers, including the former Special Branch cop, Don Lane, have been gaoled for rorting expenses. Allen Bulger was given a twelve-year sentence and another Licensing Branch senior sergeant, Noel Kelly, five years.

The police who had all insisted they would never protect the drug trade should take note that the chief beneficiary of their protection, brothel king Hector Hapeta, is now serving a lengthy sentence for heroin trafficking. The other brothel and casino kings, Gerry Bellino and Vic Conte, were also gaoled and the list goes on.

Others, like Sergeant Harry Burgess, Assistant Commissioner Graeme Parker and the main architect of 'the joke', Jack Herbert, received indemnities from prosecution in exchange for breaking ranks with the brotherhood. There is continued grumbling about whether the likes of Herbert, Parker and Burgess have been properly punished for their public disloyalty and greed.

I have no idea whether all have been properly punished. But the taxman at least has ensured that the wages of sin have been withdrawn. Those with a bent for punishment might also take comfort in the knowledge that the informants are all outcasts to the brotherhood. I doubt if any of them would believe there is profit in deceit.

Some credit is also due. The next time there is an important public inquiry others might not feel so cautious about breaking the ranks of brotherhood. Whatever the motives of Herbert and company, their decision to accept the indemnities means that in future, telling the truth could be seen as a better option than the usual one of maintaining the fiction.

Of course there is also a list of people who have been punished unfairly by 'The Moonlight State' and the Fitzgerald Inquiry. Some of them are well known to me.

The witnesses we encouraged to participate have mixed views on the benefits of having done so.

Nigel Powell has been cast into a career no-man's land. He has tried tertiary study, journalism, the law and even a tilt at politics. But society still seems to have a little trouble finding a proper vocation for acute principle.

John Stopford has not been in touch since the Fitzgerald Inquiry gained momentum. I doubt that he would take pride in his role in the programme or his place in history.

Peter Vassallo left the police force after stress-induced heart trouble. He now has a good job in private enterprise and although I know he is still sometimes persecuted by his former brethren he does his best to keep this from me and makes no complaints at all.

Dave and Josie Moore have also had to duck some abuse for the considerable support they gave to me. The police forces of Australia could do with a lot more Moores.

Jim Slade equally suffers because he dared to talk to a bastard from the media. His unsinkable good nature, as always, transcends the villainy. Jim continues to be a natural cop. His wife Chris continues to be a marvellous moral ally. It is a wonderful thing that they were not corrupted. But at the time of writing, I am sad to say, the natural cop is talking of giving up his career in the Queensland Police Force and taking his labour elsewhere.

Happily, at least one of the helpers appears to have been

rewarded. I can now reveal that the unnamed police officer interviewed in the programme was another police prosecutor, Garry Hannighan. Garry has since been well placed in the watchtower, having won a job as secretary to the new Police Minister.

I will also say some words about another confederate in the enterprise, Phil Dickie. It is widely believed that *Four Corners* followed up Dickie's *Courier Mail* report on the Brisbane brothel scene. This is not the case.

In Dickie's book he says our first contact with Jim Slade was in February 1987, after his first report. In truth I first spoke to Slade five months earlier, on September 27, 1986, the day my mother died. The Slade report, an important indicator of organised crime in Queensland, occupies some space in Dickie's book. He received the report from me **after** 'The Moonlight State' went to air.

By this stage I was a little disenchanted with my confederate. Sources I had worked hard to cultivate and protect, were being approached by Dickie, after he learned of them though mutual contacts.

When he appeared outside my office in Sydney after our programme was broadcast, seeking legal backup for the reports he had already published, I was in no mood to help. Later, back in Queensland, a good friend and fellow troublemaker, Quentin Dempster, sensibly counselled me to subdue my anger and jealousy, and pass on some of our research to Dickie. He thought it was to Queensland's benefit that the *Courier Mail* remain on the side of the angels.

Quentin was right. It is good to see the *Courier Mail* encouraging and rewarding investigative journalism at last. I had every reason to doubt that the *Courier Mail* would have published Dickie's later reports on corruption in the Brisbane Valley, if they had not known *Four Corners* was about to broadcast a similar story.

Still, in the end, it was better that we ultimately cooperated with one another, rather then set about tearing each other to bits.

In the years following there has been strident claim and counter claim about who can legitimately grab the credit for triggering the Fitzgerald Inquiry.

Neither camp can be as objective as Tony Fitzgerald who had this to say:

'During December and January 1987, the *Courier Mail* newspaper published a series of articles concerning vice and police inactivity which were written by a young journalist, Mr Philip John Dickie.

'There was nothing particularly unusual about this. Similar controversies had surfaced and subsided from time to time for many years. The spokesman for the Police Department routinely ground out stereotyped denials and hit back at critics.

'... However, on 11 May 1987, the Australian Broadcasting Corporation's *Four Corners* programme telecast 'The Moonlight State', a television documentary compiled by another investigative journalist, Mr Christopher Masters. Events which had been filmed raised the possibility that the Police Force was lying or incompetent or both.

'... On the day following 'The Moonlight State' telecast, the Acting Premier, Gunn, announced there would be an inquiry.'

For Shaun and Debbie and me, it took some time to start feeling good about the experience. Making the programme was exhausting and demoralising for us all. I know I seriously considered giving journalism away because I thought no work should be this difficult. And there was always the terrifying concern that the public did not want to know anyway. There was always the unnerving proposition that Mum's confidence that basic human decency would triumph was all serene self-delusion.

I can identify the first moment when I began to feel our

work might have been worthwhile. In December 1987, while on a bushwalk with my family in the Binna-Burra National Park, in Southern Queensland, a woman walked purposely towards me. As she passed on that remote bush track, she said, in a matter of fact way: 'thank you for what you did for Queensland'.

By then the Fitzgerald Inquiry was well under way. The inquiry succeeded so well, I believe, largely because of the skill and unusual dedication of the Fitzgerald team. But there was some luck too. Had Sir Joh Bjelke-Petersen not been distracted at the time by his campaign to enter Federal politics, there is a possibility at least that Fitzgerald might not have been allowed to gain such momentum. If there had not been some jostling for power by some of Joh's pretenders, the National Party itself might not have been so supportive of Fitzgerald.

But I should not be too cynical. Sir Joh's Deputy Premier, Bill Gunn, and the successive Premier, Mike Ahern, stood by the inquiry, even when it became clear that they had commissioned a report that would virtually guarantee their own political demise.

I think 'The Moonlight State' worked too. Our programme succeeded because it was strong and it was accurate. I would have to say there was also a probably fortuitous choice of subject matter. Journalists had proved public corruption in Queensland in the past. But perhaps Queenslanders then were not so disturbed by the idea of politicians gaining commercial advantage because of their elected position. It was seen, I suspect, not so much a sin but a sinecure — a privilege of office.

But the exposition of that Bangkok flesh trade in the Brisbane Valley was something else. In Sir Joh's moral heartland, such brazen ungodliness could never be forgiven. Another important reason that helps explain the programme's success, is that it was believed; and it was believed because it was fair. The public has acute sensitivity to even the most subtle twist and imbalance in an argument. I had always known it was important to be fair. Now I could see that fairness was a strength.

4

'FRENCH CONNECTIONS'

Investigative journalism, I am glad to say, isn't always miserably difficult. The thrill of discovery is hard to beat. When you combine this with the fun of film-making you have to quietly admit the job is not so bad after all.

What other job allows you to enter the homes of complete strangers and, with the barest hesitation, ask them the most penetrating questions? It is amazing, but the fact is that they mostly answer. Furthermore, there can't be many jobs where personal creativity is encouraged and rewarded.

There is one story I worked on that was made in heaven. There was nothing unpleasant about the experience except the origin of the story, a tragedy. And that in itself is telling of our profession.

The tragedy was the death by drowning of a Portuguese photographer, Fernando Pereira. Pereira was killed when two bombs sank the Greenpeace ship *Rainbow Warrior* in Auckland, New Zealand on July 10, 1985.

I loved the *Rainbow Warrior* story and I suppose that makes me a parasite, but I won't waste time apologising. Journalism had a worthy role to play in exposing the French public service terrorists. I am glad Peter Manning sent us there.

Five days earlier I had farewelled our executive producer, Jonathan Holmes, at a party at Lane Cove, Sydney. We thought it Jonathan's best farewell party so far (he agonised for some time about leaving) and hoped it would not be the last. It was not.

Jonathan's natural successor was Peter Manning. Peter had worked fractiously as Jonathan's associate producer for a year or so. Peter was a bit like the Paul Keating of current affairs. Being second-in-charge did nothing for his temperament or our peace of mind. We were all a touch relieved when he finally moved into the corner office.

I was between stories at the time. A promised tale of corruption in local government in Queensland faltered and was swiftly abandoned. Then an air strike stranded me so I used up a week or so of valuable research time with nothing to show for it.

We like to think these detailed investigations are the result of meticulous planning. But random circumstance can be just as important. If everything had gone to plan *Four Corners* would have had no reporter available when the *Rainbow Warrior* was sabotaged. Peter Manning would not have assigned me the story. The whole remarkable affair might have been consigned to the vortex of a million untold stories.

There are considerable differences between the objectives of daily and weekly current affairs programmes. In daily current affairs, news sense is tuned to the breaking stories. Reporters develop skills in anticipating the story of the day and reacting swiftly when it breaks.

In weekly current affairs programmes, news sense is keyed towards the future, and for that matter the unknown. The skills developed are more to do with anticipating what will be an important story one month ahead of an initial and often abstract concept. Workers in weekly current affairs lack practice in reactive journalism. While our over-the-horizon radar remains comfortably vigilant there is a good chance we will miss the story that breaks on our doorstep because the local lookout is fast asleep.

This is what made the report on the *Rainbow Warrior* bombing all the more unusual. It combined reactive journalism with our more usual slow-fuse approach to the work.

When news of the bombing reached me I was giving a speech to a roomful of information officers from the Indonesian Government. The news made little impact on me, but this was not the case with Peter Manning. His years before the typewriter had given him greater ability to anticipate important stories.

The bombing did not arouse such intense interest in the beginning as it would much later. There was no clue at first that the French were involved. Most speculation put it down to the work of a lone madman. But Manning thought otherwise. Terrorism is not often seen in the South Pacific and Greenpeace seemed an unlikely victim. He sniffed the makings of an unusual yarn.

Bruce Belsham was asked to produce the story. Bruce is an Aucklander so was pleased at the prospect of a homecoming. The New Zealanders are said to be a well-balanced lot, with a chip on both shoulders. Bruce had an even, affable personality without a trace of rancour. His local knowledge would be invaluable and he was a good companion. He took no notice of my early attempts to torment him with my limited range of New Zealand jokes.

For the early stages of a story a researcher is normally assigned, but on this occasion Bruce and I would work as a two-man team. Getting comfortable with a team approach is often the first problem to conquer for journalists transferring from print or radio. They are used to herding their story towards the publication gate all on their own. But in television nobody has ever made a good report alone. Film-making is a corporate creative medium. It works best when we all work congenially together, snatching and improving each other's ideas. Bruce was the producer and I was the reporter but essentially we were two journalists working indivisibly.

The first step was for Bruce to make a few phone calls to New Zealand while I headed to the esteemed *Four Corners* library for the newspaper clippings file on the New Zealand economy. Peter Manning was, somewhat characteristically, backing a long shot in sending us off in the wake of the *Rainbow Warrior*. Our fallback story was to be on the New Zealand economy. When we boarded the Qantas flight on July 13, this seemed the more likely option.

I read the New Zealand economy file on the plane and began to sweat a little at the prospect of having to fake an interest in finance journalism.

When we got off the plane we were greeted by a memorable scene. A man who had evidently been away for some time was happily, noisily drunk. In the busy airport reception area he greeted his wife and children with gusto and passion. Alcohol and relief from loneliness brought on a marvellous indifference to his countrymen's reserve in public places. We drove off through the rain, and in the half light, on the highway, I saw him stopped, on his knees with the car boot open, pulling the gifts from suitcases he had opened on the road. He could not wait.

The first day away is the worst day for melancholy. The scene, inexplicably, improved my mood.

Bruce and I were booked into the Sheraton Hotel. This was unaccustomed luxury and beyond the reach of our modest public service stipend. We found another, cheaper hotel, but not before making our way down to Marsden Wharf where the *Rainbow Warrior* lay dead in the water.

For the following day, Sunday July 14, my diary records we spoke to the *Rainbow Warrior* captain. I must have got a hint of something. 'A story there', it says. But I was still obviously having two bob each way, because that evening it has me talking with a New Zealand businessman about the economy.

The next day we visited the Greenpeace office. Someone was heating lunch on a single burner kerosene stove. There were bicycles in the hallway. The Greenpeace staff were sad, pale and peaceable, hardly the conventional targets of terrorism. Steven Sawyer, one of the Greenpeace directors, gave us some time. Steven was from the United States. The *Rainbow Warrior* had recently sailed from the Marshall Islands near the old US Atomic testing range. While in the islands Greenpeace helped the locals protest about nuclear contamination and the continued US military presence. Sawyer was sure the intervention would have angered Washington. He was confident the US Central Intelligence Agency was more than capable of swift, merciless retribution. This did not seem so likely to me but even so I began to sense that the *Rainbow Warrior* was unlikely to have been the victim of a lone madman.

From the way the investigation was being mobilised you could feel that this was important. At Police Headquarters there was the static electricity of excitement in the corridors. Bruce and I were forced to wait impatiently in the public reception area. While we were there a drunk lurched towards the counter and badgered the receptionist, babbling incoherently. The young Maori policeman handled the drunk with patience and courtesy, more than I could ever have mustered. I began to like the New Zealand police.

The investigation was headed by an expatriate Scotsman, Superintendent Alan Galbraith. Galbraith was so parsimonious with information, the local journalists called him 'Lockjaw'. He told me nothing but I held no grudge. I was treated with the same courtesy as the drunk.

They had an important, sensitive inquiry which might not be helped by the size twelve footprints of the media. Besides, it was going to be more fun finding out by ourselves.

The local media knew they had a good story. There was energetic competition. When we opened the paper the next day we found that a couple travelling with false Swiss passports had been detained. Once again random circumstance had figured in the arrest of the couple, who called themselves Alain and Sophie Turenge.

We did not know it at the time but a local vigilante committee was watching Auckland harbour on the night of the bombing. They had been bothered by pilferage from the boats moored in the harbour. The watchers saw an inflatable French 'Zodiac' dinghy come ashore. They saw a campervan drive to the scene, and were suspicious enough to make a note of the number plate of the van before it departed. This was extraordinary good fortune for the police and bad luck for the Turenges. Police detained the couple when they returned the van.

By now a few French clues bubbled to the surface but the conventional wisdom among journalists and some of the people in Greenpeace was that the French government was unlikely to have had direct involvement in the bombing. It was just too obvious. The Turenges, it was presumed, were mercenaries who were now being disowned by an unknown employer. We also learned that police were asking questions about a French yacht, the *Ouvea*, which had left the North Island of New Zealand and was now at Norfolk Island.

That evening I struggled with an antique telephone, making numerous calls to the island. I reached a friend who had once taught school on Norfolk Island and she gave me a list of names of locals who might help. I phoned them all. It was exciting work. I began to get a picture of how seriously the New Zealand police were treating the French connection. They had flown to the island, questioned the sailors and conducted a forensic examination of the yacht. My last call told me the *Ouvea* had just sailed for Noumea, the capital of France's colonial possession, New Caledonia.

I stuffed the New Zealand economy file in the bottom of my suitcase. Bruce made plans to head for New Caledonia. We checked the airline schedules and found that there was plenty of time to arrive well ahead of the slow-moving yacht.

The next morning we were up early to call the office, organise the flights and make a quick trip to Whangarei. The

North Island seaport is a few hours drive from Auckland. It was from there that the *Ouvea* had sailed a week or so earlier.

We questioned some people who lived near where the *Ouvea* was moored. They remembered the unusually neat French sailors well. One thought they had a certain military bearing. Bruce and I separated. He went doorknocking at the rental car agencies. I checked at the Port Authority and the Customs Office.

I was there for about half an hour, and I left with a spring in my step. One of the customs officers was rude and grumpy and told me to piss off. Another man, perhaps offended by his porcine colleague, presented me with a precious clue. The *Ouvea*, I learned, had made an initial illegal entry to New Zealand in the remote northern Parengarenga Harbour. It had thereby evaded initial customs inspection.

I could not wait to tell Bruce. I found him in one of the back streets rushing towards me equally bright-eyed. Bruce had been chatting with the local 'Avis' agent and was now equipped with a long list of all the vehicles the French sailors rented and all the distances covered.

If the French had hoped to remain inconspicuous they had managed a hopeless job of it. We had little trouble building a detailed portrait of the movements of the four saboteurs. Whangarei was alive with gossip. Xavier, Raymond, Jean-Michel and Eric had been eager consumers of all that the seaside community had to offer. Some gentle womenfolk extended considerable hospitality. The French had been charming enough to encourage them to stay for breakfast and gauche enough to boast about it afterwards. Bruce and I flew out of New Zealand wondering whether this was a current affairs story or a comedy.

We stopped at Sydney airport to collect the film crew and change planes for Noumea.

At the time of writing, *Four Corners* continues to prefer the use of film over videotape. The quality of footage shot on tape has for a long time been unequal to the texture and range of vision drawn from the film camera.

The gap has now been closed to a degree where tape footage shot can often be mistaken for good film footage. The most obvious argument for using tape is that it eliminates the expense and delay of processing the footage.

Even so, *Four Corners* argument for continuing to shoot on film is a stronger one, mainly because of the question of duration.

The telling advantage of film appears at the editing stage. When a report is compiled the vision will be juggled and rearranged over and over again. The longer the report the more the changes.

Film has a similiar technological advantage to the advantage the word processor has over the typewriter. With film you can insert a section without having to re-edit the entire report and with every new generation there is a general loss of quality.

For daily current affairs where the reports are brief, the changes are likely to be few and speed is imperative, tape is a clear winner. For reports of twenty minutes or more that are not turned around on the same day, film appears to have the edge.

When the film crew arrives they bring with them an extra burden to the budget. Air travel, accommodation and expenses suddenly double so there is a natural obligation to make use of them. But I have also learned that rushing off and filming before you are completely ready is false economy.

Once in Noumea, Bruce and I gathered up a few more scraps of information about *Ouvea* and its crew, and I headed back to the hotel to prepare a shooting script. Our film crew was given the afternoon off. As far as I can remember they did not complain very much.

The best advice I can give any prospective current affairs journalist is to take the step of preparing the script early. The advice is mostly ignored. From outside the industry there is frequent criticism of journalists making up their minds before they even begin the research.

From inside the industry there is a school of thought that says you cannot prepare for the news. You must not chain yourself to preconceived notions. You must be flexible enough to flow with the moving tide of events.

But that school of thought is full of malingerers. I can see few excuses for not preparing a shooting script for a current affairs story. If you are there on an important and expensive mission, one presumes you know why you are there. You must have some idea what the story is about. This being the case, you should be able to write it down. And when you do write it down you discover that the very process encourages good ideas.

It is better to have the ideas before you start filming than afterwards in the editing room when it is too late. There is no reason why you can't alter the script to suit changing events. At least you have something to change. Keeping on top of a story is a bit like riding a spirited horse. You must keep a tight rein and a loose rein. The tight rein is the intellectual control, the loose rein is the creative control. We must be disciplined, searching and vigilant about marshalling the facts. And we must also try to be accommodating of the creative energy that will let the story lead you to its own bright corners.

Writing your script as early as possible is the best way to maintain intellectual and creative control. Another advantage is that everyone on the team has a copy of the script, so there is no mystery about what you are doing.

One of the eccentricities of film crews is that the camera operator and sound recordist, generally known as the 'camera pointer' and 'sound catcher', always occupy the front seats of a car. The producer and reporter, who are known as the 'blowflies', or 'blowies', sit in the back. The only explanation ever offered for the latter nick-names, is that to the crews, journalists are people who hang around bad smells and always get on your back.

The explanation for the seating arrangement is that if the cameraman sees something worth filming they can respond more swiftly to the circumstance. The best thing for the reporter, sitting in the back, is that when you have the script completed and the crew begins to whinge about what the story is about, you can lean over and tell them with undisguised pleasure to 'read the bloody script'.

The next day was Sunday July 21. Bruce and I were up early. We had booked a radio telephone call to the yacht *Ouvea*. He and I were waiting anxiously for an interpreter to arrive. Both of us had only schoolboy French so we were counting on the presence of the interpreter. Unfortunately, the call came through before the interpreter arrived. We managed only a few words before they hung up. I am not sure whether they were shocked more by our attention or our French. It was the last public contact with *Ouvea*. We did not know it at the time, but soon after, the French agents scuttled that pretty little boat, sending it to the bottom of the Pacific. They were picked up, presumably by a submarine, and secretly hurried home.

While this was going on, the French Government was still indignantly denying any involvement in the sinking of the *Rainbow Warrior* and the death of Fernando Pereira.

We gathered up the camera and headed off to do our filming. A yacht hire company, Noumea Yacht Charters, had rented *Ouvea* to the four Frenchmen. We took the sister ship *Lifou* to sea to reconstruct the beginning of the voyage and we interviewed the owner of the company.

Following the interview I asked him how he wished to be described in the report and how to correctly spell his name. In my book I wrote the name 'Roger Chatelain', and how he wished to be designated.

In television we can not only quickly lose our literacy and our grammar, we can also forget how to spell. One of the few small, but important occasions when we need to be sure our spelling is correct, is when interviewees are designated and captioned at the bottom of the screen. Asking for the correct spelling, or better still, having the interviewee write the name for you is a useful habit to acquire.

The habit of captioning itself has a mixed following. Programmes like *Sixty Minutes* avoid captions, evidently believing they distract a viewer from the mood of the report. *Four Corners*, ever anxious to cram as much information onto the screen as possible, is a frequent user of captions. My own bias is definitely towards their use. The written word on the screen does catch the eye. It should not be overdone, but information that is captioned can have greater impact than the same information delivered as narration.

When we returned from Noumea Yacht Charters we found that a reporter and photographer from the *New Zealand Herald* had arrived. The *Herald* hired a plane to go searching for *Ouvea*, and very generously allowed our cameraman, Paul Costello, on board. The aircraft returned after a few hours having sighted not a trace of the yacht.

The *Herald* team was reporter, Karen Mangnall and photographer, Ross Land. We dined with them that evening. They brought news of another development which had broken in New Zealand. Before the bombing a Frenchwoman had attached herself to the Auckland office of Greenpeace, working for some weeks as a volunteer. Another newspaper, the *Auckland Star* was now suggesting the woman, who called herself Frederique Bonlieu, was not who she said she was.

While the rest of us chatted buoyantly about this latest news, Karen Mangnall excused herself and left the table. When she returned she looked liked she had been ill and for the rest of the evening seemed close to tears. We did not realise why until much later.

Frederique Bonlieu was in fact a French agent, Christine Cabon. Mangnall, as it turned out, was a victim of an appalling coincidence. The journalist and the Frenchwoman had become aquainted back in New Zealand and now Karen had to cope with the shocking news that her friend was a spy. No wonder she now looked like she had been raped.

I am sorry for Karen now, and feel a little guilty that I did not show any sympathy to her that night, but at that time I did not know. The full picture had not formed.

I have to say French New Caledonia was not a great place for forming the full picture. Enquiries at airline offices and hotels about the French sailors' movements were often met with steely glances and Gallic shrugs. A couple of New Zealand policemen assigned a similar mission were having as rough a time. I sought them out for a consolatory drink. Their lips worked perfectly when it came to drinking beer, but not for speaking. They were evidently afflicted by the same condition as their superior.

We had a little more filming to do on the yacht. The hire company, thankfully, was pleased to cooperate so we picked up a few shots as they motored the yacht across to the Club Mediterranée wharf to collect some Japanese tourists.

I waited at the wharf with the car while Bruce travelled on board the yacht to direct the crew. He wasn't exactly dressed for the occasion. Bruce must have come from the New York end of New Zealand. When he is not working with cameras he plays saxophone. He is fond of pointed shoes, dark jackets and the blackest sunglasses. He cut a striking figure, standing at the bow of *Lifou* as it edged towards the wharf. Bruce's normally excellent timing was faulty. He stepped for the wharf as the yacht bounced back. My producer swooped like a well-dressed cormorant into the ocean below. The Japanese tourists, ever polite, clucked in sympathy for a full few seconds, before their reserve broke and they collapsed with laughter.

We left Noumea for Auckland the next day. Bruce's suitcase had a damp, salty smell about it. The customs officers let us pass.

The main reason for returning to New Zealand was to complete our filming. But that did not mean the research phase was at an end. Another benefit of a prepared script is that the crew can continue filming without a need to be constantly directed. The producer or reporter is liberated to continue research or handle the considerable logistics problems which arise.

One such problem was the mobilisation of the New Zealand Police Force. The script called for detailed reconstructions of the police reaction to the bombing and subsequent investigation.

In my experience public service organisations are not automatically disposed to help the media. They are more inclined to treat us with suspicion. You become conditioned to expecting refusals. With politicians, it is the other way around. We are an important line of communication to their electorate, and they know it.

So I telephoned the Police Minister to ask if the Police Commissioner could be persuaded to allow us to film with some of his people. They were very helpful.

We also needed to follow closely the passage of the French as they blundered Clouseau-like through the bays, forests and bedrooms of Northern New Zealand. Bruce managed to rent the very vehicles they used, including one of the campervans.

We drove north to Parangarenga Harbour where we filmed the first point of entry of *Ouvea* and interviewed Hec Crene, the local ranger who had questioned the Frenchmen. Further south, we interviewed shop and motel proprietors who dealt with them, all the time scavenging as much extra information as we could.

In many current affairs reports we have the opportunity to 'cast' for interviewees. If there is a choice then there is a bias towards choosing people who are energetic and articulate. The dull, the bland, the nervous and awkward give way to the dynamic. In this respect we cannot pretend to be honestly representative. There is a lively and chatty 'type' that is favoured by television interviewers, often less for what they say than the way they say it. But in this exercise, it was the report and not the reporter that determined the cast.

Back at Whangarei, Bruce discovered another choice detail. The sailors had attempted to make contact with the 'Turenge' couple in the Topuni State Forest. It was our first evidence of an attempted convergence of the two teams.

The French seemed to believe the backwoods New Zealanders would be no match for their sophisticated European spy training. The reverse was true.

New Zealand was like a village. The villagers were nosy in the nicest possible way. They noticed everything unusual. Two forest workers spotted the French and, like the bay watchers, were suspicious enough to make a record of the vehicle number plate.

Sometimes a story seems to want to work. On the drive back to Auckland, as the sunlight faded, a perfect rainbow appeared on the horizon. We filmed the campervan, the same the French had used, driving towards the rainbow, just as it had done weeks earlier, towards the *Rainbow Warrior*. It was a flawless image.

Our cameraman Paul Costello was working on his first ever shoot for *Four Corners*. He had been a touch nervous, but now Paul and sound recordist Nick Wood were beginning to smile.

We next interviewed a man who could tell us about the sighting of the 'Zodiac' dinghy in Auckland harbour. The scene was a small but vital feature of an emerging mosaic. I wanted to illustrate the scene visually, with a filmed reconstruction.

The method of reconstructing an event from the past to satisfy the presence of a camera is often regarded with suspicion. I like the technique and have used it a great deal. I accept the very real dangers of abusing the technique by melding drama and fact, indistinguishably, but this can be avoided. It is unfortunate that the proliferation of carelessly prepared works of 'faction' has damaged the credibility of a useful technique. If there is no obvious way to tell a difficult and important story a reporter will frequently leave it untold. For this reason alone the reconstruction technique is more than justified, as long as we are careful.

Over the years I developed my own rules for reconstructions. The first rule is to avoid the use of dialogue. Even if we are certain of the precise words used, we can never be absolutely certain about the way they were used. Better not to use dialogue at all. The next important rule is to illustrate only what we were told, without embellishment. What we were therefore doing was no more than providing pictures for what an interviewee might otherwise describe with words.

The reconstructions gain credibility if we are faithful to every known detail. Perhaps they do so only in our own minds; but this is important too. You cannot expect the public to believe your stories if you do not exactly believe them yourself.

In this case we went to a great deal of trouble to locate one of the few 'Zodiac' dinghies to be found in New Zealand that was identical to the one the French used. We also had an identical campervan and a perfectly moonlit Auckland harbour.

Compared to a Hollywood film crew a current affairs team is an infant. Instead of the cranes and tracks, generators, wardrobe and makeup vans, mobile kitchens and the like, there is just one 16 mm camera, a stock of very basic reversal film and a few battery lights.

Instead of a cast of hundreds there were four of us, apart from the helpful local we used to drive the van. Bruce rowed the dinghy. Paul struggled with the fading power of the batteries. The night was so cold the camera persistently malfunctioned. We worked until past midnight. But this new cameraman with his 'Box Brownie' outfit gave us pictures every bit the equal of Hollywood. Hands frozen, and starving, we returned to the motel, too excited to sleep. We ate toasted sandwiches and raided the mini bar and talked for hours.

Soon we were back in Sydney with what was obviously a good story. I was reunited with my wife and family after a month away. I should have been content but my diary suggests I was not. 'Fidgeting. Tanya [my wife] says I am a workaholic . . . ' The problem was that I knew the story could be better.

This was an even bigger problem for Peter. I told him I should go to Paris and finish the story properly. Peter, my former producer who had always demanded we aim high and keep on working, was now my boss and the custodian of our budget. He was now hearing his own words coming back at him.

So three days after returning to Australia I was on my way to France. An economic compromise, later regretted, was that we would save money by my travelling alone and hiring a French, freelance crew. In the meantime Bruce and our own crew would pick up some extra shots and begin the editing.

You won't believe me but I was more thrilled by the prospect of finishing the story than getting on the plane. I did not want to travel, not even to Paris. This part of the work is a privilege and a pleasure but the joy of travel fades with time and I have been away too much.

The life of a travelling journalist, after a time, is caught hanging like a bad acrobat on a parabola of conflicting visions. One is the vision from the ground of an aircraft departing and the other is the vision from the air of the ground receding. We try to find comfort somewhere between the ambition to travel and the ambition to stay at home.

But I expect no sympathy. The long flight is meant to be a good time to get out the notebooks and improve the script or refine the research. This is how we are supposed to make responsible use of the twenty four hours in limbo.

It is also nonsense. Some reporters may dutifully juggle papers and pen or laptop computer on the tray table but I doubt it. Most attention drifts towards the free champagne and the movie. I find it very hard to write on an aeroplane. The words seem to slip off the armrest and become scattered on the floor, along with the crumpled blanket and uneaten peanuts. But the time is not wasted. The mind still works. It is a good time to think, and there is no underrating the quality of good hard thinking. The best thing about this type of travel is the ideas you will unexpectedly meet along the way.

The trip was slower than usual. I had waited for four and a half hours, camped on a plastic seat in the concourse of Sydney airport, because of an unscheduled delay. Somewhere between Bahrain and London I broke my glasses. According to my diary, my reading companions were Jane Austen's *Emma* and *Rugby League Week*, a worthy combination.

I missed my connecting flight to Paris but found another soon after. My bags miraculously appeared there on the rotating belt at Charles de Gaulle airport. Travellers will know too well that the sight of the Parthenon or Notre Dame compares not at all with the sudden appearance of a familiar item of luggage.

I taxied to a hotel with a view of a rusted, corrugated roof, unpacked my bag and rang Philip Brooks. Philip is an Australian freelance journalist, stationed in Paris, who was engaged to act as interpreter and general helper. And a great help he was.

I had one significant advantage over the herd of international journalists who were now forming before this story. In my possession was some good, practical intelligence collected over the past three weeks in New Zealand and Noumea.

Greenpeace held a press conference and it was mayhem. I have long suspected the value of press conferences. You will rarely discover more than they want you to discover. As soon as it finished, I sought out David McTaggart, the International Director of Greenpeace, and we slipped away for a quiet coffee.

I shared as much as I knew with David and he with me. One of the *Ouvea* crew, Xavier Maniguet, had contacted McTaggart. Maniguet, evidently suffering some remorse for the loss of the *Rainbow Warrior* crew member, seemed to be seeking forgiveness.

It was August 12. The French Government was maintaining a fixed facade of innocence. Four days earlier President Mitterand ordered a 'thorough' investigation of 'L'Affaire Greenpeace' to be conducted by a former Secretary-General of the Elysée Palace, Bernard Tricot. (Wasn't it the French who invented the farce?)

The McTaggart, Maniguet encounter converted my suspicion of the French Government's silent hand in the Marsden Wharf murder to conviction.

My private meeting with David McTaggart gleaned far more than the press conference ever could. I learned more because I had done enough homework to ask the proper questions and I had something to share. Herein lies one of the secrets of 'investigative' journalism . . . information trading.

I don't know what the rule book says about this practice but it is one I have often used. The major concern is that you might pass on something, say to a policeman or criminal, which could later cause considerable harm to someone. But there was no such concern in this case.

I was happy enough to tell Greenpeace what I could. I believed they had a moral right to know as much as I did about who was bombing and murdering them.

Even so I tried to maintain some objectivity. You can sympathise, but it is better not to take sides.

It is probably also true to say that at the time I had more suspicions and concerns about my own colleagues in the media. Correspondents hate to be beaten, so the herd hangs together, more interested in their own footprints than the horizon before them.

Print and radio journalists have a short lead time compared to television reporters who are burdened with the technical complications of processing and editing. The television reporter can discover the fact first but be a sad last getting it to air. So we are anxious, jealous and sometimes ridiculously competitive.

An ABC correspondent, Pierre Vicary, describes the process of gathering and protecting research as a bit like a squirrel preparing for winter. You stack the acorns in the tree and watch helplessly as they are nicked one by one.

There is no rule about journalists stealing each other's work but perhaps there should be. We should not be proprietorial about stories. No journalist owns the news but we have some right to be proprietorial about hard-won research. Journalists moralise about the iniquity of scientists and academics stealing research, and at the same time take pride and pleasure in unfairly scooping a rival. Too many times I have seen acorns disappear into the pockets of reporters whose line of questioning was no more sophisticated than, 'tell me what you told *Four Corners*'.

In this case I had no reason to complain. Everyone had fair access to the same story and the public was going to benefit from what was and should be healthy competition.

I was willing to pass on a little of the information we gathered but getting the trade balance right would need care. We always hope to receive a little more than we give. Philip Brooks helped me choose the journalist I would bargain with. We went for the man with the best security intelligence contacts and that was Pascal Krop.

Krop was the author of an authoritative book on the French Secret Service, *La Piscine*. The title referred to the nick-name Parisians gave the Headquarters of the DGSE (Direction Générale de Sécurité Extérieure).

The deal was done swiftly somewhere between the soup and the salad in an ancient Paris Brasserie. In return for some of what I knew about the movements of the spies in New Zealand, he would put me in touch with one of his sources.

Pascal's source turned out to be a former French spook, who kept in close contact with the old boy network and continued, as I understood it, to do a little freelance work.

We met in Philip Brooks' flat. Somewhere upstairs, sixties American music was playing loudly. The milky Paris light crept past the window boxes as the spy sat down in front of me. He was keen to talk and seemed to feel safer talking to someone from so far away. I don't think Australia counted for very much. He could not see his words boomeranging back to Paris.

The genial spook told me some of the captured agents' friends and colleagues were upset by their abandonment. They were not wonderfully fond of the Mitterand socialist government, so were not distressed by the idea of the scandal leaking. He gave me a list of names of senior government officials who he said were a party to commissioning the bombing. I recorded the conversation on tape. He agreed to let his voice be used but not his face.

I was pleased with the information but I was worried too. At the time, Paris was alive with disinformation. I was a little worried that the burly man with the moustache in front of me might not be the person he said he was.

When he walked into the kitchen to answer the call of the kettle I saw his wallet on the coffee table and reached across, opening it to reveal his identification card. I returned the wallet exactly as I found it.

Looking in the wallet was the wrong thing to do. I had gone too far and instantly felt guilty. When he returned from the kitchen he looked at me squarely and said, 'You have opened my wallet'. I shrunk into the armchair, confessed and apologised.

At least it cleared the air. He showed me his credentials and told me something of his background. He said he would like to be a journalist. Spying was a pain in the derrière. I could see what he meant.

There was filming to complete, and it was not going well. The French crew assigned to me were enthusiastic but, as it turned out, unfamiliar with film work. They had only previously handled videotape equipment, so I took the precaution of having the film processed quickly in London. When we got it back it turned out to be useless. Two days work was lost but the crew were eager to make amends.

One aspect that slightly amused me about our French film crew was the recognition that they dressed very similarly to Australian film crews, or indeed film crews the world over. Film crews very definitely have a uniform, which is generally made up of torn jeans, soiled running shoes, a T-shirt, generally with something like a cannabis leaf printed on the front, and sunglasses.

Getting them to wear anything else can be difficult, even if you are planning to interview Prime Ministers and members of the royal family. If such an interview is planned, it is well to advise them before you leave that it would be wise to pack something else besides a spare pair of thongs.

On this trip I had barely enough time to change my own clothes let alone lecture the crew about changing theirs. I saw little of my hotel room with the view of the rusting roof but I was never tired. Even after a long day's filming I would choose to walk the ten kilometres or so back to the hotel. Paris goes a long way towards explaining why the French can be so superior and arrogant.

On the sixth day I was gone, clutching my film cans under my arm, ushering them past the potentially damaging airport x-ray machine into the welcoming arms of Qantas.

I arrived in Sydney on Monday August 19. There was one week to edit. The post-production phase of a documentary is usually laboriously slow. You snip and jiggle and experiment for months. In current affairs there is no time to experiment, and although it can be exhausting I have found I prefer the discipline and savagery of the deadline. You have to get it right first time. In this sense I suppose I am like the experienced punter who is contemptuous of the 'each-way' bet. And like the hard-bitten gambler I must be a something of a masochist.

The script I had prepared back at the research stage helped eliminate some of those intermediate stages. It had also helped keep our shooting ratio to an efficient minimum. Film stock is expensive. Wading through a swamp of surplus footage adds not just to the expense but also the fatigue. But none of us can manage a one-to-one ratio. The great majority of the footage will be left on the cutting room floor.

One skill that seems only to develop with time is the ability to 'kill your babies'. Scenes that are treasured in the field can lose their glow in the even light of the cutting room. We cannot help having loyalty to a sequence that might have been won at the cost of lost sleep, muddy boots, worn temper and depleted schedule. But if they do not work they must be given a swift and merciful goodbye.

After many years I have just about lost all remorse. It may even be that I am developing an instinct out there in the field for the scenes that are heading for the executioner. There have been plenty of occasions when a particularly problematic piece of filming has caused me to wonder whether it was ever meant to be.

When we are scripting a longer report we are often provided with transcripts of the interviews. If more than say five or six interviews are recorded then it is helpful to have transcripts so that we can have an easy reference to the words spoken.

But there is a dangerous trap in selecting the interview 'grabs' or 'bites' from the text of the transcript, rather than the image on the screen. People communicate not just with words.

There is often energy and feeling in the way the words are delivered and it makes sense to watch out for those luminous moments.

Viewing 'rushes', the raw, unedited vision, is time-consuming but it is well worth making the time. It helps to see the pictures that really work so that you have a chance to write them into the script.

My editor was Mark Middis, a New Zealander and a favourite workmate. There is no doubt the best way to work with editors is to stay away from them. Leave them a comprehensive script and let them get on with it. If they do, a good editor will add a layer of creativity to your work. So I would deliver the script page by page, as Mark stayed chained to the Steenbeck editing machine, day and night for the full week.

There is one moment in that film which for me will last forever as a happy fusion of the work of the producer, reporter, cameraman, sound recordist and editor. The vision is the pitching deck of the French yacht. The narration is stretched sparely; the less words the better. Mark has let the natural sound work. The sail billows, fills with wind and snaps loudly. The timing is perfect. For a choice moment you are on that yacht on a sabotage mission to New Zealand.

A documentary film is often a collection of sequences. A sequence is a self-contained story, somewhat like a chapter in a book. The sequences are usually about five to eight minutes long, which is presumed to be the average viewer attention span. So a fifty minute documentary might have as many as ten separate sequences, each neatly linked and all building together to construct an understandable, entertaining story.

For years I carefully followed the formula and generally, it served me well. But this time I had no neat collection of sequences to thread together. All I had was a story, one story, but it was a good story. 'French Connections' as we called it, was arranged seamlessly, without sequences and transitions.

Providence accompanied us till the end. 'French Connections' was broadcast on Monday August 26, 1985. Andrew Olle introduced the story minutes after an announcement that the special investigation conducted by Bernard Tricot had cleared the French Government of any involvement in the *Rainbow Warrior* bombing. Monsieur Tricot's report soon faded to an appalling shade of whitewash.

There were many lessons to be drawn from the *Rainbow Warrior* episode. The geopolitical one is that small nations don't matter. There was never going to be any justice for New Zealand. France did what it liked and got away with it.

Despite New Zealand Prime Minister Lange's promise that New Zealand justice was not for sale, France was able to apply a bullying trade threat that ultimately forced the release of the 'Turenges' — Alain Mafart and Dominique Prieur.

The promise that Mafart and Prieur would be held in protective custody turned out to be another joke. They were soon released back to Paris after a cursory stay of detention at a military base in the South Pacific.

But I cannot really quarrel with that. Mafart and Prieur were, after all, public servants who were ordered to carry out the mission. They deserved no greater punishment than the people who sent them there. For those people there will never be any formal punishment. At least by telling the story to the world their deeds were exposed.

I later realised I had passed over an opportunity to name each of the men who had ordered the mission because the names were given to me back in Paris by our friendly spy. I did not name them for three reasons. The first was that the names would have meant little to an Australian audience. The second was that I prefer to expose the plot rather than the players. The third reason is that I had no way of checking the information, and even though it turned out to be correct, I am not sorry I left the names out.

As it turned out this was one of the few occasions when a

major international story occurred in our patch. Our British colleagues tend to be a bit disdainful of the competition down under, but this time they had no choice but to open their cheque books and buy the report. Television stations right across Europe and North America followed suit. It was good to contribute to the balance of payments for a change.

Andrew Olle, who is no 'soft' critic, told me afterwards he liked the story. What he liked was how we managed to make a film out of nothing. I knew what he was saying. When we arrived at Marsden Wharf there was the crippled *Rainbow Warrior* to film but nothing else. The rest was a ghost.

There is a convention in current affairs television that we must have a character, an event or something we can see before we can film. We look for telegenic issues as well as telegenic people. This is a blinkered attitude that denies the public important information and denies the television journalist practice in developing storytelling skills.

I came to realise that despite a common view to the contrary, television can be a good information medium. We were able to take people through this story step by step, showing as well as telling what happened. When we took them to Marsden Wharf at the end of the film, with the vision of the *Rainbow Warrior* lying helpless and the sound of the Maori keening on the wharf, people could also feel an important emotion of the story. They could feel the loss of innocence that had overcome New Zealanders, whose sovereignty had been invaded by a powerful, unrepentant 'friend'. Even for the best newspaper journalist with unlimited space to tell the tale, that feeling is difficult to convey.

So there was a lesson for the television journalist too. You don't have to be limited by the strictures of what you can see. The early work was completed in much the same way a journalist from print or radio might have done it. We collected the facts first, and once this was complete we thought of a way of filming them.

When I discovered the process worked I gathered a little more confidence in the medium. What the *Rainbow Warrior* experience taught me was this: if you have a good story you have a good film.

5

'BRANDED'

At the height of a rather nasty, protracted battle with the medical entrepreneur Dr Geoffrey Edelsten, I was privy to some advice he was offered about how to handle this troublesome journalist. The advice, eminently sensible, came from a media consultant engaged by the flamboyant medico.

The doctor was told, 'The journalist is not out to get you. He is only interested in your story. It is not personal'. But Edelsten appeared to ignore the advice. Like many others before and since, he could not see the distinction. Politicians, too, presuming everyone thinks like politicians, convince themselves media attack or criticism is politically motivated. They have trouble understanding a journalist's single-minded passion for a story. For many journalists loyalty to a story transcends just about everything. Mateship, national pride, political allegiance, home and family and sometimes our own sense of ethics and fair play can be trampled in the rush to broadcast.

At another point during the clash with Edelsten I was threatened in the conventional way. The threat came wrapped in innocence, encased in ambiguity. It was delivered by a man, Peter Walker, who was later well known for his association with the controversial 'Private Blood Bank of Australia'. Although he denied it, Walker was acting as an agent for Edelsten.

Walker would ring me and come and see me constantly with all sorts of sugar-coated warnings. He told me Edelsten knew the Painter and Docker hit man, Christopher Dale Flannery, and could not be responsible for what Flannery might do to 'protect' the doctor. He told me he also knew the NSW policemen, Roger Rogerson and Bill Duff, and warned they would come to Edelsten's aid and 'Your arse will be nailed to the wall'. He said Edelsten would sue me personally so that he would be throwing the weight of his financial backing against my own meagre personal income and that the ABC would not be able to finance my defence. He asked sweetly about my family.

I was angry, and the mention of my family made me angrier. I asked him what my family had to do with this. 'I just wondered what they thought of all this?', he said. I told him I could not take what he told me as anything but a threat. Walker nearly fell over himself in an endeavour to correct my profound misunderstanding of his good-natured, well-intentioned advice.

But like Edelsten, I ignored the advice. The story was already travelling. It had a life of its own. If I was threatened, then the threat was in all likelihood a bluff. Perhaps I was, to some small degree, exposing myself and my family to risk, but I have come to accept the risk and they have come to inherit it.

What I am saying is that it can take a lot to stop a story, and it does not always help to see conspiracy and malevolence in the journalist's motive. I do not believe in targets but I do believe in stories. Edelsten was a story.

There is a belief that the need to lop 'tall poppies' is a predominant feature of Australian culture, but I have my doubts. If there is a 'tall poppy syndrome', perhaps it refers more to a compunction to preserve them rather than bring them down to size. For every story of a tall poppy being lopped, it seems to me there are at least equivalent examples of an unsceptical media contributing to the propagation of an undeserved, exemplary reputation.

For me the Edelsten experience was every bit as bruising as

all those other encounters with the Queensland police, the NSW Government, the French Security Services and the Mafia. The prodigious effort to stop this story outclassed all others. Apart from a substantial legal effort to prevent the broadcast, the preparation of the report was accompanied by unsourced threats, unexpected obstacles and general mischief. But I am glad to stay the story was not stopped.

The origin of the 'Branded' report goes back to the middle of 1984. I was working on a *Four Corners* report about medical fraud and overservicing when I became interested in Edelsten. The Sydney-based doctor had a high profile in the society and gossip pages. He was known for his colourful Hollywood-style parties and Las Vegas-style girlfriends. He was seen as a big spender with a stable of flash cars and brash numberplates: 'MACHO', 'SEXY', 'GROOVY' and so on. He had, we were told, sponsored the Carlton Football Club cheer-squad. In short he was good for one of those regular extravagant lifestyle stories so cherished by the Sunday press.

The story on medical fraud and overservicing, 'What the Doctor Ordered', was screened on Saturday July 7, 1984. Before it was broadcast I had two important meetings which persuaded me to look at the Edelsten story. The first meeting was with Edelsten himself.

If you do this job properly you have to keep some unkind hours. Edelsten finished work, he said, about midnight and started around five the next morning.

So just before dawn the next day, I was there at his Baulkham Hills surgery, with notebook in hand, when the electric door slid open to expose the velvet wallpaper, the mink-lined examination table and the man I came to think of as the Barry Manilow of medicine.

We got on well. He seemed to enjoy an attentive audience and I am a practised, eager listener. Edelsten told me a great many things that day, much of which he would now supremely regret.

Why did he open up? An easy answer is that he is driven by a need to impress and can't help himself. That may well be true; but I think there may be another reason. I liked Edelsten, in retrospect I would say, mostly because he was a fascinating story.

A fascinated journalist with an unthreatening demeanour is obviously a thing of danger, but at the time I don't think even I realised that, let alone the good doctor.

I suspect the most successful discoverers of information are the wide-eyed and welcoming. If you hover, steely-eyed and argumentative, like a hungry barrister, then the defences are mounted, the jaw muscles tense and the information flow creeps to a halt.

While we scooted around Sydney's west in his blue Aston Martin Lagonda, the doctor opened up. All the while I made notes of the conversation which later, I would routinely type as a record of interview and file with other research material.

The doctor said a great deal; but I will focus for the moment on one vibrating anecdote. Edelsten claimed he was being threatened by a madman. The man was an unhappy former patient of the Edelsten practice who was now trying to extort money from the doctor. Edelsten thought him dangerous and sought advice about how to handle the problem.

One respectable fellow entrepreneur, he said, was believed to have such people knocked off. Another patient, a Painter and Docker, offered the same advice and had even given the doctor an on-the-spot quote for the job: '$50 000 to have him killed and $10 000 for a bashing'. Edelsten, an experienced businessman, questioned the high price of the bashing. The Painter and Docker shrugged and told him, 'baseball bats are expensive these days'.

Sydney enjoys stories like the one I had just heard. They colour the city's superstructure like neon and are part of the conversational flicker across plates of char-grilled tuna in our brasseries, bistros and boardrooms. We like to talk of these things. It is part of being grown-up. What else would you talk about in an Aston Martin Lagonda between Liverpool and Parramatta?

I was successfully intrigued, but I had heard such tales before. The story took on a more sinister complexion after the next important meeting.

By one of those remarkably recurrent coincidences I met the so-called madman who was allegedly threatening Edelsten. Through a *Four Corners* connection with a Sydney Legal Aid office we learned of a man who was complaining about being similarly threatened. He believed the threats came as the result of an action he was bringing against Edelsten.

The man, Stephen Evans, had another one of those Sydney stories. He said that some years earlier he had gone to one of Edelsten's clinics to have a tattoo removed. The laser operation, performed not by Edelsten but another doctor, was painful and unsuccessful. Evans was left with a large red scar.

He sought legal advice and was told that before a case could be made against the Edelsten practice, which performed many such operations, he would need more examples of the scarring. Evans advertised in a newspaper and sure enough a number of people with similar experiences contacted him.

The former tattoo patient was a meticulous type, who indexed and tape-recorded each telephone response. One response to the advertisement was a rough, no-nonsense voice telling him if he didn't stop running the ad he would have his legs broken. Evans the meticulous type became a nervous type, but he continued with his writ against Edelsten.

The story went on. Evans said he headed off to the bush to earn money picking fruit and found himself arrested. NSW police had travelled to the Victorian town of Mildura from where Evans was extradited and charged with 'demanding money with menaces' from Edelsten.

Evans said they brought him back to Sydney and when he

was being transported by police car through the city, the policeman sharing the back seat with Evans began punching him.

Evans said he broke free, opened the door of the car, and fled. The policeman chased and caught him, and according to Evans the punching continued. He said he was then thrown in a cell and kept in custody for a month before he could obtain bail.

Evans believed Edelsten was a dangerous man with underworld connections and some allied clout with the NSW police. He also believed that this chain of misery he was rattling before me had its beginnings with his writ against the doctor.

Edelsten, on the opposite side of Sydney, had already told me the other side of the story. He was the victim of a madman. He was being threatened and harassed by mail and telephone. Edelsten believed Evans was behind the harassment campaign. Edelsten had at least considered taking the advice of a Painter and Docker patient by denting the nuisance with a baseball bat.

I met Evans after I had first made contact with the doctor. I did not tell Edelsten that the contact had been made. To do so would have meant a breach of a confidentiality agreement I had with Evans. Even so I found myself in an awkward position and realised I was going to have to tread carefully.

Evans was very nervous about the threat made against him. He was on the verge of panic and seemed not to know where to turn. Partly in order to calm him down I suggested we record an 'insurance' interview with him.

On rare occasions at *Four Corners* we have recorded such interviews. If someone is in danger because of what they might say, then theoretically, the danger diminishes if a record of their story is held with the national media. Hundreds of people vanish without trace every year in Australia and their stories vanish with them. In this case, instead of disappearing, the story in all probability would be given prominence.

Recognition that their story is stored in this way goes a little way to improving the story tellers' chances of survival — or so the theory goes. The Evans interview was filmed and stored away, but I can't say it brought on a noticeable show of calm. He was also very suspicious, so we gave a guarantee of the arrangement in writing. So with our letter in his pocket and his story on our shelf, Evans departed.

After the first meetings with Edelsten and Evans I found myself between two opposing accounts of the same story. Both men appeared to believe their own versions. I did not know whom to believe but I knew I was in the middle of a good story.

It would not be an easy or fun story to make and there was the very real concern that the talk of threats and bashings and murder could graduate to something more real. I had also just completed a story on roguery in the medical profession and was doubtful that *Four Corners* wanted another similar story.

But the information that had come my way was unique, important and perhaps very serious. A man's life may well have been in danger. There wasn't much point in taking the information to the NSW police, particularly considering the police seemed to be part of the problem.

What I had discovered nagged me as it always does. You cannot help feeling a responsibility to pass on what you know. I took a deep breath and told our executive producer, Jonathan Holmes, I thought I should continue work on a story about Edelsten.

At the time, the now common practice that reporters work with producers on every story was not established. I had worked on my own on the overservicing story and would have to be without a producer again. Jonathan approved the story and I accepted it as a solitary endeavour.

This turned out to be a mistake so profoundly regretted that I would never repeat it. As I have mentioned before, these 'big digs', as we call them, should not be attempted alone. There is too great a chance that the mullock heap will come tumbling down on top of you, with no one on hand to hear your cries for help.

Three days after the report on medical fraud and overservicing was shown I telephoned Edelsten and repeated an earlier proposal that we make a film about him. This is part of my diary entry. 'He is depressed about programme but still keen on proposal. A bit of a child in some ways.'

An important ethical question arises about my own level of deceit in persuading Edelsten to cooperate. The question of how much to tell is one which journalists frequently encounter. I am sure that Edelsten today would say he was tricked. I don't believe that is so. But I can't pretend to be any more objective, so I will leave the judgment to you.

My plan was vaguely this. I would set my sights on the best and most revealing story. This might turn out to be a story about the doctor's association with the underworld and alleged threats on his life as well as the alleged counter threats on the patient.

But in reality it was unlikely a story like that could be completed in the assigned six weeks, even if the facts checked out. A more achievable story was one about the colourful doctor and his 'McDonalds' approach to medicine.

At our first meeting he had driven past one of the hamburger stores and told me that franchised, accessible, high volume, fast turnover medical services were the way of the future. Edelsten had a sensible argument that doctors should make more of an effort to make their services less of a bitter pill. Too many doctors' surgeries were crowded and unpleasant, with nothing more than a tatty *Reader's Digest* to keep you company during the interminable wait. It was also awkward getting medical attention outside normal working hours. There was mileage in this corner of the story.

I also thought that the story of his tattoo removal operations was well worth exploring. It was clear that a great many people suffered silently because at one point in their youth they had allowed themselves to be branded. The unwanted tattoo did a great deal of psychological damage. Fathers would not take off their shirts in front of their children. Women office workers faced a life sentence of long sleeves. There was also a good issue here.

The tattoo removal work was valuable, but Edelsten's claim of a failure rate of only approximately one in fifty was dubious. People like Evans, who ended up with a scar much worse than the tattoo, seemed to have little recourse.

Indeed, they were often drawn from the large tribe of the ill-educated and powerless who were no match for a well-heeled doctor. There was also some controversy about the amount the doctor charged for the operation. The Medicare schedule listed an extensive area laser removal operation at $182. Edelsten feared the benefit was about to be removed and therefore a great many people who could not afford the cost would suffer.

The counter view was that Edelsten was rorting the system. The number of operations being performed made it clear there was not enough time in the day for the busy doctor to do them all himself. As I observed myself, while Edelsten began the operation, it was often completed by a nurse.

The first story, about Edelsten's entrepreneurial approach to medicine, was easily achievable in our time frame. The second, sharper-edged story, about the controversy surrounding the tattoo removal surgery was a possibility, but one worth aiming for. The third story, of the threat and counter threat against doctor and patient and the doctor's association with Sydney's gangland was something I would keep an eye out for as I pursued the more achievable objectives. It was too much of a long shot to rely on, but it was as well to remain alert.

At this stage I chose not to tell Edelsten what I knew about the suggestion he was rorting the system over the tattoo removals. I did not tell him I had by now met Stephen Evans and had another perspective on the secret war between the doctor and his former client. My feeling then and now, was it did not make a lot of sense to tell everything in the beginning. When you do, artificial defences are constructed, excuses are manufactured and the light that searches out the truth is snuffed like a kerosene lamp.

I did not tell everything to Edelsten, but I did not lie. My policy is to outline the proposal accurately so that at no later stage can it be claimed I entered the story by means of a 'Trojan Horse'. I cannot think of a justification for pretending you are doing one story but secretly planning a completely different story. But clearly I was treading a fine line. If your objective is to uncover concealed information then you may have to deal with the moral dilemma of needing to conceal information yourself.

What I had to do was outline the proposal so that it encompassed the territory that I might end up covering.

I told Edelsten that I wanted to profile him, his approach to medicine, and the tattoo removals. I told him that whatever I discovered I would use, good and bad. I was careful to make sure he understood that. He said he did.

It is true I carried something of a concealed weapon when I approached Edelsten, but my approach was as open as he could reasonably expect. Edelsten should have known journalism is not public relations, and *Four Corners* is not *Lifestyles of the Rich and Famous*. He had just seen a programme I made which was critical of the whole industry of medical overservicing.

There is an argument for alerting the unwary about participating in a programme that might carry consequences. But this was one moth who should have been well aware of the flame. Edelsten, though hardly publicity shy, could not be regarded as unwary, and he had been given such a warning.

What I found was that he appeared keener on the proposal

than I was. The only problem, Edelsten said, was his fiancée, Leanne.

Leanne had arrived in Sydney from the Northern Territory. She became a face and a name in the cities, glossy and sophisticated enough; but there was still something about her manner and vocabulary that kept me in mind of the outback.

You only needed to talk to Leanne to realise she was as tough as a buffalo catcher, but still, I could not help feeling a bit sorry for her. Unkind observers were suggesting what must have attracted her to Edelsten was his wealth. But this was hardly likely to be true. Anyone as close to Edelsten as Leanne would have known that despite the cars and the helicopter and Spanish-style mansion, the doctor did not appear to be overburdened with cash.

My research ended up introducing me to a range of dispirited creditors. Edelsten had the outward show of wealth and in Sydney at least, this alone made him wealthy. If people believe you have money, they presume you are a good credit risk. If they fall into litigation they presume they will be defeated by the expensive army of lawyers that a person like Edelsten can muster.

The Sydney media, which loves stories about money, had helped propagate the myth of great wealth, by running stories on the cars and the helicopter and the purchases of the football teams and the plans to obtain a Boeing 707 to transport them. One simple question might have been asked, but for the most part was not: 'where is the money coming from?'

Edelsten would not agree but by and large I think he got a soft ride from the media and to some degree profited from our lack of scepticism. The media can frequently, unquestioningly and unknowingly, become part of the alchemy which turns lead into gold.

I remember Edelsten once telling me a lesson he learned as a young medico. A senior doctor with an expensive car would park it ostentatiously outside the surgery. The doctor told the young Edelsten that rather than offend the patient, this show of wealth would indicate the doctor was successful and the patient would want to share some of that success. The lesson must have made an impact.

Edelsten appeared to appreciate a lack of scepticism, not only in the media but in his patients too. He told me he had moved his practice to the working class suburbs out west from upmarket St Ives on Sydney's North Shore partly because the North Shore lot, 'drove me crazy by continually asking questions about their treatment'.

I met Leanne at home at the Spanish mansion. The house had a touch of *Dallas* about it, and indeed was used for a time as part of the set for a local soap opera.

A house-maid greeted us and brought us instant coffee and Arnotts biscuits. Leanne then made her entrance down the staircase. She was wearing a white leather pants suit. I remember Edelsten smacking her proprietorially across her leather-clad rear.

The echo of that meeting has followed me down the years. A year has not passed when I have not been called to give evidence or talk to lawyers and policemen about Edelsten-related matters.

The meeting preceded the arrival of our film crew. I arranged to film Edelsten and his cars and then fly by helicopter to a football match. Edelsten was contributing at the time to the sponsorship of the Aussie Rules team, the Sydney Swans.

Before the crew arrived Edelsten and Leanne and I discussed the project. The doctor was keen that I meet with Leanne's approval. I am not sure how I fared. She eyed me rather suspiciously, but there was little chance of torpedoing the filming because it had already begun. A few days earlier Edelsten had allowed us to film the tattoo removal procedure and some of the show-biz gimmicks at his clinics.

The Baulkham Hills clinic had a video juke-box in one

corner and a small plastic robot near the main entrance. The robot greeted arriving patients and directed them to the available services.

Edelsten had one legitimate concern. He feared the NSW Medical Board would view harshly any breach of the code which prevented doctors advertising their services. There had already been a problem over advertisements for the tattoo removal clinic.

I told Geoffrey and Leanne I would check with the Medical Board to get an indication of how they would react to a programme profiling Edelsten and let him know. There was no witness to the conversation beyond Edelsten, Leanne and myself. This was something I came to regret.

The crew arrived and we did a day's filming. The next day I called in on the NSW Medical Board and discussed the Edelsten project. I was told that as long as it wasn't a blatant plug for Edelsten there would be no objection. My diary records me passing this on to Edelsten that afternoon and also records his response as: 'anxious'.

I was anxious myself. I always am. I think anyone who works in television has got to be prepared to make a bit of a fool of themselves from time to time. One of the drawbacks of the job is we cannot make our blunders in private.

But I did not want to make a fool of myself by blundering in this story. Getting together a sensible, accurate portrait of the controversial doctor would not be easy. I have learned that it is next to impossible to tell all and absolutely impossible to please all.

The only way to be satisfied is to believe your story yourself, and believe you have exhausted every possible avenue of discovery. The only ultimately trustworthy method of adjudication about the rights and wrongs of your work, is through your own conscience. There is only one way I know to avoid bruising my conscience and that is to work.

I got busy drawing up a list of possible leads. I would talk to friends and enemies, Health Department officials, tattoo patients, fellow medicos, and contacts in the underworld, everyone I could think of who could improve my knowledge on the doctor and his practices.

The story was still an amorphous collection of possibilities. Although we were already filming I was still researching and had not yet achieved that necessary, certain focus.

The sharp end of the story was still the possibility that Edelsten was a party to a plot to bash or kill a troublesome patient. I learned a little more about this from Edelsten himself.

When we returned from filming the tattoo removal at his Georges Hall clinic he repeated the story about the Painter and Docker and the prices quoted for the bashing or murder. Edelsten went on to say that a senior NSW policeman had advised him the best way of dealing with the man was to have him killed. What he told me on each occasion was recorded in the buff-coloured Commonwealth Government reporter's notebook I tended to carry everywhere.

The dilemma of what to do with this information was revived. I did not feel I could comfortably take it to the police. To do so would have been a breach of confidence. There was also the problem of lack of confidence at the time in the NSW Police Force's determination to expose its villains.

But I did not feel comfortable carrying it on my own. I called the ABC Legal Department and told them what I knew. To be doubly certain I also reported what had happened to the staff-elected member of the ABC Board, Tom Molomby, who is a lawyer and a friend. While I didn't want to get too carried away, it was clearly sensible to share some of the information and thereby diminish some of the risk.

The detail of not yet having completely focussed the story was a concern but not a crushing one. I am used to stories passing through various levels of truth. At first glance you might see a subject of your story as a saint. After a day's research you may begin to see them as a sinner. After a month you begin to understand the environment which encourages the sin.

In the media we very rarely penetrate to this last, most important level of truth. Most journalists seem to complain about not having enough time to do a story properly, but few are given the time. As one of the few, I was unusually privileged. I was now about two weeks into a six week schedule, and my star was beginning to show signs of stage fright. Edelsten's will to cooperate declined in equal proportion to the ascending likelihood that the report would not be entirely favourable.

One week after our filming of him at his home and at the football, the troublesome patient, Stephen Evans, was raided by NSW police. Evans told me they searched his flat, looking for further evidence to support the charge that he was demanding money with menaces.

The search uncovered the letter *Four Corners* had written to Evans.

The suspicion that Edelsten was getting unusually attentive support from the NSW cops quickly intensified.

The next day when I called Edelsten to organise a planned interview, his staff told me the doctor was too ill to be filmed. The next day I called again and after some trouble got through to Edelsten. He told me he knew about my association with Evans.

I had no choice but to confess but did not feel a need to apologise. Edelsten was not angry. At first he tried to pretend he had discovered the association through an informant in the ABC but eventually revealed his knowledge of the letter discovered in Evans' flat. The NSW police had suspiciously, and I would think improperly, passed on the information.

The tangled web was beginning to strangle me and just about everything else in sight. Evans was in court a few days later, to answer the, 'demand money with menaces' charge. I sat in to listen to the evidence. Evans was anxious about my attention and I began to see why. It was clear he had lied to me about the case the police had mounted against him. Evans appeared to be operating a dole scam by using two separate identities.

But the rest of the evidence did not seem to establish an overwhelming case that he had been menacing Edelsten. It had always seemed unlikely that such an obviously unsophisticated man would have been the source of all the clever mischief being visited upon the Sydney doctor.

However even if Evans was not guilty of harassing Edelsten he was at least guilty of lying to me and it is not worth risking your professional credibility for a liar. I saw some sense in keeping a distance from Evans.

At the same time Edelsten was beginning to distance himself from me. I found it a little bizarre to be caught between these two small and anxious men. Both were scared of each other even though they had never met. To me they seemed timid, yet possibly scared enough of each other to do something very foolish.

Edelsten and I met again the next evening at his Baulkham Hills clinic. We had managed to stay on good terms. Oddly enough we did get on well. He has considerable intelligence and his mind races at a dazzling pace. He is an original thinker with enough good ideas to make any number of honest fortunes.

I liked to listen. It is possible to separate your personal and professional feelings but this is not always understood, particularly by Australians. The mateship ethos often defines friendship as a kind of immunity. So a mate who 'dobs' on another commits an act of betrayal.

Perhaps Edelsten felt my friendliness would guarantee a soft ride. If so this was foolish. The man and the story are different beasts. Besides by now, as with Evans, it was obvious I could not trust him.

We spoke frankly about Evans and the tattoo removals. He

told me his patients were very happy with the results, that his claim for the success rate was accurate and that he had not been sued. My own research so far suggested a different story.

It is fair to say that with the cat now out of the bag and wailing loudly, Edelsten also felt he could not trust me. The way the *Four Corners* story was shaping was not to his liking. Repeated requests for the promised interview were met with varied excuses: the doctor was delivering a baby; the doctor was having trouble with an eye operation; the doctor was ill or too busy.

I think interviewees make a mistake by refusing an interview at an early stage of a programme's research. The reporter becomes even more suspicious and with nowhere else to turn will often stray closer to the camp of the enemy. With no access to Edelsten I sniffed the campfire smoke of his detractors. Of course I would have spoken with them anyway, but perhaps not to the same degree if Edelsten had not appeared so evasive. He was not short of enemies and they were not short of words.

The focus began to form on the tattoo removal story, mainly because it was more achievable and because I was now accumulating a long list of unhappy patients.

From a local newsagent I bought a large chart of graph paper and began to write in the names of such patients and the times and details of their treatment. The first names came from the original list Stephen Evans collected when he advertised for fellow victims in a Sydney newspaper. One witness tends to know another, and so the list builds.

Listening to some of their stories was like sitting in on a horror show. I had been in the surgeries and seen the lasering and felt some discomfort as the smell of burning flesh reached down the corridors into the waiting room. But from what I could see, the lasering itself caused little if any pain. The patients received a local anaesthetic before the laser burnt into the tattoo.

These patients said most of the pain and suffering came later. Edelsten would wrap the treated area in ordinary household 'Gladwrap'. Some patients reported that the wound later began to fester. Within days they became sick at the smell of their own rotting flesh. The pain was so great that when the wound was finally unwrapped and the ink stains scraped away, they would sometimes pass out.

I began to look for other medicos with expertise in the use of lasers to remove tattoos. There were not too many and I was not optimistic about expecting much help. When it comes to self-protection, the medical community is about the worst, even worse than the police forces. They seem culturally unwilling to self-regulate and expose malpractice by fellow medicos. They seem to be driven by a 'there but for the grace of God go I' attitude, and a certain self-protective timidity.

This at least was my prejudice, but it dimmed considerably after meeting Dr Adriana Scheibner and some others in the field of laser surgery.

Dr Scheibner, then still in her twenties, was not exactly what I expected. She learned her laser surgery from Dr Bill McCarthy, a leading skin specialist at Sydney University, and had not long been established in private practice. She believed the laser technique had considerable merit, but the patients had to be treated carefully and slowly, and not in production-line proportions. She doubted Edelsten's claim that only one in fifty would be scarred by the treatment.

Scheibner, although new to the medical profession, was already in considerable demand, particularly for her skill in removing portwine stains, the disfiguring red marks some people carry from birth.

The medical community were generally uncomfortable about speaking against Edelsten. Although many of them were critical even to the point of outrage, few had the courage to speak up. They saw Edelsten as powerful and more particularly, litigious, and did not want to spend the time and money defending their stand in court.

Scheibner, knowing full well she was in for a battering, took the stand, stood by her principles, and agreed to be interviewed.

Although it was difficult getting others on camera, I spoke to a range of skin specialists in Australia and abroad. The very great majority agreed with Scheibner's doubt about Edelsten's claimed success rate, and were critical of the technique of using household 'Gladwrap' to bandage the wound.

Some 'leaked' information also began turning up on my desk suggesting Edelsten was charging the Medicare system far more for the treatment than his entitlement.

The research and the filming was conducted simultaneously. What I could get on camera was backed up by a range of documents and supportive typewritten records of interviews. I kept on telephoning Edelsten to organise the promised interview. He kept on stalling with more, transparently dishonest excuses. The more he stalled the more I was forced to turn away and find more evidence which was inevitably damning.

There is a convention in 'investigative' journalism that if you are going to conduct an adversarial interview than you leave that interview till last, so that you have time to accumulate as much evidence as possible. In a way I was grateful for Edelsten's persistent stalling. He was dealing me the time the *Four Corners* unit was hard pressed to provide.

By the end of July 1984 I was three weeks into the shoot. Geoffrey Edelsten married Leanne and departed for the United States for a brief honeymoon. I still hoped and expected he would be interviewed when he returned.

We found more tattoo patients and more evidence in his absence. We found more angry creditors, and a few people who were suggesting Edelsten was corruptly benefiting from various referrals for pathology and radiology services. We also managed to borrow from the Channel 9 *Sunday* programme a rather remarkable videotape invitation to a party Edelsten had held at his Dural manor.

The tape had Edelsten surrounded by bikini-clad models, being served champagne by a dwarf and much more. It was redolent with kitsch and in its own way revealing of Edelsten's appetite for vacuous glamour. Beyond the insight into the character of the subject of our report the tape could provide useful vision for what was becoming a picture-starved story.

The problem, however, was that I doubted I would be able to use the tape because Edelsten would own the copyright and be unlikely to grant permission. But when I called the production company about the rights they told me Edelsten did not own the copyright. He had never paid his bill and I was welcome to use it.

When the doctor returned he revived the same round of excuses.

We continued filming. I found a few doctors who had worked with Edelsten, who told me of his insistence that patients be referred for further services, like pathology and radiology. I made typewritten records of interviews of these conversations, and in one case persuaded one of the doctors to be interviewed. The doctor felt the Edelsten objective appeared more concerned with generating better business than providing better medicine.

We also found our way into a tattoo parlour to get an impression of another end of the story; why and how the tattoos were applied in the first place. The tattooist was a 'bikie' named Tony Cohen. When we were filming he told me a story.

One day a policeman strolled into the parlour. Cohen, expecting trouble, was surprised and delighted when the policeman asked to be tattooed. Here was an opportunity to inflict a bit of retributive pain. The tall policeman unbuckled his belt, lowered his trousers and pointed to his backside and asked that a tattoo of a bullseye be imprinted squarely on his bum. Cohen could not believe his luck.

The good luck continued. A week or so later an attractive woman came in and asked for the identical service. Cohen tattooed a bullseye on the lady's rear. When completed she asked how much was the charge. He suggested $20. She said, 'But my husband was in here last week for the same tattoo and you charged him $50, why the difference?'. Cohen looked at her and said, 'Well, there are arses and there are arses'.

The story, otherwise, was hard going. Edelsten was still holding out. His staff told me he was delivering a baby and asked that I send a list of questions. I sent the questions on the understanding they represented the broad outline and not the detail of the proposed interview.

Soon afterwards another interview appointment was cancelled. By now I was prepared to go ahead and put the programme to air without an interview and managed to have this communicated to the Edelsten bunker.

It was about this time that I began receiving calls from Peter Walker. Walker said he had heard I was 'after some dirt' on Edelsten and he would be happy to help.

He said he and Edelsten had been partners in a pleasure boat venture and Edelsten had bailed out owing him a lot of money. I smelled a rat — and then later met him.

Walker arrived at the ABC, looking small and furtive. He said the whole business was costing Edelsten a fortune in legal fees and he had suggested to Edelsten that he, Walker, would 'burn down the whole bloody ABC for $25,000'.

At the same time, while Walker was making direct approaches to me, alternative methods were being employed by persons who did not wish to be identified. I began to receive harassing phone calls at work and at home. The phone would ring at all hours with nothing but heavy breathing at the other end. At one point the Fire Brigade arrived at my home, claiming my house had been reported on fire.

The style of mischief I was experiencing is to some degree taking the place of the more conventional and less sophisticated stand-over campaigns. A clever harrassment campaign, inevitably impossible to trace, can ultimately exhaust the victim into submission.

By now the programme was in the editing phase. Walker was keen to see it, and keen to insinuate his way into the *Four Corners* offices. I was careful not to let this happen. Meanwhile the cat and mouse game with Edelsten continued. He would agree to an interview and then cancel.

The role Walker was playing became comically absurd. Even though he continued to insist he was not in league with Edelsten he happily acted as a go-between, delivering me a letter from the doctor. I told him I believed he was working with Edelsten. He blithely denied it, handing me the letter. Every contact made by Walker, every phone call from him, was meticulously recorded and placed in our burgeoning legal files.

I continued to research, film, interview and edit at the same time. Lawyers were called in to vet the script and view the 'rough cut' of the programme. The on-air date now loomed and we began promoting the programme as 'Branded'. Although Walker had told me Edelsten was not planning to try an injunction, that is what happened.

The programme was scheduled for Saturday September 15, 1984. On the preceding Wednesday a summons arrived. Edelsten claimed I had given him a verbal contract allowing him power of veto over the story. This is something a journalist would and should never do. We scrupulously guard the editorial control of our work.

Edelsten, Walker and the lawyers and judge viewed the rough cut of the programme. Despite the improbability of his claim that I had given him power of veto, he won a temporary injunction to stop the programme. Now the onus of proof was placed on me.

I had to prove a verbal contract did not exist. I knew it was not going to be easy. Edelsten had managed to gag the press by merely alleging he had such a contract. He also managed to win some breathing space. It would be another month before the court would make up its mind whether the programme should come under a permanent injunction.

This presented another concern. Our witnesses were now exposed to the other side, without the protection of the glare of publicity which follows publication. Soon after, two of the doctors who spoke against Edelsten reported they were being harassed by phone and through the mail. There was no proof of who was responsible.

The tangled web continued to weave, strangling and suffocating what was left of my energy for the story. Now that the tussle with Edelsten was public the phone rang louder. One of the callers, rather mysteriously, suggested that a package would be left for me with an ABC commissionaire.

The package contained a tape recording. When I played it I heard a series of conversations between Walker and Edelsten and others discussing their struggle with the dreaded *Four Corners*.

I don't think I can go into some of the things that were said, but if it was to be believed then Edelsten was prepared to sell his wife, if not to sell his grandmother, to stop the programme.

Another of the recorded conversations, between Edelsten and Leanne, has entered Sydney folk history. On the tape Edelsten tells Leanne about meeting the Painter and Docker hitman, Christopher Flannery. Here is a transcript of part of the conversation.

> Dr Edelsten: . . . this bloke will do it for 10 grand.
> Leanne: Maybe he's just charging you 10 grand.
> Dr Edelsten: Pardon?
> Leanne: Maybe he's just charging you 10 grand.
> Dr Edelsten: I don't know.

Leanne: Maybe if I asked him he wouldn't charge 10 grand?
Dr Edelsten: Oh, I think he would.
Leanne: You think.
Dr Edelsten: Yeah, I helped him and, em he just said he doesn't drop his price for anybody and that's it. He said, 'I'm a professional — its my livelihood'.
Leanne: Beats people up . . . is that all he does?
Dr Edelsten: He kills people.
Leanne: Yeah.
Dr Edelsten: Yeah, nice young feller.
Leanne: Yeah.
Dr Edelsten: But um, I think he is a professional killer.
Leanne: Has he got a nice house . . .

Meanwhile the voracious appetite of the schedule had to be satisfied. The month stay of execution was no reprieve for me. *Four.Corners* wanted a story so I was sent off to cover the final days of the Costigan Royal Commission in Melbourne.

For the next month I did my best to concentrate on this different can of worms, all the time more than a little awkward about the prospect of returning to Sydney to appear in court to debate the injunction.

I was not, and never have been, happy about entering the witness box. The adversarial system is such that, quite reasonably, a witness's evidence must be tested and tested thoroughly.

A consequence of this is that the witness becomes a defendant. You can tell the truth beautifully, but still receive a caning and be made to look a liar or a fool. Like everyone else, I cannot think of a better system, but still your sense of fair play is offended from the very start. The system requires that a witness be punished in a sense for performing his or her civic duty. No wonder it is so difficult getting witnesses to come forward.

Beyond this, a reporter has another fear, the fear of being pressured into revealing a source. The other side knows our position and most likely will be happy to embarrass us into contempt of the court and disdain of the presiding judge or magistrate.

My major concern however, was the one of trying to prove that a verbal contract did not exist. I had no witnesses. Edelsten had Leanne. If it came to my word against his I wondered whether the court would lean towards the reputation of the doctor rather than that of the reptile from the press.

In mid-October, the day arrived. As expected, I sat with a pitcher of water, a bible and a verbal onslaught before me. Edelsten's detractors say he might have a problem settling other bills, but he never stints on lawyers. They are paid well and he pays for the best. I fidgeted and swallowed and stretched at the seams of my fatigued David Jones suit. My heels were so far dug in they must have dented the ceiling below.

But I did have one good moment. Edelsten's barrister attacked the proposition that I had checked a wide range of experts who questioned Edelsten's claims about the merit of his tattoo removal treatment. Edelsten argued there were very few specialists in this field with more expertise than himself. I was asked to identify the people I consulted. Even though I had provided a typed list I was not allowed to refer to it.

I don't know where it comes from but I do have a memory that surprises me in its capacity to deep-freeze and later defrost the clearest recollections.

The memory rose to the occasion. I closed my eyes and began to reel off the names. After naming about eighteen such people I was asked to stop. I opened my eyes and could not help noticing Edelsten looking a bit ill.

But generally speaking I did not perform well. I was much too anxious, too suspicious of the other side not to look suspicious myself. In the end I was saved by an even worse performance from Geoffrey and Leanne. They could not resist the urge to add further strain to their version of events.

The Edelstens went into detail about a visit they claimed I

had made to their house. They told the court that on the visit I had agreed to give Edelsten power of veto over the program. The date was identified as Sunday July 8, four days before the filming began. They said I arrived early in the afternoon. Leanne remembered I had worn a brown suit.

I did not hear the evidence and was asked about it later by the ABC lawyers. I told them the meeting was a myth and produced my small blue pocket diary to prove it. On the afternoon in question, I was playing tennis with a group of neighbours . . . and besides I would not be seen dead in a brown suit.

There was a lot of fuss about that little blue diary. I had reason to regret its introduction as evidence and confess I did not properly understand what was happening at the time. For all of that, it performed a miraculous service.

The people with whom I played tennis were all summoned. There were quite a few of them. They mostly remembered my being there (I am a conspicuously hopeless tennis player) and my name was found in the tennis court register. Some even had diary entries of their own putting me there, on that afternoon, at that very different court.

Now Edelsten's evidence was beginning to look a bit sick too. He offered to cease proceedings and pay the ABC's costs. We bargained over conditions. We asked that he be available at last for the long awaited interview and were able to set the time and place.

He asked that a non-disclosure clause apply to the proceedings. In other words, no one would know whether we had won or lost. We were not happy about this, but agreed rather than carry on an expensive legal fight. The fact that the programme could now be broadcast was itself evidence of a win to the ABC.

The interview was scheduled for Sunday October 21. By now, all vestige of goodwill between Edelsten and myself was extinct. He arrived, with Leanne, at an office we had set aside in what is known as the 'Fort Knox' building. 'Fort Knox' was the home of our television executives. It is therefore considerably more spacious and tidy than the cluttered mess of the *Four Corners* office. (I can't think of any profession with more untidy work conditions than those tolerated by Australian journalists.)

We assigned two camera crews for the interview. For what it is worth, any prospective interviewee can forevermore regard this as a clear signal that the experience is likely to be unpleasant. Usually interviews are done with one camera. When the interview is complete the camera operator turns the camera around to shoot what are known as the reverse questions and the shots of the reporter listening attentively which are known as 'noddies'. We also film what is known as the 'two shot'. This shows the reporter and the interviewee sitting together. After a savaging by the reporter, an interviewee is unlikely to be in a cooperative frame of mind to stay for the extra filming, so the pictures are collected at the start. The two cameras are also there to catch the action if the interviewee chooses to walk out.

In this case Edelsten needed no warning the interview was going to be a tough one. Just before it began he disappeared into the toilet with Leanne and emerged minutes later looking primed for battle.

We went at one another straight away, like a pair of Queensland blue heelers. In most interviews the toughest questions are politely saved for near the end, but there are occasions when a reporter will show no mercy and attempt to unsettle the interviewee at the very start.

This is common in the 'live' studio interview when you know a well-practised politician will calmly deflect the toughest line of questioning. One rude question at the very beginning can unsettle the politician's reserve and produce an honest and probably unflattering response.

Richard Carleton's first question to Bob Hawke when

Hawke replaced Bill Hayden as ALP leader, 'Can I ask you whether you are a little embarrassed at the blood that is on your hands?', is a good example.

I must say I have never had a great deal of faith in this sabre-charge style of journalism. I think in reality few people with something to hide will break down and confess, no matter how clever or rude the question. The celebrated Royal Commissioner, Frank Costigan QC, used a tactic, which, it seemed to me, had a greater likelihood of success.

Costigan knew many of the suspected murderers and drug dealers who appeared before him were not the types to be conscience-stricken about telling lies. If you ask them whether they were in Hong Kong at the time of a drug transaction they are likely to say 'no'. If you then produce the air ticket and hotel booking showing they were there, it is hard to maintain the fiction.

I tried something similar with Edelsten. Edelsten was charging the government a fee for the tattoo removal which was greater than the proper entitlement. I had a copy of a letter sent to Edelsten by the Health Insurance Commission telling him of the proper rate.

I asked Edelsten about the fee he charged and then asked whether he had ever been told not to charge the fee. When he said he had not received any such advice I produced the letter which suggested otherwise.

The mood of extreme tension did not improve from that moment. My hands shook with fear and fury. Edelsten spat his replies with undisguised contempt. Someone should have thrown a bucket of water over us. It was not a good interview, generating more heat than light, but in the vernacular, it was 'good television'.

At that very moment, it is probably true to say my determination to get the story told had over-ridden my sense of fair play. Something told me we should try again. With much of the fury spent, there was a chance a second interview would be calmer and more reasoned. But Geoffrey and Leanne decided against a retake and headed for the lift.

I was not to see him again for some time, but he rarely strayed from my attention. The following week I completed the report on the Costigan Royal Commission which had just wound up. This meant the other story, 'Branded', had to wait an extra week. It was finally screened on Saturday November 3, 1984, four months after it had begun.

The harassing telephone calls persisted. My wife reported that our house was being watched. The ABC Managing Director, Geoffrey Whitehead, very kindly put myself, my very pregnant wife and my family up in a hotel that weekend. The kids had room service icecream at the taxpayers' expense. To this day the memory revives a ridiculous fusion of gratitude and guilt.

For the next month or so my diary records some tidying up after the 'Branded' story, preparation for a trip to Ethiopia to report on the famine and the birth of our son, Timothy. From Thursday, December 13, the entries cease. The year was 1984, an appropriate time for the arrival of the 'Thought Police'.

When I had produced my diary in court back in October, Edelsten became aware of the prospect that it contained information about some of my sources. He complained to the Australian Federal Police that the information I collected must have been collected illegally and presumably informed them the diary might contain clues to the alleged source.

It is true that I did have copies of correspondence between Edelsten and the Health Department. The letterheads and contents of the documents suggested they were authentic and this had been confirmed after discreet inquiries.

It is also true I did talk 'off the record' to various Health Department officials about Edelsten. I did not know who had leaked me the documents. I had followed a common formula in making sure I did not know. When digging deep we often make it known we would like to see these things. The papers will sometimes arrive, almost always in a plain envelope with no accompanying note. The envelopes are discarded. The papers are photocopied and the originals thrown away.

I cannot be too ingenuous and pretend to be a totally innocent party in this arrangement. In the minds of many people, by receiving the documents I had invaded someone's privacy. In the minds of some I had possibly broken the law. In my own mind I felt my actions were justified. The matter I was dealing with was of public importance. It was about allegations of medical malpractice and a dubious practice that was costing the Commonwealth a fortune.

This issue seemed much bigger than one of a reporter receiving a 'leak'. But the Australian Federal Police appeared to think otherwise. If my receiving the Health Department information was an offence, it was deemed a Commonwealth offence, so it became a matter for the Australian Federal Police.

On December 13, I arrived home to find a small team of embarrassed police perched in the living room. My wife, a country girl, was trying to be hospitable, juggle the baby and understand what was going on.

The cops said they had a search warrant and they wanted my diary and reporter's notebook. I don't know whether I was more angry than sick. I told them I was astonished they would allow themselves to be used in this way. One of the cops sheepishly explained that they feared there might be a Royal Commission so they thought they should be careful to do this by the book. They were acting, I suspect, not out of common sense or corruption but because they were frightened. I have found that when you can strip away the conspiracy theories, so much human mayhem has common fear as a shallow inspiration. So the Feds struck at the minnow while the mackerel swam lazily away.

I gave them the diary and the notebook rather than have them search the house and upset my wife. They would have found them anyway. It was not until later that I learned they had also blundered with the warrant. Lawyers told me it was invalid.

The police took away my private thoughts. This is something I thought Australia was above, but the fact is that many worse things happen in Australia every day.

It was a good lesson all the same. So much about being a journalist is prying. We like to think we trespass with care and good reason but we will obviously make blunders of our own from time to time and I suppose it helps to know what it is like to have our own privacy invaded.

The diary was eventually returned. A range of complaints, including those relating to the tattoo removals, was heard by the NSW Medical Tribunal. After lengthy deliberation and a further appeal Edelsten was barred from medical practice in NSW. He was also later charged by the NSW police with conspiring to assault a patient.

Every year since the programme was completed I have spent hours and weeks being interviewed by police and lawyers and being grilled in court over Edelsten-related matters.

It would probably be fair to say there is only one person more sick of the Edelsten affair than myself, and that would be Edelsten.

In 1985 during a rare breathing space in a procession of Edelsten related court hearings the doctor bumped into my brother Roy. Roy was standing on a Sydney street corner during a bus strike searching for a taxi when one pulled to a halt beside him. The taxi already had a passenger who offered to share the service. The generous passenger was Geoffery Edelsten, who had recognised my brother.

There was faltering conversation in the back of the cab. Roy offered the information that I was in the Northern Territory making a different film. Edelsten interrupted, '. . . let's hope he gets eaten by a crocodile.'

Edelsten was convicted in July 1990 for soliciting Christopher Dale Flannery to assault Stephen Evans, and for perverting the course of justice, by rendering medical treatment to Flannery with the intention that Flannery avoid a trial. When he was released in 1991, the case against Stephen Evans was revived after five years, and Evans was acquitted of the charge of demanding money with menaces. I hope that brings the chapter to a close but I doubt it will.

Much attention in the various court rooms has been given to the legality or otherwise of the tape recordings that were delivered to me at the height of the struggle. I did not know it in the beginning, but I learned later that the recordings were made by a Sydney private detective, Rex Beaver.

Rex is a curious fellow, a non-drinking, non-smoking, non-swearing, church going private inquiry agent. He found it useful in his line of business to collect intelligence by listening to a radio scanner in his spare moments. The scanner picked up random car phone conversations. Although the people talking by car phone presumed their conversations were private, this clearly was not the case. To some extent the conversations were being broadcast on a publicly accessible frequency. The courts and Telecom have since moved to plug this loophole.

As it happens the tape recordings were not essential to my proving the story we broadcast. In fact I have never relied on tape recordings as a research device. I find it is generally a waste of time as you end up having to listen to a conversation twice. There is no substitute for good note-taking. Somehow the physical act of committing the words to paper also helps commit them to memory.

Good notes are also generally respected by the courts as valuable contemporaneous evidence of a conversation, whereas there are endless arguments about the possibility that tape recordings are not original and may have been corrupted in some way.

The notes should be as verbatim as possible. It is better to write down the actual words that were said, rather than the words you think were said. I find it is better to keep all notes in one book and transfer key conversations into separate typed records of interview. It is better to do this work as close to the time of interview as possible, while the memory is still fresh.

I find it a practical help to keep a list of names and telephone numbers in the inside front page of the book as a ready reference guide. I have also learnt not to write down names of people who are unattributable sources.

The Edelsten experience reinforced for me the importance of good note-taking. The original scrawling in my reporter's notebook and the typed records of conversations helped me to concentrate on a maddeningly complicated and elusive story. The notes were used as important evidence in the many courtroom dramas which followed the report. And I have to say that little blue diary, despite having caused me immense trauma, went a long way to saving my skin. Since its return I am inclined to look at it fondly.

6

'BANNED AID'

I am fond of the Henrik Ibsen quote, 'A man should never wear his best trousers when he goes out to battle for freedom and truth'. I suppose it suits my innate daggery and concede Ibsen and I are probably pretty much on our own. Wardrobe consultants are creatures of power and persuasion. It is not hard to understand why young reporters would prefer their advice to mine.

When prospective reporters approach me, faces shining like the cover of 'TV Week', revealing in an instant their ambition to be as famous as Jana Wendt, I find myself devoid of sensible advice. Jana Wendt is a successful television journalist, first because of her talent, and second because of her experience. True she also looks good. But an attractive airhead with exquisite dress sense might find career longevity on *Wheel of Fortune*, not on *A Current Affair*.

What we say has always been more important than how we look. Our stories have always been far more important than ourselves. Well, that's what Henrik and I reckon, but we are becoming a little hoarse in the wilderness.

An excellent example of the competing tensions of style and content was evident in another wilderness, a famous one, which attracted tribes of reporters like myself in the expiring months of 1984.

The BBC reporter Michael Buerk, on his way back to Britain from South Africa, stopped off in Ethiopia. His cameraman, Mohammed Amin, encouraged Buerk to go bush, and there they recorded scenes of mass starvation. (There is a sad postscript to this story. When Colonel Mengistu's military government was finally overthrown in 1991, the rebels advanced into Addis Abbaba. Mohammed Amin lost an arm and sound recordist John Mathai was killed while filming the explosion of a munitions depot. Mo Amin had been there at the beginning and he was there at the end.)

We, in the developed world, were Christmas shopping at the time the first Buerk/Amin reports were screened. The pictures were shocking, exhausting and compelling. Money was diverted to the various aid agencies and more reporters diverted from their daily rounds to board the extra flights for Addis Abbaba.

Here was television journalism at its best and worst. Television took the Western world to those refugee camps so the indescribable could begin to be described. The speed and visual impact of television enabled those starving people to speak directly to the Western public. Television made the wheels of aid spin a little faster so that saving some of those people became not just an issue, but a reality.

What was also seen by the descending tribes of journalists, was a possibility they could obtain for themselves some sort of degree in compassion.

Reporters, well coiffed, scarf arranged at the perfect angle, and brow set with an appropriate show of personal distress, queued up to be filmed with dying babies. One respected colleague was observed asking a raggedly pathetic funeral procession to retrace their footsteps, so a second take of a 'piece to camera' could be recorded.

The 'piece to camera', sometimes called the 'standup', is as common as litter. This is when the reporter speaks to camera, either walking, sitting, standing, descending from a parachute or hanging from a helicopter. Reporters will go to uncommon lengths to get their faces on screen, hopefully in the most dramatic circumstance. They will, quite literally, talk under water (believe me it has been tried) in the quest for the most memorable 'standup'.

The Ethiopian famine was a subject rich with opportunity. The story was undeniably important, far more important than the storytellers. But how many of us felt we had the time or the inclination to even take the clippings file on the aeroplane so we could begin to use those compelling pictures and our own craft to tell the story properly?

I was one of the reporters to board a flight for the Horn of Africa. I did take the clippings file and some extra reference material, but that is to *Four Corners'* credit rather than mine. There is an insistence at *Four Corners* that reporters have a competent understanding of the subject before they start spending the budget.

Most reporters, not so privileged, are forced to operate within the confines of inflexible deadlines. This means they can do little more than report the obvious. There is barely time to cover the story. The experienced win perhaps a little more time to project some analysis; but few are given time to cover, discover and analyse.

A news reporter might have only hours or even minutes to meet their deadline. The time they have to compile the report is frequently much less than the time they must give over to coping with the considerable logistical problems of obtaining and meeting a satellite booking.

A reporter on a daily current affairs programme might have a little more time, but much of it can be exhausted looking sideways at the competition, rather than forwards at the story.

Producer Allan Hall, cameraman Chris Doig, sound recordist Guntis Sics and I had five weeks to complete one story on the famine. There might have been moments when we thought it a questionable privilege but that was then. Looking back I doubt if any of us would regret our time there. It's surprising how quickly you forget the inside of a five star hotel room, but none of us is likely to forget what it looked like inside a famine.

Our approach to the story was straightforward. We would trace an Australian aid convoy from origin to objective, from the rattle of a can in a Melbourne Shopping Mall to the scratch of a plough and the creak of a windmill, on an East African hillside. Public suspicion about the aid industry tends to focus on whether the money gets through, so we would follow it all the way, if possible.

One of the first depressing lessons we learned was that the aid industry is often cowed by the frailty of public sentiment, just as journalism is sometimes cowed by the frailty of public opinion.

Schemes which sought to sponsor one child from a village invariably seemed to attract large donations. But a scheme to supply an entire village with a clean water supply, despite the fact that it would contribute more to the lives of all the villagers, children included, will struggle for support.

We decided to film with 'Community Aid Abroad' which had just such a worthy and unglamorous project in mind. They wanted to transport an Australian drilling rig and some mechanically operated Australian water pumps to the province of Tigray, in Northern Ethiopia.

Australians are good at drilling for water; we have had a lot of practice. We also make a useful water pump, one that does not need petrol to keep it going, nor crates of spare parts to cope with perpetual breakdowns.

It seemed like a sensible project and the destination also made sense. Most of the aid to Ethiopia was going through the front door where it could be distributed under the watchful gaze of the Government of Ethiopia.

But Ethiopia was at war. Eritrea had been fighting for its independence for decades. The neighbouring northern province of Tigray was also battling with the Central Government — the 'Dergue'.

Unlike Eritrea, Tigray did not seek independence from Ethiopia, but a voice in a new democratic government. This was more of a civil war, but ultimately as indistinguishably bloody and costly as the one next door in Eritrea.

We planned to slip into Ethiopia with the aid convoy through the back door, to report on the famine from the other side of the battle line. It was not going to be easy. We knew we would have to enter Ethiopia from the north, through the Sudan.

When we checked with Sudanese car rental agencies it became quickly clear they were not going to let any of their vehicles across the border into a war zone. We scratched our heads and ended up with what seemed the perfect solution.

We worked out that the cost of renting an appropriate four-wheel-drive vehicle, even if it was possible, would be greater than the cost of purchasing the vehicle tax-free in Australia and shipping it to Sudan. Best of all, when we were finished with it, the vehicle could remain as part of the aid package.

A sturdy Toyota Landcruiser was purchased, equipped with some tents and cooking equipment, and hoisted onto the freighter, the *Golden Venture*. The ship was due to sail from Port Adelaide with a principal cargo of 6000 tonnes of Australian wheat.

We would travel more comfortably, via Qantas, some weeks later. With us went the customary 14 cases of filming equipment, a portable generator, our personal luggage and a month's supply of food. We could hardly ask the starving people of Tigray to find food for us that they could not find for themselves.

On my way through Sydney airport I bought a small Sony shortwave radio, which became in subsequent years as close a companion as my pocket diary. Shopping is a regular pastime for travelling film crews. It is a kind of therapy, far more popular than drinking and a little way in front of tennis.

I played with my new purchase on the plane, fretted a little after the brief stop at Singapore airport, where I saw the same model selling more cheaply, but recovered by the time we got to Bahrain. There is a reference in my pocket diary to: 'studying up on poverty, somewhere between choice of cognac and port'.

In Bahrain it was the turn of our cameraman, Chris Doig to fret. Chris had bought a bottle of duty free Scotch. When he learned 'shariah' (Islamic religious law) was in force in the Sudan, and that possession and consumption of alcohol attracted some unpleasant penalties, he decided to leave it in the airport toilet. I can still see his forlorn look as he exited the cubicle, and have sometimes wondered what happened to that bottle.

There was confusion at the Bahrain Departure Lounge and we somehow managed to board the wrong flight to Khartoum. Instead of arriving in the Sudan we found ourselves in Saudi Arabia without appropriate visas. There was another twelve hours delay as officials organised an escort to our proper destination. By the time we arrived in Khartoum the four Australian travellers were looking a little ragged.

Finding our way through Khartoum Customs and Immigration brought to mind the camel and the eye of the needle. There was a black sea of bodies. Our 14 cases could be seen bobbing above like flotsam from a shipwreck, as they were transported hand over hand across the top of the crowd.

One traveller was on his hands and knees on the floor as officials searched through volumes of Western magazines in his opened suitcases for any evidence of bare flesh. A *Playboy* magazine was an even more dangerous possession than a bottle of Scotch. Now the entire crew was looking forlorn.

As it happened, all we lost was the film from our sound recordist, Guntis Sics', stills camera. Taking photographs at the airport was also prohibited.

When we emerged, after another three hours delay, the four of us were fallen on by taxi drivers. We had arrived too late to change our money at the bank, and were too tired to haggle. The smallest currency we held was a US $20 note. There was one brief betrayal of ecstasy on the face of the driver, before the doors slammed shut and we rattled off into the night.

The next few days were occupied by meetings with aid workers and representatives of the TPLF (Tigray Peoples Liberation Front); the routine of form filling; and facing up to the merciless Sudanese telephone system.

When Allan Hall at last got through to Australia, he was told of the prospect of an Ethiopian Government military offensive into Tigray. We were advised that should we be caught, the Australian Government could offer no protection. It was fair warning. Journalists will go to a lot of trouble to have themselves filmed within sight and sound of the smoke of battle. What is sometimes overlooked is that they risk not only their own lives but those of the accompanying crew.

There is every chance that the gung-ho journalist will drag his film crew to a dubious martyrdom, on the umbilical cord of his own ego.

When we are working on a local story the realistic dangers are few, even when we are in pursuit of crooked cops and drug traders. At home, we know the jungle. If there is a risk there is also generally a warning.

But when we travel the dangers can significantly intensify. If anything the risk of reporting in foreign war zones is probably understated.

In November 1979 the ABC's London correspondent, Tony Joyce, was shot while on assignment in Zambia. With the cameraman, Derek McKendry, Joyce had rushed from London to Lusaka, following a report that Zambia had declared war on Rhodesia.

Joyce and McKendry had little sleep during the 36-hour trip, but even so, felt compelled to get to work, and took a taxi to a bridge which had been bombed by the Rhodesian Air Force.

On their way back from filming the Chongwe bridge, a gun shot, fired from the bush, struck the taxi and caused it to stop. They were then surrounded by a group of armed men, most wearing military uniforms. Joyce and McKendry were stripped of their shirts and shoes. The contents of their pockets were taken and the two men accused of being 'white imperialists', 'Rhodesian rebels', and 'spies'.

A police car then arrived, and Joyce and McKendry believed they were saved. The men were ushered into the back seat of the police car where they sat while their filming gear was transferred from the taxi.

At this point, the apparent leader of the group, a man wearing only a pair of black trousers and carrying an automatic pistol, fired his pistol through the open window of the car. The bullet struck Tony Joyce high on the forehead.

The blacks returned to the bush and the police took Joyce, now in a coma, to the hospital. After considerable obstruction by various Zambian authorities, he was finally allowed to leave the country. But Tony Joyce never regained consciousness. He died in a London hospital in February the following year. His murderer was never brought to trial.

This absurd incident took Joyce from his family and cost the ABC its best reporter. It was compelling proof, if proof were needed, that there is no immunity from angry rebels, drunken border guards or patrolling helicopter gunships. To the contrary, well-fed whites can make attractive targets.

There was time in Khartoum to contemplate the risks, and to decide how best to proceed. We all talked it through and although the debate was tainted by the usual degree of innocence and optimism, there was no overt foolhardiness.

There was turmoil instead in my stomach, but this was the result of a different war. A particularly vicious strain of bacteria began a prolonged assault on my digestive system. My habit, inherited from my mother, is to be stoic about illness. But this time there was no way I could ignore my tormentor. The pain was no amateur. This was a bacterial Gestapo, at its ruthless and efficient best.

When it didn't go away after many hours I was exhausted and frightened and began to doubt that I could cope. I telephoned the hotel desk and asked them to send a doctor. Within an hour or so an Indian-born general practitioner arrived, apologised for the standard of local hygiene, which he presumed was responsible, and asked if by chance I had brought any drugs with me.

I showed him the small kit of medicine my wife had pushed into my suitcase. He stared with wonder at the little bottles and packets as one who suddenly encounters unimagined wealth. He prescribed some anti-bacterial medication and pain killers, returned his own small packet of Aspirin to his kit, and departed.

For the next four days I lay on my back, in a darkened room, eating nothing. I sipped occasionally from a large jug of orange juice and listened to the shortwave service of the BBC. This was the worst illness I had ever experienced. The only thing good about being this sick was that the trauma swept away conventional tension. My accustomed good health was challenged to a point where all other everyday worries were suspended. But all the same, I was glad when the pain was gone, and my conventional tensions returned.

Some hundreds of kilometres to the south thousands of men, women and children lay in the dirt, with illnesses far worse. Their opportunities to reflect on a brave recovery were also far less.

We found a van and a driver to take us to them. The plan was to film at the Sudanese refugee camps near the Ethiopian border, and then carry on to collect our vehicle and other supplies at Port Sudan, when it arrived with the aid shipment from Australia.

When we drove out of Khartoum the Sudanese van we had hired was straining under the weight of our equipment and the impotence of the local fuel. A merchant sitting outside the hotel with one broken watch on a rag between his knees patiently watched our departure. He and the watch would still be there when we returned.

Beyond the city limits the highway swept into the desert. My window was a slide show of flashing images . . . impossibly overloaded buses and ancient trucks, the bones of dead animals pointing at us from the desert, and the security police with their large guns swinging towards us as we approached.

I don't know whether other travelling Australians are as discomforted as I am by the sight of violence buttoned into an official tunic. I have never got used to it and hope I never will.

After two days of getting lost and breaking down we arrived on January 12, at the refugee camp of Wad Kaulli. The van expired once more within sight of the camp so the final leg across the dry riverbed was completed on foot.

We walked in to the sounds of tents being hoisted, officials being busy and children chattering and laughing. It was not so different to arriving at the camping ground on the NSW South Coast, where I usually spent this time each January. It was not what I expected.

I have often had cause to doubt the value of first impressions. They are a trap for many journalists, and regrettably often an unavoidable trap. The truth we understand today is not always the truth we understand tomorrow.

The camp appeared to be coping and if I had no more light to cast on the story than this first light, that is what I would have reported. People naturally want to show their best side. Even at the camp, where some benefit could be obtained from putting the misery on display, human habit prevailed.

The spirit of optimism and survival hung by the front gate while the hopeless were quietly hunted to the darker corners of the camp.

For the first day or so we hung by the front gate ourselves

and listened to the stories. A handsome, well-educated woman who had lost her entire family offered with considerable dignity, politeness, and no trace of self-pity to cook for us. A simple man with a plain, honest face told of abandoning his desolate landholding, and with a child on one shoulder and his possessions on the other, walking hundreds of kilometres to replenishment.

He talked of returning to his landholding and some modest prosperity, with, I would have thought, undue confidence. But the confidence and the courage were inspiring. There are times when humans can be enormously impressive.

We went on to the temporary hospital where one English doctor stood before a thousand sick and dying faces, all patiently waiting their turn. The 'triage' system, used in the battlefields of France during the First World War, was being revived. The doctor moved among the refugees separating them into the ranks of the saveable and the unsaveable.

For a journalist there is acute discomfort every time we find ourselves pointing our cameras through the keyhole of human misery. At least I hope there is. Sometimes the best we can do is recognise the intrusion and behave with appropriate sensitivity.

But on this occasion the issue of our presence was no mere emotional dilemma. It was an issue of life and death. The solitary doctor was there to save lives. Should we interrupt him and rob him of valuable time, some of those lives might not be saved.

We decided not to interrupt the work. There would be no retakes. Usually in circumstances like this, the same scenes are shot over and over again, so we can get different angles, and wide-shots and closeups of the same people. It is a tedious, time-consuming business but necessary for the film editor to pull the scenes together into a cohesive, visual story.

We tried to stay out of the way of the doctor and cover the action as best we could. It proved difficult. Wherever we went the doctor followed. After a little time it became embarrassingly obvious he was anxious to be filmed. One of the great mysteries of television is the enormous appetite it provokes in people to claim their place in recorded history. We did some quick filming and moved on.

Back at our camping space we were cheered by the arrival of a BBC film crew. There was the prospect of company and comradeship and by the look of their gas-powered refrigerators, some comfort as well.

We looked on with envy as they unpacked. British television current affairs teams are far larger than their Australian equivalents. Beyond our complement of producer, reporter, cameraman and sound recordist they had a researcher, a camera assistant, an electrician, and a cook. There were two drivers for the two impressively equipped Land Rovers.

Ever anxious to soak up information I insinuated my way into the company of the person most likely to help, the researcher. The operation was not entirely a cynical one. The researcher, Chris Terrill, apart from being well informed, was also pleasant and interesting, and we seemed to get on well.

Australian film crews are probably a bit like the Australian military. At the small unit level they work very well. They seem to have the common-sense attitude of taking advice from the person with the best advice to give, regardless of rank . . . or so the story goes. It has always pleased me that outsiders seem to have trouble working out who is boss.

But the British were very different. Their habit of respecting rank, whether or not the respect is deserved, seemed evident with this film crew. There was an obvious hierarchy and my deference to the lowly researcher seemed not to be appreciated by their producer and reporter. The British crew worked longer, and although we wondered at the necessity of some of the labour, I have to concede they worked to a higher standard.

Because we were so much smaller, we seemed more efficient and more mobile. For the next few days we found ourselves arriving ahead of them, at the various locations, and after a few days they seemed too busy to be friendly.

At another camp for Eritrean refugees, Wad Sherrife, we ventured beyond the front gate. The lament was the same. A constant stream of the sick and hungry arrived daily to discover that at journey's end, there was not enough food and medicine.

A Canadian nurse explained that children were the most prominent victims of famine because they did not have the body weight to resist disease and malnutrition. An Eritrean father who had been turned away beckoned me to follow him to a shanty at the back of the camp. He opened the flap to show our camera his dying children. I have never felt more useless.

One of the unspoken rules of reporting on the aid industry is you don't criticise. The reasoning is that by revealing the flaws in the aid business you give people an excuse not to make donations. But without the criticism there are fewer checks and balances and perhaps a lesser standard of competence than might be expected from equivalent costly enterprises.

I was given to wondering on occasion whether the distribution of aid might not have been a great deal more efficient — but I did not say so in my report. I stuck by the unspoken rule. After all, who was I to attack Florence Nightingale?

We made our way to the border city of Kassala and found a hotel. As usual, the first thing I unpacked was my radio. The first story on the nine o'clock BBC news reported a blunder with particular personal significance.

The Ethiopians had seized the Australian aid shipment bound for the rebel regions in the north. How had it happened? The *Golden Venture* was supposed to sail for Port

Sudan. At the last minute, for reasons I have never understood, an extra cargo of 'World Vision' wheat was dumped on top of the rebel shipment, and the ship was ordered first to the Ethiopian port of Assab. It was a bit like the Allies sending supplies to the French Resistance via Nazi Germany.

The clearly marked bags of wheat and the ship's manifest made no secret of the *Golden Venture's* intentions. It was hardly surprising that the Ethiopians would sight the supplies bound for their enemy, and seize the entire cargo.

Our chances of pursuing our own intention of following the cargo to its rightful destination were instantly eliminated. I have never learned what happened to the brand new Toyota and all that camping equipment. In all probability the ABC cargo quickly became a proud possession of one of the favoured sons of the Dergue.

I rushed into the neighbouring rooms to tell the others. We gabbled and gesticulated and walked around in circles for a while in the way humans do when confronted with an unexpected dilemma. The REST (Relief Supply of Tigray) people appeared at our door soon after having also heard the BBC broadcast.

They were a little perplexed by the idiocy of the Australians but remained polite. Instead of the drilling rig, water pumps and 6000 tonnes of precious wheat, they had four overfed whites to present to their starving people.

However, they offered to find space for us on another relief supply convoy. We could accompany the convoy into Tigray, and report the famine from the rebel side, from behind enemy lines.

We decided to accept the offer, and began arranging our kit for departure. The loss of the camping equipment gave us an excuse to go shopping. But at the local market our eagerness to spend was well and truly outclassed by the vendors' eagerness to sell.

'Howeja', they called as we passed. This was the local word for foreigner, and in the delivery it seemed alternatively welcoming and threatening. If we produced a camera the mood swung towards hostility. If we produced the pictures the camera took of our own home and family, there was instant friendship and flattery. A small family photo album is one of the best passports you can carry to the Third World, often enabling a swift and useful leap across the language barrier. A Polaroid camera is even more effective, but carries with it the risk of provoking a riot. On one occasion in North Vietnam I did just that, when I began handing out photos to people who could not afford a mirror, let alone a camera.

In the Kassala markets we kept our lens caps on and our wallets open. We purchased blankets and a small fuel cooker. Ever nostalgic, my eyes scanned the produce for a hint of Australia. At last, I saw it, a small packet of Kraft Cheddar cheese which had somehow found its way from Port Melbourne to Port Sudan and another world. The cheese is a long-time favourite of my children. It reminded me of them, and the arguments at dinner time, inevitably about a surfeit of food, the food they would not eat.

Back in our hotel room we waited for the REST people to tell us when the convoy was ready to go. We passed the time with a pack of cards. We should have been the right number for 'Five Hundred' but regrettably we were three and a half, rather than four. I could never get more than half-interested in the game and this drove the other three crazy. When I made yet another hopeless bid, they rolled their eyes and looked for something else to do. It was the perfect opportunity to produce my battered set of Travel Scrabble again. Scrabble was my game, but they too, were weary of defeat.

There was one moment in the waiting game, when the monotony was broken by the appearance of a French photo-journalist, on his way back from Eritrea. He told us to watch the skies. The Ethiopian MIG fighters were conspicuous and dangerous. A few days earlier they had attacked a column of refugees.

The Eritreans monitoring the pilot's radio transmissions from the ground, heard the pilot report to base his reluctance to fire upon innocent civilians, and then the command from his base to do so.

The photographer told of a MIG attack on his vehicle. If they miss the first time, you have time to abandon the vehicle and hide, as it takes over a minute for the fighter to turn back. There was no such chance with the helicopter gunships, he warned. They could hover above the target and shoot until their ammunition was exhausted. For these reasons the convoys travelled at night, when the Ethiopian airforce was asleep.

A few nights later we got the call to go. REST packed our camera cases on top of old Italian trucks, already laden with bags of sorghum. We were separated and squeezed into the already crowded cabins of the trucks. When we arrived at the Eritrean border the number plates on the vehicles were changed.

As soon as we crossed, weapons were taken on board. A Tigrayan 'fighter' climbed into the cabin with his Russian AK47, the all-purpose weapon of the liberation fighter the world over. A belt laden with hand grenades bumped and jolted beside me.

I strained for comfort and distance. There was no hope of the slightest relief, no chance of sleep, but I was far too alive to rest anyway. The heavy trucks bashed over rocks and sand. The headlights sprayed through billowing clouds of dust, illuminating the dead landscape, and bringing to life the occasional image of an armed fighter, standing at guard by the makeshift roadway.

We stopped frequently. There was rush and activity and for us, confusion, as we climbed down from the cabins and huddled together. From the darkness we heard 'Howeja' before the speaker was seen moving shyly into the light to shake our hands.

The stoppages were mostly caused by vehicle breakdowns, but once by an exploding enemy mine, which paralysed a lead truck. The many guards along the roadway were there to protect us not so much from the Dergue, as from rival liberation fighters.

The Tigrayan convoy was moving towards home territory through Eritrea. Though the Eritrean Peoples Liberation Front was fighting alongside the Tigray Peoples Liberation Front, splinter rebel groups sometimes attacked, adding extra bloodshed and confusion to the twenty-three year old struggle.

At dawn the vehicles disappeared. It was a magic trick which impresses me still. There is little cover in the desert, but what there was was used so effectively, it was as if the entire convoy was neatly folded into the map. The vehicle tracks were swept as dawn fell and fatigue pointed us towards our bunks.

We slept for the few hours it took before the heat and glare aroused us. I heard Guntis playing with his small 'Walkman'. Guntis is a musician, and guarded his tape player, tapes and portable speakers, as assiduously as a child with a marble bag. I took out my shortwave radio and searched fruitlessly for Radio Australia. Guntis and I eyed one another and cautiously exchanged toys, but only for a few minutes.

The TPLF brought a meal. We were embarrassed they had spared precious food for us, and so were doubly obliged to enjoy it. It was a chili and chick pea dish served on 'injera', a bread made from fermented dough. It would have burned the bum out of a rhinoceros, but we did our best to look pleased.

At nightfall, the convoy moved off once more. We bounced about in the cabins like sandshoes in a washing machine, quickly regretting our lack of sleep. As it turned out, the vehicles were even more exhausted than their occupants, and breakdowns persisted through the night. The drivers effected ingenious temporary repairs, which would have done an Australian bush mechanic proud. But the delays were costly and dawn arrived with us still one hour short of our destination; the rebel held town of Sheraro, in northern Tigray.

There was a great deal of shouting and repacking and for us, once again, confusion. The convoy leader decided to pack us into one truck and send it on ahead to Sheraro while the rest of the convoy stayed hidden in the desert.

They were acting as if there was no time to waste. The four of us quickly recognised this moment, and this decision, as a critical turning point in our fragile lives.

We tried to tell them to let us stay and sweat the day out with the convoy, but we were pushed into the cabin. The accelerator was pressed to the floor and the vehicle sped into the desert.

There were seven people in the cabin. We had barely room to breathe and there was little or no talk. First light was a favourite time for the MIGs to attack. Sheraro was a favourite target.

The plume of dust created by the roaring truck could have been spotted by a MIG pilot from the other side of Africa. I was inwardly furious that I could so stupidly allow my life to settle on whether or not an Ethiopian pilot felt like sleeping in.

After half an hour we spotted the distant steeple of the bombed-out church at Sheraro, and concentrated our collective will on moving it closer. There was still no talk.

And then I spotted a large hare. It was bounding away across the desert and was the first evidence of wildlife I had seen. I pointed out the window. 'Look', I said. The other six hearts stopped for a moment, restarted and powered a chorus of loud complaint. I had not meant to, but I had almost caused six grown men to shit themselves. They thought I was pointing at a MIG.

We scooted into Sheraro. The truck was squeezed between two small buildings and a false roof was pulled over it even before the dust settled. We emerged white and creaking from the cabin and were shepherded to a nearby hut.

There were cool rooms and clean bunks. In the minutes before I fell asleep I forced myself to try Radio Australia once more. After twiddling for a few seconds I heard the distorted racket of the Radio Australia kookaburra, followed by the Australian news bulletin. Paradise!

Later in the day Allan and I went exploring. We were back soon to gather up the others for some filming. We had seen a camel-train arriving with an interesting cargo.

At the doorway of a local merchant we filmed the protesting camels as they were forced to their knees, so the cargo of European Economic Community milk-powder and Canadian wheat could be unloaded. The food, given as a gift to Ethiopia, was being peddled on the blackmarket. The Ethiopian Government was at war with its own people, and here in Tigray they had to pay, even for charity.

Early that evening the food convoy we were accompanying arrived, paused to collect us, and then set off on the final leg. The truck that Allan and I climbed into proved to be an unfortunate choice. After an hour of bashing over sand drifts and small boulders the steering collapsed. The front wheels had to be manhandled every time we needed to make a right turn.

Some time after midnight, in the middle of nowhere, we stopped again, but this time with a flourish that suggested journey's end. Allan and I stepped into the blackness and were guided by torch-light down a bush track into an underground bunker which was REST headquarters, in rebel-occupied Tigray.

The REST people, having learned a little of the decadent ways of the Australians, had gone to a lot of trouble to collect a small supply of beer from the Dergue lines, and smuggle it across as a welcoming gift.

We are fond of nick-names at *Four Corners*. I had dubbed the sound-recordist I usually worked with, Tim Parratt,

'Talking', as in the talking parrot. I had dubbed my usual cameraman, Chris Doig, 'the dog with one eye'.

Now 'the dog with one eye' was found stretched back in a relaxed canine pose, the eye a little more glassy than usual. Chris was not one to make little of the fact that his choice of truck was far more sensible, and he had arrived while the beer supplies were more sumptuous. There were two small bottles left for Allan and I. We sat, and sipped, and sulked in the darkness.

When we awoke I had a quick look around. TPLF headquarters was big, as you would expect, but the whole camp had been camouflaged so that it was next to invisible from the air. TPLF fighters, each wearing khaki shorts, shirts, sandals and carrying a bandolier and AK47, were well in attendance.

They managed to look both friendly and formidable at the same time. We later learned they were an elite commando corps. Many were young women, and their orders were to look after us, and follow us wherever we went.

Having just awoken, the place I wanted to go to was the toilet. The young, female TPLF fighter, was insistently obedient to her task.

Back at the bunker I set about washing my clothes. A cut-down 44-gallon drum arrived, with a small quantity of precious water. I threw my clothes in, mixed a little detergent and began handwashing them. I saw my guard look disapprovingly at a bright red T-shirt.

It was now about 6 a.m. and I was hanging out my clothes when we heard the shriek of an approaching jet fighter. The young woman moved gracefully towards me and in one fluid motion lifted a khaki garment from the washing, draped it over my red shirt and was gone before the jet flashed overhead. The MIG was on its way to Sheraro, where we had arrived about the same time the previous day. I said my thanks and assigned the red shirt to the bottom of my bag.

From the headquarters we were allowed to branch out and

film the various food supply centres and medical clinics which had been set up along the refugee escape route.

In the TPLF-controlled areas, people were starved of the majority of aid being sent to the south, where the Dergue was in control. The TPLF maintained they were happy for their people to travel to the Dergue areas to avoid starvation. But the Dergue, they claimed, was deliberately starving the people in an attempt to depopulate the rebel regions.

The Tigrayans, they argued, had no choice but to head north and cross the border to the refugee camps in the Sudan. The food they were bringing in was just enough to fuel their people's northern journey. The refugees looked well enough, so much so, we were told, that an American journalist who had preceded us, complained angrily that there were no starving children to photograph.

The refugees travelled on foot and by night. To escape the preying MIGs they sheltered in dry creek beds during the day. We filmed them in their transit camps, by now well aware that they were better fed here than they were likely to be when they arrived in the Sudan.

Unfortunately they had no choice but to keep moving. REST could only hope that international aid to the Sudan would improve by the time the people arrived.

We moved among the refugees collecting stories. They told us why they would not go to the Dergue townships. The Dergue, they claimed, would not feed them anyway.

They spoke of 'show' food supply sessions, where food would be given, in the presence of members of the international aid community. After the foreigners had gone the food would be taken back. They told heartbreaking stories about the government's resettlement policy.

A woman told me how she had gone to a Dergue town, with her three children, looking for food. The soldiers, she said, took her and her children and put them on a plane bound for the south, separating her from her husband.

At the resettlement camp, she said, they were being starved to death, so she escaped. The woman spoke impassively about arriving at a state of exhaustion, and for the sake of the survival of the others in her family, having to abandon her small baby in the wilderness.

A man told me of returning home from the fields to find his wife and children gone. When he searched for them he learned that they too had been seized and forcibly resettled. I asked when he would rejoin them and he said, 'How can you find someone who is dead?'.

There were many such stories. I was persuaded they were genuine. Meanwhile the Australian Government was giving support to the Ethiopian Government's resettlement programme. An Australian aid representative told me later they had visited the resettlement camps, but only briefly.

Our next destination was the Boccano Mountains further to the south. The Tigrayans were labouring to build a road across the mountain to extend their supply route. It was another night journey and this time it would be on foot.

The Tigrayan commandos hoisted our filming equipment on to their shoulders and charged off through the bush. We Australians had only light clothing, sturdy footwear, and a small kit of personal supplies to burden us, but keeping up was extremely difficult. The fast walk was of Olympic pace. They later told us a company of Dergue soldiers was attempting to encircle us but thankfully we knew nothing of this at the time.

It was a 25 kilometre walk and the unfitness of the Australians began to show. Our condition would have been average for Australian city-dwellers in our mid-thirties but we certainly were not used to using our own muscles like these people.

I kept my head down, careful about wasting energy by lifting it and finding the sight too dispiriting. All I could see was the black bulk of the mountain in front of me, and some stars blinking in the small space above. Whenever I looked up, we appeared no closer to the summit. Allan, a smoker, was struggling for breath and vowing to kick the habit.

It was early morning before the pace seemed to ease, and through the gloom, a small stone fence and pathway emerged. The path led us to the smell, sound and finally the sight of a goat pen. We stumbled through the retreating animals towards the shape of a shelter and there we collapsed on a stone floor. Despite the discomfort we all fell into the most deep and precious sleep of our lives.

In the morning the TPLF fighters woke us. One, with the face of a child, handed me a large mug of tea. We learned of the Dergue attempt to encircle us and were reassured that the fighters protecting us were more than capable of doing so. One, I was told, was a famous hero. I asked which one. Our guide Tecklewoini said, 'He is the one who brought you your tea'.

We were hurried to our feet, so the final walk could be completed before the sun was too high. We were drenched with sweat well before we arrived at a scene that was straight from the Bible.

When a television reporter describes a scene there is a minimal use of words. The components of a television report are pictures, narration, interviewees talking in vision, interviewees' voice over pictures, reporters talking to camera, actuality (that is, spontaneous dialogue), music, sound effects and natural sound.

All or some of these ingredients converge in the telling of a story. When we debate whether the words or the pictures come first I am inclined to say there should be no struggle for precedence. The ingredients should be arranged harmoniously.

When television writers accept that it is neither the words nor the vision that should drive the scene their scripts begin to work. One of the most important writing skills is the one of understanding when **not** to write.

The scene I was now looking at needed no words. My work as a television reporter has deprived me of practice in the use of words alone to describe a picture. Usually the camera does it for me and Chris Doig has unparalleled skills in capturing such a scene.

He abandoned the tripod and walked among the workers and became part of their toil. Current affairs work seems to appreciate a 'from the shoulder' look. There is also a bias towards shooting 'tight', that is, in 'close-up'. There is something dull and uninvolving about pictures that keep their distance from the action. But tight, from the shoulder work, requires acute concentration; and there is a higher risk that some of the footage, at least, will be unusable.

So encouraging the cameraman to abandon the stability and security of the tripod and go in tight is often a problem, but Chris needed no urging. His camera remained well framed and in focus, collecting small scenes that when later pieced together, would tell the story of that labour.

He followed workers in drab brown rags, struggling to roll large boulders down the cliff, as others chipped at the hillside with primitive tools, or their bare hands. There was the steady drone of industry as a work gang of a thousand men and women moved like a locust swarm up the hillside, leaving a naked trail behind them.

Every 'close-up' has to have a context. There is a sensible rule that at least one 'wide shot' should be captured at every location. At the summit Chris put his camera on the tripod for the 'wide-shot'. In doing so he managed to connect the scene we had just shot to the distant scene of another work gang, on the other side of the valley. In the distance we could see an identical scene, as another section of the road snaked slowly towards us.

Work, we were told, stopped only on Sundays, and when the Ethiopian helicopter gunships arrived. It was not difficult to see there would be little hope of surviving the latter, as there was absolutely nowhere to hide.

We walked back to the hut through the midday sun and once again fell exhausted on the stone floor. I remember, through the mist of a deep sleep, hearing one of the farm animals protesting loudly about my occupying its space. From the tone of the voice, I could tell the animal had some authority around the farm, but I was too far gone to apologise or feel any regret.

We slept for two hours, were awakened once again, and set out on the 25 kilometre return journey. By daylight we could see the mountain we had crossed in the dark. It looked even more intimidating, but we struggled over it, and I was beginning to feel proud of myself when a girl of no more than six years of age, carrying a large pitcher of water, walked effortlessly past me.

In these regions, the women are by tradition the water carriers. One of the evils of the drought was that it made their work far more difficult. Instead of a ten minute journey for water, they might have to walk for hours.

Soon after, a small boy appeared at my elbow, wanting to relieve me of my knapsack. His persistence overpowered my reluctance, and for the last ten kilometres I walked unencumbered. At the end he returned it to me, politely refused my efforts to reward him, and hurried back to his farm duties.

That night we camped in the open, the four of us huddled together under one slim blanket, too cold to sleep. At dawn I discovered Allan had rolled onto my radio and broken the aerial.

I let go with a withering burst of temper which was interrupted only by the arrival of an Ethiopian reconnaissance plane flying directly above us.

The fighters gathered us up and we were quickly off again, to be collected by a Toyota and returned to the base camp. On the way, we were told there was a battalion of the TPLF in training which we might be able to film. When we stopped I searched the horizon for evidence of the force and saw nothing.

I turned and asked the commander where they were. He raised his rifle, fired a single shot and an army suddenly appeared, as if from the ground.

We filmed the military exercise. Guntis, in a singlet and baggy bloomer shorts, wanted some additional sound of the troops running over the flinty desert surface.

A few men were selected to run up and down the hill with Guntis flailing and flapping alongside with his squat, grey boom microphone glued like a fat daschund to their heels. The entire army roared with laughter, falling down all around us, rendered impotent by mirth. Anyone who could neutralise an entire army that swiftly deserved great respect. Our good friend Guntis, we quickly realised, was worth millions.

We headed back to base in the Toyota, while the sun was still reasonably high. We knew that travelling by day was risky, but that the risk was moderated by the presence of a fighter acting as a lookout on the roof. In time we learned to search for the comforting shadow, skating alongside, of a lone figure looking skyward.

By the light of the lamp that night Teklewoini, our guide, suggested he and I play scrabble. Teklewoini was bright and affable and a reasonably good communicator but his command of the English language, it would have to be said, was only fair.

Be that as it may, I was prepared to accept the challenge.

In less than an hour Tecklewoini punched his last tile into a board illustrated with the most amazing collection of words I have ever seen. The words were all legitimate, just as Tecklewoini was the legitimate victor. Our guide, it transpired, had learned his English by committing the *Oxford Dictionary* to memory. I made him a gift of my Travel Scrabble kit and looked for something else to restore my ego.

Guntis was showing two of the female fighters how to play Five Hundred, Australian style. Guntis and I were each teamed with one of the women, and we began to play. My partner was tall and strong. Across her face was a cruel scar, the result of an attack by helicopter gunship. The scar made her no less impressive or attractive.

Even though we had no language to share I could quickly tell that my partner had a keen competitive streak. She was unlikely to have much patience with my usual illogical, sloppy game. I worked up an enormous sweat concentrating on that stupid game and for the first time in my life managed a win.

Next on the itinerary was the Tekeza River. This was the one patch of green in the entire region that the Tigrayans hoped could be made more fertile with the help of Australian irrigation equipment.

The problem was the farmland was like a green bullseye for patrolling Ethiopian pilots. The market-gardens were attacked constantly and the orchards just as frequently reduced to fruit salad.

We arrived, accompanied by a small Danish medical team which had just joined the convoy. The team comprised a doctor and his assistant. The pair of them managed, with understandable pride, to contain in their two backpacks all their personal requirements and an entire mobile surgery. The two men were a walking aid package 'par excellence', and they were cheerful companions to boot. By now we were about four weeks into our travails and we were probably a little tired of each other.

The Danes had never met Australians before and the only Australian they seemed to know about was Rupert Murdoch, so we began talking about the newspaper baron. They were amused by some of the famous Murdoch headlines like 'Headless Body in Topless Bar' and 'Terror from the Skies', a story reputedly about frozen toilet waste falling from aeroplanes.

We did a little filming around the farm, stepping around the large bomb craters, which peppered the area. The guards, ever anxiously looking skywards, soon ushered us to the cool shelter of a large underground bunker complex, which was dug into a nearby hillside.

The Danes and I resumed our conversation as a large tray of fresh fruit and salad arrived. For the past weeks we had lived mainly on tinned and freeze-dried food, so the prospect of fresh food was appealing.

But my tender stomach was not impressed. There was sudden pain and a pressing need to find a toilet. I rushed out of the bunker expecting to run into the usual female fighter intent on accompanying me, and to my great delight found myself alone.

I pushed up the hill along a beaten track to another joyous discovery. There beneath a hessian shelter was a classic Aussie two-holer dunny. It was the first proper toilet I had seen in weeks.

I wasted no time and was comfortably positioned when some raw instinct caused me to hesitate. I stopped, held my breath and listened. Drifting up from below, Tigrayan voices could be heard in earnest discussion. I was directly over the main command bunker and the unsuspecting top brass of the TPLF.

With trousers at half mast I thundered towards the nearest bush, away from what was, in fact, a ventilation shaft. Soon after I hurried back to the Danish medical team to report what happened.

As I left them to find the crew one of the Danes was seen rocking back and forth giggling and repeating the words, 'terror from the skies'.

Beyond the interviews recorded, and sequences filmed, we also collected a series of 'pieces to camera'. There is a theory energetically promoted in commercial television that the audience wants to see the storyteller. You will frequently see the reporter appearing at the head of a report, like a tour guide at the head of a journey. In public television there is a lesser adherence but even in the ABC the 'piece to camera' is a ubiquitous feature of all news and current affairs reports.

In commercial television, in particular, the theory is elevated to the presumption that a reporter's energetic, luminous presence is enough to save an otherwise dull story. The reality is that very few reporters are that interesting. Furthermore, I have little doubt most reporter's performances in front of the camera add nothing to their reports or their reputations.

But convincing myself of this, let alone convincing others, has never been easy. Journalists, like most people are poor judges of their own public appearances.

I am lucky in a sense. I have never been one to love the camera and I would not have it any other way. The reporters who are fond of looking at themselves can easily fool themselves into believing everyone else shares the same warm feelings.

The one thing a reporter speaking to camera can do, however, which is not so easily achieved by other means, is reveal something of how they feel about a situation. Some of the best reporter's pieces have emotion and sincerity. They are almost always brief, never gratuitous, and work best of all when the reporter has an honest keenness to speak the words.

By now with all the filming completed, including the 'pieces to camera', we turned for home. On February 1 1985, we rejoined the empty convoy for the return journey. It was another rugged trip and after four hard weeks most of our good humour had been ground into the dust.

At one point Chris and I quarrelled furiously about who would occupy a seat in the cabin of one of the trucks. I lost, and was shunted back to the open tray. While I was brooding mightily over this slight, a Tigrayan fighter, permanently assigned to the rear of the truck, gave me his cotton shawl to protect me from the monsoon tide of dust.

Further on, when the night was blackest, and exhaustion

complete, a flare exploded and the truck immediately lurched to a halt. The driver extinguished the diesel engine, and in the silence the fighter beside me could be heard switching the safety catch on his rifle.

The next noise was the stutter of a two-way radio conversation. There was more silence, and then finally a second flare was fired to signal we could proceed. The brush was with friendly Eritrean resistance fighters.

The next evening they found space for me inside one of the cabins. I slept upright and while asleep my glasses were jolted from my nose and broken somewhere on the floor.

There is a photograph of the four of us, soon after we arrived back in the Sudan. I can be seen holding my broken glasses, with my three companions alongside. In our eyes is the thousand-yard stare we sometimes see in the faces of the people we film. It is the look of an acquired experience which enters your consciousness as an emotional debt, which from that time on, can never be ignored.

It is true there had been friendship and good humour, we had lost some weight and shed some innocence; but it is hard to remove from your senses the feeling of the small hand of a child who is alive no more.

On February 6 we flew out and connected with a Qantas flight from Bahrain. The sight of a Qantas steward and the sound of the honest friendship in the unmistakeable Australian voice is a genuine tonic.

We had gone to cover a drought and returned with a report about a politically manipulated famine. The Mengistu Government in Ethiopia was spending 15 times more on armaments than on agriculture.

The Soviet Union supplied the weapons which improved the efficiency of the bloodshed, and secured Colonel Mengistu's otherwise doubtful right to rule. Meanwhile the United States maintained its powerbase in neighbouring Somalia, which was also skirmishing with Ethiopia.

Such was the absurdity of this superpower puppet-play that in preceding years the alliances were neatly switched. Before the present conflict, the United States had a toehold in Ethiopia while the Soviet Union retained influence in Somalia.

The TPLF and the EPLF insisted they received no outside military assistance, instead outfitting their resistance with weapons captured from the Dergue. There was no clear evidence to disprove the claim, although we were mildly suspicious of the American-accented, military-looking civilians, hanging around the camps on the Sudanese border.

Although it was hard to resist feeling a natural sympathy for the people protecting us, I was reluctant to be swept up by their cause. From what we could see the TPLF were careful to treat their prisoners-of-war with humanity and were doing their best to care for their own civilian population. But there was also the faint odour of Stalinist rectitude about their leadership.

There was also a depressing sense that after decades of struggle the ploughshares had been irretrievably converted to weapons of war. Tigray and Eritrea were so conditioned to the mechanics of a war economy you wondered whether there were still the skills to survive if peace was ever achieved.

The best reason not to take sides when reporting from a war zone is that you simply don't know what is happening beyond what you can see. And most of the time you can see very little. While military censorship blinds one eye, political censorship often blinds the other. We can never tell the full story and one of the worst mistakes is to pretend you have done so. The worst mistake is to report war as an adventure.

Our report was much less about the cause of the TPLF than it was about the plight of the people denied aid because they were on the wrong side of the battle line.

What could be said, with conviction, was that the famine was not just the result of drought and locust plagues. It was as much a politically induced famine. The people Colonel

Mengistu could not shoot he could starve, or at least he could try.

Across the entire African continent there was the smoke, litter and barbarism of a dozen such conflicts. The record of the Western world in improving peace and prosperity on the African continent has never been wonderful.

Even the business of granting aid can be counterproductive, if Western nations insist on applying their own complex economic principles to subsistence societies. As the reformed economies gear up to pay for imported oil and consumer goods, grain crops give way to cash crops.

When the economy dips, as it inevitably does, the peasants can't eat the tobacco which now sprouts where the corn once grew.

Even the provision of services like new paved roads can be harshly regarded by the peasantry, if all they are seen to do is bring the government soldiers and tax collectors a little closer.

Now the West was having a lot of trouble importing enough food and medicine to meet one emerging crisis. The media's response to the crisis was probably no more efficient or creditable.

One conspicuous fault in the media is that having put our work to air, the story no longer exists. There is a lot of talk of the need for follow-ups, but not always a lot of action.

I am glad to say that was not the case with this story. In 1989, reporter Mark Colvin led another *Four Corners* team back to the Horn of Africa. Mark spent a further five weeks, travelling deeper into Tigray. His moving report, 'The Forgotten Famine', showed that while the Tigrayans had gained ground in their military struggle, the struggle for life in the civilian population was no less desperate.

Devastated by the large number of people who died while on the long march to the Sudan, the Tigrayans resolved, this time, to stay where they were and hope that help would come. The result was that, while they did not have to die of the cholera and typhoid and other epidemics the camps engendered, they were forgotten by the world. And once again, few among the world's media had the funds or the determination to go and find the story.

The earlier report, my own 'Banned Aid' was broadcast on March 5, 1985 and the aid coffers were instantly swelled. There was a similar reaction a few weeks later when the programme was screened in New Zealand.

When we were editing the programme I was troubled by a piece to camera I recorded in a refugee camp. It was a stream-of-consciousness lament, and I had argued for its exclusion. I was embarrassed as usual by my customary dagginess, but more than that I think I was awkward about having revealed a little too much of myself.

When a reporter manages to encourage an interviewee to lower their guard and produce an honest outburst we are delighted. But we are curiously hesitant about revealing the same in ourselves. Andrew Olle and Jonathan Holmes thought the piece to camera helped the story. They ignored my bleating and I went to air, warts and all.

Although it might seem perverse to talk about personal performance against the backdrop of a famine there is a point. Artifice is an uncomfortable feature of television reporting and is easily detected by the viewer. The artifice is all the more evident when it is cast among the suffering.

The important lesson is this. The reporter's presentation is there to improve the story. The story is not there to showcase the reporter's presentation.

And in our presentation we should be prepared to be as honest as we try to be in our journalism. If it means revealing a bald patch, an unfashionable collar or an honest emotion there is a chance it might even strengthen the story.

I learned a great deal from my trip to Tigray and although it was hardly the most important lesson, it was good to realise that being a bit of a dag can sometimes help.

7

'THE DEAD HEART'

The most popular stories we do are almost invariably local stories. There is not much mystery about the ordinary person's greater appetite for knowing what is going on in their street, their village, their city, their state, or their country, before they seek information about what the rest of the world is up to.

Thirty years ago the very sight and sound of an Australian reporter standing under a fur hat before the Kremlin was a guaranteed attention grabber. In subsequent years many Australian current affairs programmes have sought to establish their 'big time' credentials by sending their reporters to all corners of the globe. It was a way of showing how grown-up we all were.

But in the 1990s the well-travelled Australian is a familiar figure. A great many reporters have puffed the hot breath of Australia in Red Square. A great many more members of the Australian viewing public have been there themselves. So the requirement to appear grown-up is taken care of by the natural process of maturing.

Fortunately there are many exotic locations to be found not far from our own front gate. I found one in the middle months of 1987, while I was seeking refuge from a bushfire I had helped ignite in the state of Queensland. The new shoots of democracy were yet to sprout there, but revival was on the way.

The reporter too was in need of revival. I was in a dreadful mess, having just emerged battered and blackened through the smoke. The Queensland experience had taken the last reserve of my depleted energy. I had stayed too long at *Four Corners*, where there is little choice but to maintain a Jesuitical conviction to the work, and little time for anything else.

The worst thing about investigations is the unavoidable reliance on the unknown. Critics of an investigation that did not 'make it' rarely give much thought to the possibility that good fortune was not in attendance or that there was nothing much to discover in the first place.

As any gambler will tell you, there is a lot of stress associated with the wait for good luck. And there is a twin evil in the fact that what you are waiting for is often a revelation of another act of turdish behaviour by your fellow man.

This was all probably not much good for my soul, let alone my good humour and even temper. As my diary recalls, I was so tense I had barely enough time to stop for a compliment. What I needed was a way to make these stories without so much reliance on revelation.

When we set out to muster the facts, not all the beasts oblige. The most cunning will stay buried in the scrub. But you return from the muster wiser for the experience. If you work at it it you may also find a way to pass on some of what you have learned. Besides, stories are not just facts. Beyond the collection of information, there is a hinterland of perspective which should be observed and explained.

On June 23, 1987 I packed for the hinterland, and wrapped a present for my eldest daughter's birthday. Packing a suitcase had developed into something akin to my own version of the Japanese tea ceremony. For an hour or so there was a quiet, absorbing ritual of choosing and placing garments and treasured home comforts. It was a soothing act that helped perpetuate the myth of an orderly life.

As the poet, William Blake, asked:

What is the price of experience?
Do men buy it for a song?
Or wisdom for a dance in the street?
No. It is bought with the price
Of all that a man hath, his house, his wife, his children.

There was enough time the next morning to see my daughter unwrap her present before the sound of the taxi caused me to bend, and hug, and step through the torn, coloured paper, into the next story.

Two boys, James Annetts and Simon Amos, had gone missing in north-Western Australia at the height of the previous summer. The mystery of their disappearance was partially, tragically resolved, four months later, when their remains were discovered in one sad corner of Australia's dead heart.

An overflying aircraft first sighted the vehicle they had been driving, stranded near the apex of a sand dune. The 1983 four-wheel-drive Nissan utility had suffered for months from a broken front drive-shaft. It would only operate in two-wheel-drive. The roof of the cabin would have been like a hotplate. On it the boys had carefully arranged a collection of tools to form the letters, 'SOS'.

The vehicle belonged to their employer, Peter Sherwin. At the time, Sherwin was Australia's largest private landholder. The cattle properties he controlled in northern Australia were larger than the land mass of Tasmania. One sizeable lump of his land sat like a saddle on the fence of the border between Western Australia and the Northern Territory. Sherwin had five huge properties on the eastern fringe of the Kimberly, about 500 kilometres north of where the boys were found.

On these properties Amos and Annetts worked their first and last season as jackaroos for the Sherwin Pastoral Company.

The boys' bodies were found an exhausting 20 kilometre walk further down the track from where the vehicle bogged.

Simon Amos, who was just sixteen years old, was beneath the sparse shelter of a small desert oak tree. He had been killed by a rifle bullet, most likely by his own hand. Seventeen-year-old James Annetts was about a kilometre further on, where the road faded into the desert. James had walked away from the body of his mate, to die an unimaginably agonising and lonely death, a victim of heat and heartlessness.

Not far from James' body was an empty water bottle, and scratched in the plastic was misspelt a poignant epitaph: 'My follt'.

But these few clues did not erase the mystery of why the boys travelled such a long distance in the maddening summer heat, to such a perilous location, and why young James took the blame.

Clearing up the mystery would need luck but the journey seemed worth it because of the ground we would be forced to cover. There was more to explore than the story of the deaths of two boys. Beyond that mystery there was an issue of child labour, of working conditions for the young and unskilled in the bush. There were questions about the hospitality of the bush and its people, and there was the story of our continuing battle with our own frontier.

When I had made the customary browse through the *Four Corners* clippings file I had found a crowd of paper which told of the legion of lost travellers who perished annually in the Australian Outback.

The taxi stopped on the way to the airport to collect the producer for the story, Paul Williams. Paul is an old workmate from the *A Big Country* days. There in the Rural enclave of the ABC, he used to chide me about my inappropriate city footwear, as he stretched back in his chair and banged his R. M. Williams riding boots on the desk.

He was perfect for the story, a good hard thinker, a clever television craftsman, and a good mate. 'Willo' also knew well the language of the bush.

We flew first to Griffith to see the Annetts family. When I picked up my bag, I saw people staring at me and as usual found myself checking my fly. No matter how many years I work in television, I doubt I will ever get used to the business of being recognised by strangers.

Paul and I drove to see Les and Sandra Annetts at their small, rented farmhouse out of town.

James was the number one son. His mother had arranged his possessions neatly in a large trunk. In that flimsy fibro cottage, the trunk was a shrine. I had never met James but I came to know him and, in a small way, to share the sense of loss.

An earlier generation might have been kinder to James. He seemed to enjoy the outdoors, hard work and sorting the world out with common sense and a firm grip. He was awkward in a schoolroom, and a little shy about authority. But he was keen to do well in his own way.

His money was saved not for clothes and movies but books about the bush, scout jamborees and camping trips. The letters he had written spoke about his first job with touching pride and restrained disappointment.

Les and Sandra Annetts were bereft, not just at the loss of their son, but at their own helplessness. When James went missing they didn't have the means to mount an expensive search. They told of encountering hostility when they questioned the station manager, Giles Loder.

After persistent telephone calls to the police, they said, they were treated like pests. Not all Australia was unmoved by the tragedy. There were dozens of cards offering support and expressing sympathy. But from James' employer, the Sherwin Pastoral Company, there was nothing at all.

Paul and I flew on to Adelaide where we tried to make contact with a representative from the Sherwin company to enlist some help.

We were not encouraged. Sherwin had a hermit-like

reputation. He was a bushie who had worked his way up from the drover's saddle to the baronial throne. But the bush baron had not forgotten his droving ways. Sherwin's minions, and many of his neighbours, were terrified of his frontiersman's approach to settling disputes.

One former neighbour told me that after a quarrel Sherwin chased him across country in his plane. The neighbour was forced to stop his vehicle when the plane suddenly landed on the road in front of him.

When Sherwin advanced with a pistol the neighbour grabbed his rifle from the cabin. No complaint was made, because, as he told me, 'I had a gun too and mine was bigger'.

Sherwin was not always on friendly terms with his neighbours. Although respected for his toughness and his remarkable mustering skills, he was also seen to be hard on his cattle and his workers. The harshest criticism we heard was that Sherwin would use his talent for mustering to discover cattle the previous owner did not know were there. He could then strip the property of the cattle and use the proceeds to buy another property. In this way, his critics claimed, he had created his empire; but it was a rather run down empire. When Sherwin finally fell into a $47 million debt to Elders Finance he was bailed out by a public float. The float was oversubscribed, proving that, although he had his critics, he had a great many supporters too.

We presumed, quite reasonably, that Sherwin's regard for journalists would rank below most people, down among the dingoes, or perhaps even some of the government inspectors with whom he regularly tussled.

The cattle baron was well into his sixties but this did nothing to lessen respect for his punching ability. I spoke to a lot of tough men of the bush who were obviously very frightened of Sherwin.

Adelaide was also the home of Simon Amos. He was from a broken family and had lived with his grandparents. We called them but they did not want to see us. We learned that other media had been given the same answer. We tried again, out of a wish to be persistent rather than to pester. But their will to be left alone was clearly unshakeable, so we did not call again.

There is a vague rule, more popular in commercial television than the ABC, that if you can't get the main 'talent' you can't get the story. This could translate as a brief to the reporter to move heaven and earth to smooth-talk someone else into telling a story they should be professionally capable of telling themselves. If you take the role of the storyteller seriously, you could be forgiven for taking offence.

What a reporter needs more than 'good talent' is a good focus. If you can find a simple, original focus to the story then you have a valuable reference point which helps you with every decision you are likely to make about whom to interview or what to film.

The best focus is a simple phrase or perhaps even a word which stands in your mind as a headline for the story. What began to form in my mind was a strange, clumsy expression I was not used to using. It was the word 'heartlessness'.

Paul and I set about finding out every detail possible about the short, unhappy careers of Simon Amos and James Annetts. We did not have the cooperation of their employers, but there were many workmates who also laboured on the Kimberley properties.

The 'jackaroos' were now labouring under the less romantic name of 'stationhands'. Finding them would not be easy. Many of the stationhands were itinerants. There were few permanent addresses and even fewer telephone numbers. There was a false trail of bogus names and addresses from others anxious not to be found.

I bought a large sheet of graph paper and began entering the names of the known workers and their period of employment. When we made contact we asked them for the names of other workmates. When we had a new name and some notion of their home town, we would tap into the bush telegraph and as often as not, track them down.

And so the little squares in the graph began to fill and slowly a pattern formed. The young workers would arrive at a Sherwin property like 'Flora Valley'. Some would stay, sometimes only for weeks or days or even hours. Many complained of ill-treatment. Some were unceremoniously dumped at the gate.

Annetts arrived at 'Flora Valley' on August 20, 1986, after a three-day, 5000 kilometre bus trip from Griffith. Simon had arrived a month earlier. By the end of the year they were some of the few to remain. The two novices emerged as two of the stayers.

Before leaving Adelaide, we made a stop at the local office of the rival Seven Network. One of their reporters, Chris Warren, had done some good work chasing the story. There is a lot of jealousy and competition in the media but I am glad to say there is great generosity too.

Chris let us view his tapes and passed on much of the benefit of his own research by telling us who would cooperate and who would be difficult. He gave us more names of people who had worked the Sherwin properties. In doing so, this rival journalist saved us days of work.

What is difficult for us to understand sometimes is that we cannot own a story. There are understandable tensions when journalists compete for information before a story breaks. There is understandable annoyance when one journalist profits from another's labour and manages to receive the credit. But in the end we are all better off if the public is better informed. Chris Warren, who had already broadcast his report, helped me in the way I hope I would help other journalists.

One thing we discovered was that many of the Sherwin workers found their way up from Perth; so we organised our flight to the Kimberley via the western capital.

A couple of stationhands who knew James and Simon reasonably well agreed to be interviewed. With a film crew borrowed from the ABC Perth office, we headed off for a morning appointment with one of them. He was traced to a squat littered with dismembered motorbikes, beer cans and dog shit. He was asleep on a mattress on the bare floor. A bleary eyed, tattooed mate led us to him, pointed and stumbled away.

So our first interviewee, Jim Ghilotti, woke to the sight of four neatly dressed authority figures standing over him. It took a little while but when he realised he was not being arrested but merely questioned for national television, he relaxed and gave an exemplary performance.

There was another interview, and some questioning of the local rural establishment about the Sherwin way, and another flight, this time to the north.

On the way we played the memory game. Paul would ask me questions like: 'what was the number plate on the Ford Zephyr your father drove in 1954?' I would answer 'AHH-754', and he would move on to something like: 'what colour underpants were you wearing on the day your oldest daughter was born?' He would write down the responses and question me again a week or so later.

When I answered correctly he would bellow with laughter, no doubt impressed by this glimpse into one of the great minds of television.

We stopped in at Broome. Here was the office of the Commonwealth Employment Service which helped organise jobs for many of the Sherwin stationhands.

We understood they had also received some serious complaints so we were keen to know more. Following the complaints, the office had placed a ban on providing employment to Sherwin's Kimberley properties.

On a jetty pointing into the Indian ocean we talked with a contact. The water was the bluest I had ever seen. As we talked, mackerel the size of dogs could be seen leaping and tumbling below.

It was that vision splendid which helps explain why the great majority of Australians cling to the coast. But we had no choice but to leave. The story took us inland towards the sunlit plains. We paused at Derby and tasted a first generous helping of country hospitality.

Clan Constructions, the survey company that constructed the network of roads where the boys perished, was helpful.

The owner/manager, Gerry O'Driscoll, told us how and why the roads were constructed. His company had been contracted by an oil exploration team to create what they called a seismic survey grid.

To properly picture the scene you would need to be way up in the sky in a jet bound for Singapore. What you would see is a lattice-work of red stripes, like the red welts from a whiplash, across the broad brown back of the Great Sandy Desert. The stripes are graded roads, networked like city blocks.

From the ground the roads appear so well made you could be easily convinced they were meant to lead somewhere. You would be wrong. The cross-pattern construction on the surface is there for the sake of the seismographer, not the traveller. Once in the grid, the traveller is caught like an ant on a barbeque, trapped in a lethal maze. The only way out is the way in.

Gerry O'Driscoll offered to help us find our way there and back again. Apart from a small number of Aborigines, his men were some of the few humans who could find their way around this part of the country with any confidence. We arranged to team up with one of his men before attempting the desert trek.

The next stop was the office of the Royal Flying Doctor Service, which was said to have monitored some of the last radio messages made by the boys when they were working at the Sherwin properties. The former policeman who ran the place seemed to regard the communications as having the status of top level KGB intercepts. He showed us the door.

We moved on to Kununurra, the northern inland capital of the Kimberley. The Kimberley is a popular resting spot for the caravans of retired Australians who have patiently waited sixty years or more before stepping out to have a look around.

But I don't mean to sound disparaging. It is a wonderful thing to see. The Kununurra locals joke that all the caravanners seem to notice is the different price of 'Omo' between one stop and the next, but I doubt this is the case.

The Kimberley is another land, a blazing bushfire of colour, a permanent sunset of spectacle. There is nothing like the Kimberley and its exclusivity seems also to be reflected in its people. They take on some of the brooding character of the muscular red hills.

We found one of the caravan parks where one of the former Sherwin stationhands was said to be temporarily settled. At the reception office I asked his whereabouts.

A red-faced woman caretaker with a baby on her hip yelped at me with the timid viciousness of a tormented spaniel. I am not sure what she said — she spoke an incomprehensible camping ground dialect — but I could tell it was not pleasant.

From time to time we could not help notice that the southern media was not always popular. There are people in the outback who hate the bleeding-heart reports on blacks by people who never have to live with blacks. They hate the attention and they hate the inattention and they just hate.

We managed to find the young stationhand, and some neutral territory, where he could be interviewed. He had the same story, of poor food and poorer conditions. He told of being bullied, but being too scared to leave. He remembered one of the boys being struck by the overworked station manager, Giles Loder, when the boy chose to resign.

Late that afternoon there was welcome relief from the bleakness of the story and the ugliness of our reception so far.

A decade earlier, Paul had made a documentary about one of the pioneers of the Ord River scheme, Ian Oliver. The scheme was a response to the Menzies era call for Australia to 'populate or perish'. The theory was that Australians would follow the water and that by creating another Snowy Mountains Scheme, we would open up the north and provide food for the hungry Asian market.

Instead the sudden flush of green, in the mostly barren north, fed every hungry insect in sight. By the time the dam was finally and officially opened, many of the settlers had already left.

Ian Oliver was one of the last to leave. But although forced from his landholding, he stayed on in the Kimberley where he now ran a large stock and station agency.

Ian took us for a short cruise along the Ord, and then treated us to a barbeque at his Kununurra home. There was a great unbuttoning of tension, and I found myself, as is common on these occasions, doing what I have come to call my 'corruption rave'.

Corruption is more a feature of the cities than the bush. In smaller communities it is harder to get up to conspicuous mischief. But in large communities normal social controls become confused and disoriented.

There is a wide-eyed fascination with the secret sins of our neighbours, and I have managed to spoil many a social occasion for myself by being encouraged to talk up.

But there must be some therapeutic value in letting it go. I have seen enough to know Australia is an appallingly corrupt country, with none of the excuses that helps explain corruption in the Third World.

Here we are corrupt not because we are hungry, but because we are greedy. I am sure this would be less so if more people knew what was going on, and were more conscious of the pain that corruption causes, even to themselves. The only reaction I cannot bear is: 'I wish you had not told me that.'

There was no such reaction this night, and not a great deal of comfort when we returned to the story the next morning. It must be obvious by now that I am easily charmed by swimming holes and gumtrees, by country cafes and School-of-Arts halls, frocks and hats, louvres and verandahs, woodheaps and watertanks and all other soothing recollections of my own bush childhood.

The trouble is, my romance with the bush was feeling as battered as a well-worn Akubra. This is the place of open hearts and narrow minds. On the way to every Ian Oliver, a brown snake lurks somewhere in the long grass.

We drove on to Halls Creek. At a garage we asked about the search for the boys. The proprietor snarled about the time wasted and the tyres worn. He attacked the boys and then turned his sights on *Four Corners*. Andrew Olle had been here previously, he said, and gone back to the city with a whole heap of bullshit.

It was a stupid lie. Andrew had never been to Halls Creek, but there was no point in arguing. The garage proprietor who complained about reporters not wanting the facts to get in the way of a good story clearly did not want the truth to get in the way of a good grudge.

Paul and I drove away, turned a corner and were stopped by two members of the Western Australia Police Force. We were booked for coasting through a 'Stop' sign. There was not another car in sight. We were driving slowly and carefully and we were no danger to anyone.

The two policeman glared at us. We said nothing (and later paid the fine), but inwardly I was furious. The fact that I was unpopular with police was hardly surprising. But I am not supposed to be the enemy; the public is not supposed to be the enemy.

An obvious breeding ground for police corruption and a

police state is at this most common point of contact with the public. It is possible to be booked fairly by a courteous policeman and feel the appropriate degree of repentance. It is possible to be random-breath-tested by a pleasant policewoman and be thankful that she is there to protect us from ourselves. I can think of experiences, almost exclusively drawn from Victoria, where this has happened.

Where the self-esteem of the police is obvious, there is reciprocal public respect and the vicious cycle is broken. But when the public begin to hate the police, the police begin to believe they are justified in acting like criminals, and the viciousness persists.

I had seen it in Queensland and in my home state, New South Wales. I had received plenty of invitations to come and have a look at South Australia and Western Australia; but for the moment the wise course was to put as much distance between myself and the constabulary as possible.

Oddly enough, that was precisely the motivation of a lot of the people who came this way. We headed out of Halls Creek towards country known as 'The Underworld'.

This was the territory for a refugee column of maintenance dodgers and bail jumpers. In this part of the world people get used to asking no questions. It was tough country, and particularly so for a pair of inquisitive journalists.

We drove out to a place known as Carranya Station, where there was a small store and camping ground for the tourists who braved the Tanami track and stopped to look at the large meteor crater neatly punched into one corner of the property.

Paul and I learned that Simon and James had taken to making surreptitious, dangerous visits to the store in their final weeks at the Sherwin stations. James would make a six-hour round trip from 'Nicholson Station' in order to cash a cheque and buy a small pocket knife or, on one occasion, a stylish bush hat.

Simon, too, had managed to sneak away from Gordon

Downs station for another long journey to satisfy his boyish appetite for sweets.

We also heard that one of the former workers at the Sherwin properties, who had known James and Simon, might be now employed at Carranya. We were keen to talk to him.

The worker seemed to have a generous collection of names but the one he was most commonly known by was 'Spook'. That night, by the campfire, with a cold stubby in hand, we asked through the darkness about the whereabouts of Spook.

The smoke inevitably swung towards the interlopers from the city, stinging my eyes. Through straining eyes and with the help of the irregular illumination of the fire I detected amusement at the station.

No one could help with the whereabouts of Spook. Somehow the movements of those two boys were elevated to the realms of a state secret.

The culture of silence in the bush encouraged caution — even when it came to something as innocent as their shopping for sweets. We were not making much progress.

And then while ducking a new gust of campsmoke, through the titters I heard the shape opposite me referred to by one of the many pseudonyms used by Spook. The penny dropped.

The man opposite me, so regretful about his inability to place the whereabouts of anyone called Spook, was Spook himself.

Paul and I finished our beers and excused ourselves. As I left I said my goodbyes, saving a special farewell for Spook. The tittering ceased, leaving only the crackle of the campfire and the triumphant beating in my breast. It was a rare victory for the city over the bush and Paul and I were excessively pleased.

After stopping and talking to other property owners and fellow-workers we made our way back to Halls Creek and Kununurra in time to greet the arrival of our crew.

Along the way we set about collecting some necessary

props to enable us to reconstruct the last journey of the two boys. In doing so we saw another side of the bush.

A different garage proprietor in Halls Creek let us borrow some fuel drums and a large jack identical to the ones the boys had used to try to free the bogged vehicle. It was a touching act of trust and generosity.

The most difficult part was finding the correct vehicle. White 1983 Nissan utilities were not common in this part of the world, but no other vehicle would do. Filming reconstructions is a perilous business. It does not help to have the audience's faith further weakened by inaccurate props.

Eventually Paul located an appropriate vehicle which, fortunately, belonged to a generous owner who agreed to rent it to us for the following week. We clubbed together the other necessary props and asked our design department in Sydney to manufacture a set of number plates identical to the ones on the original vehicle.

On Monday, July 6 1987, our crew arrived. Chris Doig, who had accompanied me to Ethiopia, Queensland and a dozen other danger zones, stepped confidently from the plane. Behind him was a sound recordist new to my acquaintance. Chris Alderton or 'Waldo' was good humoured, easy-going and, like many of his ilk, a confirmed music lover and part-time musician.

Most sound recordists are good at their work. You rarely have to abandon footage because of bad sound. It is probably therefore a little too easy to take their work for granted, and this is a big mistake.

Part of the texture of any scene is good, honest sound. The sound catcher has to choose and place the microphones out of sight of the camera and create a kind of portable studio with the minimum of equipment so the sound can be mixed and balanced on site. It is a complicated business, so the sound catcher has to be given time to do it well.

The sound recordists who stand out tend to be the ones

with a surfeit of personality. A sound recordist who is bored and indifferent when an interview is being filmed can kill a scene stone dead without even trying.

But a sound catcher who is interested, enthusiastic and does not see his work as confined to catching the sound alone, can be a tonic to everyone, on both sides of the camera.

There was not much accommodation in Kununurra so Paul and I found ourselves sharing a two-room unit in one of the motels. While he sorted out some final details, before we began filming, I set about finishing the shooting script.

My self-imposed discipline dictated that the script had to be completed by the time shooting began, and like most writers I moved with reluctance and unease towards pen and paper. The best excuse for leaving the writing until last is that it gives you maximum time to chase the research.

By now the research was in reasonable shape and the excuse was spent. The broad sheet of graph paper was coated with information which formed a pattern of life on the Sherwin properties over the past six months.

I wrote into the night, and when the eyelids began to sag the alarm was set and the lights turned off. The fresh of the morning is a better time for me to work. Somehow in the solitude the mind seems far more eager. During that night I snored loudly, disturbing the sleep of my companion in the next room.

At 5 a.m. I returned to the notepad to find my concentration broken by loud roars of return fire from the next room. Paul was farting. It sounded like the diesel engine of a truck that had not been started for months. He crackled and banged and roared for hours. In volume and repertoire it was truly remarkable. There was no shortage of wind in Willo.

As the roars subsided, and with the fresh of the morning in determined retreat, the script moved towards completion. After a quick pack and the routine of paying bills, we were under way.

Willo had worked out a filming schedule to account for the massive distances we would have to cover.

There is an art in creating schedules. A properly planned schedule can make the difference between success and failure. One of the great sins of the business is having to go back and re-shoot something that confusion or lack of planning caused you to miss the first time. Filming assignments are very expensive. The travel budget alone for this project was in the range of $20 000. A producer guilty of botching a schedule, and having to go back and do it again, would be unlikely to hang on to the job for too long.

The secret of organising schedules appears to be never to overcrowd them. It is a bit like the art of packing a suitcase for a long trip. You include only what can be sensibly used and leave room for the unexpected treasure.

An overcrowded schedule is a tedious burden. When there is too much to do, nothing is done well, and good luck keeps a nervous distance. But Willo had planned with care. We would have full days, with a little spare time, and there would be no panic.

After driving out to Lake Argyle to interview another of the stationhands, we made our way slowly to Halls Creek, stopping to collect more information along the way.

At Halls Creek we were to coordinate with the representative from Clan Constructions, who would be our guide in and out of the desert.

There was a last meal at the local motel. This is the time of day we most often look forward to. Film crews not only have a uniform (faded jeans, motif T-shirt, dirty running shoes and sunglasses), but a language of their own. The film crew's version of grace goes something like, 'I could eat a low flying duck' or 'I could eat the crotch out of a rag doll' and other less refined expressions.

The pre-meal incantations were heard many times as we bumped shoulders on the long march to a thousand dining rooms. On this evening I was amused by the generosity and candour of the waitress who made a point of not recommending the pie.

Our guide, Peter Carter, arrived on time the next morning. On the back of his Toyota was a reserve of fuel, oil and water, and plenty of tools. In the cabin was the requisite two-way radio.

At Carranya, Chris Doig fitted his camera to a waiting light aircraft to shoot the aerial footage. We were not sure whether the small plane would be able to climb high enough to properly show the lattice-work of roads but we needed at least to show the sheer vastness of the country.

While I drove on ahead in the Nissan, Chris took to the skies in the Cessna. We also wanted to film some scenes of the vehicle on its southern journey into the desert.

Alone in the Nissan, jolting and sliding over the sandhills, I got some sense of the boys' daily routine. Their main job was to patrol the huge properties, completing what was known as the bore run.

If the pumps which fed the dams broke down, cattle might perish for lack of water. Making sure the bores continued to operate was an indispensible regulation of station life.

When Nicolson station was part of the Vestey empire it employed as many as 200 workers. They had teams of stockmen, mechanics and cooks. There was even a barber shop. Under Sherwin the Nicolson workforce was reduced to one seventeen-year-old boy, with no driver's licence, and no experience.

A large part of the practical responsibility of keeping Nicolson station operating had fallen on James Annetts' young shoulders. James would take all day to complete the bore run in a vehicle that could not operate in four wheel drive and had a persistent fuel feed problem. He would drive for 500 kilometres all day and see no one.

As I peered ahead along the sandy track I began to

understand a little of how his young life must have become attuned to the monotonous clatter of the diesel engine. It was easy to see how James could have allowed himself to drift beyond the reaches of his overconfidence, into the danger zone of his inexperience.

My reverie was broken as the aircraft burst into view only metres above, the sound and the slipstream buffeting me as it soared away. I carried on as the plane turned back to return our cameraman to the other vehicle which was to meet me further down the track.

Driving through the space and solitude of Central Australia is a captivating experience. I have never known a coastline that will conquer tension as comprehensively as the desert. The size and the silence take stern command of the beating heart, and you become part of the stillness.

The more often I go there, the more convinced I am that a compulsion to desert the coast and move inland will eventually overwhelm many Australians. If I could look into the future I might see cities out there. Instead, I was about to look into the past.

When the boys took the same route, in early December 1986, they drove along public roads for over 500 kilometres without being seen by anyone. Australia is still large enough for a traveller to do that.

After driving for hours without seeing another vehicle I was surprised to sight, in the distance, a dust cloud moving towards me. It took minutes before the vehicle preceding the cloud, came into view, and creaked to a halt beside me.

The first thing that was unusual about this particular bush vehicle was the large kangaroo protruding from one of the rear windows. The dead kangaroo competed for space with the surprising number of Aborigines these vehicles are able to contain.

The Aborigines were from the Yagga Yagga outstation. A small community had removed itself from the larger, and often troubled, Balgo settlement, to seek the sanctuary of the desert and the past.

The small community had taken one step back to a more primitive way of life. Among their number was the inevitable anthropologist. He was tall and fit and engaging. We stood between the two vehicles as he introduced me to his companions.

One of the Aborigines with blue-black skin and a multi-coloured shirt, stood staring at the earnest, bespectacled white man. If he was fascinated then so was I. The anthropologist explained how this Aborigine had come in from the desert only a few years previously, and had not seen many white men.

Some of the roadmakers out here reported finding their water supplies diminished overnight and sighting human footprints around their camp. The idea that the footprints had stepped from the stone age was less likely than the probability that the makers of the footprints were in temporary exile from one of the communities.

Whatever the explanation, this encounter was as close to a first contact as would occur in my lifetime. My work brings many privileges, and standing and staring into history on that day, was one of them.

We shook hands and said our goodbyes. The anthropologist promised to watch the programme when he got back to Canberra. As they continued north I headed south, moving closer to that point on the map where the boys had perished.

Although James and Simon must have driven directly past the Yagga Yagga outstation, the settlement, as the Aborigines explained, was empty at the time. At the height of summer this country was too hot even for them. They had packed up and left, probably only a day or so before the boys came through.

After driving for five hours I reached the beginning of the

network of roads which made up the seismic survey grid and stopped to wait for the other vehicles.

We needed the assistance of the guide Peter Carter, to find the correct road in. Before long all three vehicles converged, and in the last hours of daylight we pushed ahead to make camp near the scarred sandhill that had ended another journey.

In the fading light we could see the furrows where the vehicle bogged. The evidence of James' scout training was also to be seen. Three long pieces of timber had been dragged into position to form an arrow, pointing in the direction they would take on foot.

What now seemed likely was that James and Simon had travelled this prodigious distance by night. This would explain why they took no hats with them, and one had only thongs for footwear.

They may well have planned to be back on their stations in time to make their bore runs the following day. But instead the fault in the fuel pump had appeared, at the worst time, just when the Nissan needed a last surge of power to carry it over the sandhill.

The boys worked very hard to free that vehicle. As the sun rose, the heat would have been intolerable. The fair skinned, freckle faced Simon must have been in agony. Despite the heat they used the metal jack, which would have burned at the touch, to try to free the wheels.

They tried repeatedly to restart the engine and power their way out, exhausting first one and then a second battery. When the last sob of energy drained from the last battery they must have felt their lives slipping away.

For us, the day had been long. We crept into the deep comfort of our swags and were asleep well before the embers of the campfire faded to charcoal and dust.

The next morning was a busy filming day. It was July 11, 1987 — Federal Election day.

We worked all day, reconstructing the boys' struggle for

survival. In the final scene they walk away from the vehicle, carrying with them a heavy canister of water, some tinned food, fly spray and a rifle. They must have had some cause to believe something was ahead. The road was well-made. It is a reasonable expectation that such a well-made road would lead somewhere.

They crossed a hundred sandhills, walking approximately 20 kilometres, before the road vanished into the desert. Simon Amos' life was ended with a bullet. James Annetts had to wait for nature to appear as his executioner.

According to police, he lived on longer, before he, too, was claimed by dehydration, exhaustion, hypothermia and the dead heart of Australia. There was still evidence of the bodily remains, scattered in the shallow scrub.

We replaced everything as we found it and made ready to leave. There was very little talk. Somebody struggled with the radio dials, and through the static we learned Labor was returned to power.

On the long drive back to Halls Creek, we stopped for a bit more filming and some interviews.

One of the witnesses to station life, Sherwin-style, was a sensible young woman from the city who, like James and Simon, had sought a vocation in the bush.

Debbie Davis, like so many of the Sherwin employees, had decided to take her loyalty and her labour elsewhere. She was now employed as a cook on another Kimberley property.

I had already spoken to Debbie on our earlier visit to Halls Creek, so when we arrived at the station to record the interview there had been plenty of time in the interim to think and prepare.

We were greeted politely on the verandah of her modest but conspicuously tidy cabin. Her husband's muddy workboots were lined up outside. We took the cue and removed our own and began the often disrupting business of preparing to film the interview.

Film crews can sometimes be a little ungracious about moving into someone's home and switching the furniture and the pictures on the walls to best suit the camera. The sound recordist will ask to turn off a noisy refrigerator and, on rare but embarrassing occasions, forget to turn it back on. We did our best not to offend, having learned to work hard at preserving the natural atmosphere of the home.

There is a ridiculous convention in television interviewing that the most important feature of the job is asking clever, punishing questions. The best interviewers, I believe, are the ones capable of asking the tough questions, but also capable of asking the gentle question; in other words interviewers who can manage a range of subjects and adjust the emotional temperature accordingly.

But mine is not a common view. The interviewers most often respected by our peers are the ones with a talent for rudeness and self-promotion.

For these interviews the television studio is the perfect environment. The hot, sterile lighting and the friendless environment ensures, for the uninitiated, acute discomfort and an awkward, defensive performance. They will be caught like a kangaroo in a spotlight, and dispatched accordingly.

But what is often overlooked is that the great majority of interviews we do are not adversarial. The objective in most cases is to get the premium performance from the interviewee. Although this might seem obvious to outsiders, it is surprising how many reporters seem to regard the interview as a contest.

The most serious work in interviewing occurs before the cameras roll. Here the concentration is on relaxing the subject so they will be as natural and honest and enthusiastic as if the camera was not there.

The most common arena, the studio, is probably the worst place to get a relaxed, natural performance. A cleverly worded question will never guarantee a cleverly worded response.

A clear advantage of interviewing in the home is that this

is where the interviewee is likely to be most comfortable. The interviewee tends to take the cue on the way to answer from the manner in which the question is asked. A show of curiosity and enthusiasm in the tone of the questioner is likely to provoke an equally energetic response.

Debbie Davis spoke with passion and conviction about her disappointment with giving their best to the Sherwin company and feeling only indifference in return. She spoke with warmth for the boys, smiling at Simon's mischief, and his pride in his newly acquired car. Her description of James, and his quiet, shy, sensibility was equally affectionate.

To listen to this unaffected description was as far as we could go towards knowing those boys. When she spoke, she spoke as if there was no camera in the room, and no reporter asking questions. She spoke as if she was talking in the living room of the viewing public.

I have interviewed thousands of people in my time. There have been world leaders and brilliant raconteurs among them. I am not quick-witted enough to be a overly skilful interrogator. This is not what I search for as much as that wonderful moment when the interview lives because of a spontaneous, natural and honest response.

For me, it is a reaction I am more likely to get from a woman. This is probably because women seem to be less self-conscious about their weaknesses, and more honest than men. And as it happens, among the thousands of interviews I have filmed, a definite favourite is the one with a 22-year-old station cook, somewhere east of Halls Creek.

Debbie gave us a cup of tea and we said farewell, remembering to turn on the refrigerator on the way out. A few hours later we were back in Halls Creek, to find the only accommodation available was a tiny caravan in the local camping ground.

It was a dispiriting return. Through the tall fences with the string of barbed wire along the top I could see the drift of the urban blacks. It was like looking through the wire of a concentration camp.

There was not much of a show of integration in the local pub. The blacks wallowed in alcoholism in one room, the whites wallowed in alcoholism in another.

Many of the Aborigines still wore their stockman's gear although few had permanent jobs in the pastoral industry. The introduction of equal pay provisions forced Aborigines to swap one form of discrimination for another.

Instead of being unpaid they became unemployed. More than one station manager, ever respectful of the skills of the black stockman, suggested to us that the deaths of the two white boys were a further penalty of the blacks being pushed off the stations.

It was the Aborigines, they said, who taught them their bush navigation. Many a story was told of the black stockman who, in the dead of night, guided the bewildered young jackaroo back to camp.

At sunset I sat at a table in the pub with a microwaved meat pie and a beer in front of me. A few metres away a fat man perched on a bar stool surrounded by a small forest of glass. He was wearing shorts which had ridden down, exposing the large cleft of his bum.

It was an unholy sight, so appalling it captured your attention and held it against your will. It was like someone turning on a bad television programme at a dinner party. You don't want to watch but you can't help it.

I left the defrosted pie and walked back to the camping ground with purpose in my step. A theory had formed in my mind about why the boys made that unlikely journey into the desert, and I knew this night was perhaps the only chance there would ever be to prove the theory.

From numerous discussions, it was clear James was keen to continue working in the Kimberley, but not with the Sherwin enterprise. He wanted to go back to his family in

Griffith for the Christmas break, confident he could return to a proper career.

But young James, imprisoned on the bore run, had no opportunity to canvass other job prospects. Like many a seventeen-year-old, he was also impressionable and easily persuaded by the talk of some of the older stationhands.

One of them, a former workmate of James, happened to be temporarily settled in the neighbouring caravan. The fact that we were assigned to the van next door was a coincidence, but he did not know or believe that. Within seconds of the ABC arriving, his suspicious nature accelerated to pure paranoia, and I knew it would not be easy.

My new neighbour had worked for a time with the oil exploration team down in the desert. I could see him boasting about the work and the money and lighting a fire in the wide-eyed James.

James was not someone capable of writing a dazzling job application and was too shy to manage a confident approach by telephone. But he presented well. There was trust and reliability written all over the boy. James had a better chance to win a job by showing himself to a prospective employer.

My theory was drawn from an uneasy mixture of evidence and intuition and could only survive if this crucial witness cooperated.

The trouble was, apart from being suspicious and uncommunicative, he was also a hopeless drunk. As I found my way to his caravan, I carried with me a bottle of Bundaberg Rum, something of a passport in these parts. I was also carrying an opportunity to prove another theory I have heard put by investigative journalists.

The theory is that pubs, clubs and all other drinking establishments are good places for collecting information, in the same way the U-bend in a sink pipe collects sediment. The further theory is that the secrets can be easily unclogged by the application of a favourite brew.

A favourite brew in this part of the world is 'Bundy'. I am fond of 'Bundy' too. It has an appealing, gamey fragrance that for some reason puts me in mind of women. But with a physical and mental constitution attuned to moderation, I had to be careful.

The problem is that moderation is not a characteristic of the north. 'Bundy' is so prominent a feature of the landscape it is even used as a measure of time and distance. A journey is measured by the amount of bottles consumed along the way, so a trip to Alice Springs might be a six 'Bundy' trip. A notorious stretch of wet road was known by one outback traveller as an eighteen 'Bundy' bog.

My bottle of Bundaberg Rum, eagerly proffered, drew scorn. A woman was dispatched for another. She struggled back with a bottle the size of one of those milk cans dairy farmers leave on the side of the road. I was amazed and more than a little frightened.

The drinking began and the talking tentatively followed. I don't think he said anything but by the time I left I had no idea what he said.

The theory of alcohol as a liberator of secrets was, for me, disproven. What one drunk has to say can't be taken seriously. In fact if the receiver of the secret is another drunk, it can't be taken at all.

The next morning I was very sick. Paul asked me how successful I had been. I could not answer. For the next four days I said and did very little. I suppose I could have pretended the sacrifice was made for the sake of journalism, and although this was true enough, there was nothing noble about my suffering.

We filmed a muster and some other scenes of station life on the way back to Kununurra. I was capable of very little, other than the odd brief speech about the evils of strong drink. I was lucky Paul was there. In fact for the next weeks it was Paul who found the fortitude to push ahead as I began to wilt.

We had a few days left in the north to tidy up the programme before flying back to the maelstrom of the Fitzgerald Inquiry. More than a month had passed since the announcement of the inquiry, and back in Queensland the police were remaining tight-lipped. Crucial witnesses were still being intimidated into silence. There was no cause to relax.

Paul and I washed and cleaned the Nissan and returned it, gratefully, to its owner.

We were about to head on to Darwin, a favourite town where I tried to be at least once every year. There were more interviews to record and there was the last chance to snag an audience with Peter Sherwin. Sherwin, we learned, was now enthroned at one of his Northern Territory stations, 'Walhollow'.

I had put in a bid to interview Sherwin earlier with no success and now it was time to try again. My diary records me calling twice. 'Last call answered by rude woman who tells me not to call again. They act like the royal family.'

If we had believed the maxim that you have not got a story if you have not got the star player we would have been defeated. But Paul and I were foolish disbelievers. It was possible to tell the story of the two boys without their presence; and it was possible to tell the story of Sherwin without his cooperation.

When a company, a company director or the like is caught in an unflattering pose before the media spotlight, the simple refusal of cooperation is often enough to prevent the story being told. If not, it will at least blunt the media's interest. Editors frequently tell reporters, 'we need to see a villain'. They want someone to blame. They want a scalp to dangle before the camera.

Programmes like *Four Corners*, however, are less likely to be so easily deflected. In our case, non-cooperation can not only fuel the suspicion that the story is there, but also fuel our determination to tell it.

From a public relations point of view, it seemed ridiculous to me that Sherwin was not cooperating, if not with us, then with the rest of the media. The Aussie battler-cum-cattle baron who took on neighbours with his fists, and bureaucrats with his scorn, was just the type of story the media love. There might well have been sympathy and a soft ride if he had come out of his Walhallow bunker.

But while Sherwin stayed hidden, a revealing image of the Sherwin way was brought to light. When in Darwin, we heard about a startling piece of videotape which revealed something of the harshness of Sherwin. We were told Sherwin mustered a herd of cattle for mandatory TB testing at his base station in the Northern Territory.

Unfortunately, once the cattle were penned there was a rainstorm. The normal practice, we were told, is to release the cattle so they don't become injured in the inevitable quagmire produced by the rain.

To do so, of course, means that the costly and time-consuming exercise of mustering and penning the cattle has to be repeated once the weather improves.

The cattle were not released, despite the protestations of government officials who were present. Someone was believed to have videotaped animals suffering and dying while Sherwin held his ground.

It was this type of behaviour which cut Sherwin off from his neighbours and therefore the bush telegraph. And the problem of the Sherwin properties not being plugged into the conventional bush telegraph could well have contributed to the loss of the boys.

I was struck at the time by how the bush could accommodate two directly contradictory principles. There is the neighbourhood watch principle, where everyone keeps a quiet eye on the welfare of each other — and there is the dingo principle, where every bastard looks after himself.

It was now close to our air date and we were running out of

time so Paul and I divided the remaining work. The producer would chase the videotape while the reporter chased more interviews.

When we got back to Sydney we switched again. Because I was forced to stay with the editor and write the final script, Paul had to travel back to Griffith, without his reporter, to record the important interview with Les and Sandra Annetts. We had not filmed the interview on the earlier visit, first of all because we had no film crew, and secondly, because we had not collected enough facts.

Paul returned and the parts of the interview were cut into the film with his questions left on the cutting room floor. Anyone watching would have presumed the interviewer was me. Although that is almost exclusively the case, and I would have preferred it to be so, I had no reason to feel anything but pleased. The questions were sensitive, the answers moving and the fine line was trodden that exposes, rather than exploits human grief.

The last stage we had now reached, the editing stage, is supposed to take two weeks, but we had left ourselves only three days. I asked my boss, Peter Manning, for an extra week but Peter was doing no favours.

The ABC Senior Legal Officer, Bruce Donald, arrived to vet the script. With the Fitzgerald Inquiry gaining momentum I was seeing quite a lot of Bruce.

Bruce wanted some changes. Not many, but enough to annoy me. The scene of myself stomping petulantly back to the typewriter is a familiar one. The flaws Bruce identified in the script had to be dealt with.

The strange thing is, this new and aggravating task set me by our lawyer produced the best writing in the entire script. This had happened so many times I wondered why I bothered to be annoyed. It also made me realise, yet again, that the media–law alliance can be a very profitable one.

It was now the eleventh hour and, none too soon, Paul's

efforts at chasing the videotape of the cattle perishing in the Sherwin yard paid off. The tape turned up, in the familiar plain brown envelope. The pictures were graphic and telling and a last-minute rearrangement was made to include a segment of the tape.

The last thing we were inclined to think of at *Four Corners* was what we would call the film. I wandered up to the tiny office occupied by Andrew Olle, carrying with me a list of suggestions.

Andrew has a talent for titles. 'The Dead Heart,' he said, 'You won't do better'. I think he was right.

When we set out we were not sure what story we would come back with. In the end it was a story of many textures, but significantly a story about youth employment.

We would often talk about tackling such an important subject but give up for lack of an original angle. Now, without our realising it, the angle found us.

Simon Amos and James Annetts were lost, I believe, on the employment trail. In the end they were separated from salvation by the harsh side of the land and the people; by the dead heart of Australia.

Although I had some confidence that the motivation for James and Simon travelling to such an unlikely location was James' innocent belief there might be an opportunity for work, I did not say so in the report.

There is little room for speculation in journalism. You must stick with the information you have, ever conscious of the prospect that a new herd of facts might be waiting beyond the horizon. I did not have all the facts. I still don't, so I could not be definitive.

As it turned out, it took the Perth Coroner four years, the longest such inquiry in Western Australian history, to finally determine that the boys died by accident. The Coroner, David McCann, found that 'the two boys set off on an innocent adventure and paid for it with their lives'.

But even though we discovered nothing that comprehensively proved what inspired the adventure we were able to give the tragedy some dimension. The best lesson was learned with considerable relief. I could now see it was possible to complete an investigative report without producing the smoking gun evidence.

'The Dead Heart' was screened on August 3, 1987. As it happens this was the birthday of another daughter, Laura, and things were looking up, as for once I was home.

But the reprieve was temporary. The next morning a taxi called at 6.30 to spirit me to the airport and back to Queensland to attend a public hearing of the Fitzgerald Inquiry. They were all never ending stories.

8

'TWO CONFESSIONS'

At the end of 1987, in my twenty-first year at the ABC, I made a decision to leave. Despite the long-term loyalty to the one employer, I have always been a restless person. My father was the same. As soon as he finished the garden he would want to move. Once he moved just five houses down the street.

Dad was a schoolteacher, a profession which satisfied the competing desire for permanence and impermanence. He could be a nomad with job security.

In many respects the ABC did the same for me. I had the security of a job with the Public Service, but it was a job which had changed many times and taken me to many places.

There is a long list of reasons why I decided to work in commercial television: I was tired; I needed a fresh start; I could at last seize the opportunity to make an unusual amount of money. The list goes on and it is mostly boring, but there are two more reasons worth mentioning.

The first is that I wanted to see what commercial television could teach me. Learning has always seemed a lot more fun than knowing, and the anticipation of knowledge a more spirited source of energy than knowledge itself.

The next reason was more altruistic and less formed in my consciousness. I presumed, with my customary naivety, that on the journey to commercial television my standards would travel with me. I expected, when I got there, that if anything was going to change it was the medium and not me. One of the best things the ABC does is challenge, and perhaps even raise, the standards of its competitors. So I was hoping I could do a bit of teaching and learning at the same time.

Others had managed to do just that. Good journalists like Ray Martin and Mike Carlton, both apprenticed at the ABC, raised their own standards, and the wisdom of a great many more Australians, when they slipped into the impure depths of the commercial media.

There are some deep running tensions between the two camps. Defectors from public broadcasting to the commercial media can be looked upon as traitors. The defectors in turn become petty and defensive, often acting as if they can't forgive the ABC for getting on without them.

Meanwhile their erstwhile mates at the ABC behave with equally exasperating preciousness. The presumption within the ABC that the commercial media has nothing to teach those who have not yet deserted the monastery is plainly silly. What the commercial media obviously does a lot better than the ABC is to understand and speak the language of the common man and woman.

I accept that this is not necessarily a respectable skill. Attracting a mass audience is not always difficult. Just ask any organiser of a public execution.

But I had the idea that good journalism and a large audience were not mutually exclusive. I felt that most people liked a good story, and that applying storytelling skill to respectable subject matter could work very well, even with a mass audience.

The main theme of the mutual sniping is that the ABC is only interested in dull and worthy stories while the commercials are preoccupied with 'sexy' stories. My own bias has always been unashamedly to the worthwhile but even so it always seemed a mistake to be too much of a snob about stories. It is not always easy, but whatever stories we are assigned, we should approach with enthusiasm and determination to give the subject some useful meaning. As it happened I was quite looking forward to a slight change of diet.

So I was a willing enough conscript, as long as the job was right. There had been some offers in the past, enough to teach me that competition between the ABC and the commercial stations was nothing compared to the rivalry between the commercial stations themselves.

The Network bosses behaved like bushrangers and no opportunity was lost to bushwhack the opposition. When I decided that an offer to join a new current affairs programme on the Ten Network was right enough, there was some furious counter-bidding from Channel Nine.

Nine offered me six months off work on full pay and an overseas holiday for my family before I would even have to report for duty. The main problem, however, was working out what I was supposed to do when I got there.

I could almost see them dusting off the shelf space. Channel Nine already had a first–rate current affairs team. It also had a reputation for purchasing and warehousing talent. I could not help feeling they had more of an interest in me not going to Ten than joining them, and this more than anything steered me to the double figure.

The job I accepted was supposed to be reasonably similar to the one I departed. I was to be a reporter on a new 'serious' current affairs programme.

The programme was going to allow for thorough and important journalism, but beyond this it seemed slow to develop an identity. In fact it was slow even to develop a name. One of the first assignments we were given was working out what we would call the show. A case of Bollinger champagne was promised to the author of the most inspired title.

I scribbled furiously. 'Whistleblowers' I liked, 'In Camera' appealed, but 'Inside Story' was the station favourite. The champagne, it seemed, was mine. We rushed off to register the title and in doing so had to cross the battlefield of network rivalry.

We found that Gerald Stone, the founding Executive Producer of Nine's *Sixty Minutes*, had registered the title some years before. When Ten showed an interest in using 'Inside Story', instead of letting it remain buried in a Registry Office, Nine hastily exhumed the title. So 'Inside Story' had a brief life headlining an early morning finance programme on the Nine network. When Ten was forced to come up with something else, 'Inside Story' returned to the crypt.

In this way, *Page One* was born. I think the title was the work of my new boss Richard Carey, but he didn't boast about it, and I don't think he claimed the champagne.

Richard and I had already talked about what I was supposed to do. He told me he wanted me to do exactly as I had done at the ABC, but preferably with a bit more speed.

I told him that even though programmes like 'The Moonlight State' took three months to complete, they were still 'quick'. I doubt if he believed me. There is a presumption that ABC workers are dozy, and ABC management, untalented and ill-disciplined. I would have to say I probably shared some of the prejudice; but this would change.

My experience turned out to be unpleasant and, to be fair, probably atypical of the commercial media. At the time I said 'yes' I should have sniffed the madness in the air, but somehow I missed it. It was a time when, all across Australia, the scent of money overpowered the dry taste of reason even more effectively than usual.

The new management at Channel Ten were carting haystacks of money towards the semi-arid field of ratings, and there was I, on hand with a pitchfork. The spending lunacy led ultimately to an economic seizure throughout the once profitable business of commercial television.

I have no particular pride in the role I played in all the madness. I should have known better.

What should have been foremost in my mind was the recognition that in television a connection between big dollars and big success has never been certain. Success appears to follow hard work and hard thinking more consistently than it follows hard spending. A generous budget certainly helps, but it does not guarantee critical or ratings rewards.

At the ABC, where the budgets are rarely generous, workers and managers have practice in spending carefully and thinking hard forced upon them. From what I could see, in my experience of the commercial media, this practice was sorely needed.

But I was every bit as ignorant of the realities of commercial television and the depth of my ignorance was revealed by my choice of a first story. The story was 'Two Confessions', a report on the wrongful imprisonment of a 22-year-old Mt Isa man, Kelvin Condren.

At the time, 1988, Condren was serving a life sentence for the murder of his girlfriend, Patricia Carlton. After six weeks work we managed to collect enough evidence to cast reasonable doubt on Condren's guilt. Among the more compelling evidence was a second confession to the one murder.

As the details emerged the dimension, drama and importance of the story expanded. I came to think quite often that it was easily as significant an issue of injustice as that of another Mt Isa Australian, Lindy Chamberlain.

Nevertheless the choice was a poor one — in public and commercial terms — for one simple reason; Kelvin Condren is black.

The most common question I am asked is: 'How do you find your stories?'

The answer is that stories are found in many different ways. Sometimes they emerge from a tipoff, sometimes as the result of pursuing an original idea, and sometimes because of an instruction from the boss. But mostly the collection of stories is like the accumulation of yeast, one story grows into another, and another, and another.

That is what happened in this case. Following the broadcast of 'The Dead Heart' I learned from a colleague in Perth, Jan Mayman, that the white boys, Amos and Annetts, were not the only ones to go missing from the Sherwin properties.

Jan said it was believed another worker, an Aborigine, Fabian Butcher, had also left the property some years earlier and was later found dead, hanging from a windmill near Turkey Creek.

When Jan began chasing the story it led her to the Aboriginal boy's home town, Mt Isa. When she started questioning Aborigines in Mt Isa about the story, they told her of the Condren case. Jan in turn told me and I pitched the Kelvin Condren story, with great enthusiasm, to my new Executive Producer, Richard Carey.

The selling of a story to a boss is an important feature of this work, and sincere enthusiasm for the story is probably the most important feature of the salesmanship. If the reporter is enthusiastic, there is a good chance the enthusiasm may be infectious enough to carry to the audience.

Richard Carey bought the story, but I have no recollection of him appearing particularly thrilled. Richard had a way of waiting until you disappeared before letting his true feelings known.

It wasn't until many months later, in an argument about another Aboriginal story, that he muttered something about the public not being interested in that sort of thing anyway, before tearing off into the night.

The fact that Aborigines were not prominent on the commercial agenda was something I was a little slow to recognise. If this had been pointed out to me it might have been debated and a lot of time and effort saved, but debates and committees and meetings were for the 'wankers' at the

ABC. In commercial television you just got on with it, so get on with it I did.

Jan Mayman, who worked freelance, agreed to continue chasing the story from her Perth base. David Margan was assigned to produce the report. David had a hybrid background, having done his early training at the ABC before moving to Channel 9 and now Channel 10.

The theory was that, having survived the cross-breeding with most if not all motor skills in place, he could pass on the benefit of his experience and help me to walk and talk at the same time. I know that sounds facetious, but it is only partly so.

Walking and talking at the same time is, you would think, a fundamental human ability we can take for granted. But it is amazing how swiftly it deserts reporters the second they are put before a camera.

When 'action' is called, the limbs start to behave like stick insects and the mouth like a megaphone. Reporters jerk towards the camera at unpredictable and varying speeds, their voices lurching between a yell and a whisper.

Behaving normally in front of a camera can take a lot of practice, and there is just a chance that complete success is next to impossible. David Margan, my new animal trainer, was keen to do his best.

With a story like this there are three important stages of initial research: telephoning, talking and reading. We phoned and made appointments with key players like Condren's family, lawyers and witnesses.

Getting information over the telephone is never an ideal way to work. Talking face to face, usually in many separate conversations, gives you a much better feel for the quality of the information.

Whether the camera is rolling or not, people communicate with more than their voice, so it is helpful to be in a position to receive all the signals. Giving trust to a journalist is also obviously a lot easier for the witness if the journalist is a person rather a voice over the telephone.

I like this 'people' work and usually launch myself into this phase quickly. The purists prefer to do the reading first, so they can get on top of the available information and not fail to ask important questions when they do catch up with the people. But in practice, because there is never enough time, the reading and the talking mostly occur simultaneously.

We obtained transcripts of the Condren committal hearing, the trial and the Voir Dire (the court's preliminary examination of evidence), and then plotted through them. On a piece of graph paper I charted the important times and dates. In this way the necessary detail soaks into the memory.

Our first stop was Brisbane. We were booked into the Sheraton Hotel which was a little dazzling for someone who nearly went mad staring for three months at the wallpaper in one of the more modestly priced hotels nearby. At the ABC, the daily travel allowance was such that it helped to have a taste for cheaper motels and hamburgers. We were paid a daily rate, of about $100, out of which all expenses had to be covered.

But at Channel 10 my spending money alone was about $100 a day. On top of that, my hotel was paid for and I carried a company credit card which could be used for any extraneous purchases.

As part of the contract the company had already given me a car and a petrol credit card, holiday travel, free clothing and an entertainment allowance. It was all very different. I would return from my travels with wads of forgotten money in various pockets and the vague feeling that something was wrong.

For all this I was supposed to work every day of the year, if required, at full capacity. I secretly thought they could not possibly get me to work harder than I had done at the ABC, but I was wrong about that too.

In Brisbane we spoke to the lawyers who handled Condren's recently failed appeal. One of the witnesses used at the appeal was a Queensland academic, a language expert, who had given evidence that Condren's signed confession used language uncommon to an Aborigine of his background.

Dr Diana Eades was at the Darling Downs College of Advanced Education at Toowoomba. It was a long drive and I was surprised, when I arrived, to find a small delegation of lecturers and a class waiting for me.

I have never been able to resist invitations to speak to journalism students. I can remember few people, when I started, who were prepared to stand behind me and nudge me in the right direction.

I am well aware of the fact that my own youthful idealism and energy could easily have been left to wither. So I never miss the chance to tell the newcomers that it is right to labour for something more than money, and it is proper to care about your work.

Afterwards Diana Eades and I had a small cup of tea and a long conversation. She, like everyone I came to meet who knew the Condren case well, was completely convinced of his innocence.

Dr Eades took me through his signed statement pointing out the many examples of odd phraseology. In the statement, Condren described the pole used to kill Patricia Carlton as: 'silver and eight feet long.'

This she said was uncharacteristic. An Aborigine was more likely to say something like: 'it was longer than that rake over there', or, it was 'shorter than that post'.

I drove back from Toowoomba puzzling over why Condren would sign a statement that would in all likelihood put him in gaol for life. How and why members of the Queensland police would strip a man of his liberty on the strength of manufactured evidence was not as much a puzzle as it should have been.

I had been through all this before. Probably the worst consequence of a corrupt force is the tolerance of 'verballing', the invention of confessional evidence, and 'loading', the planting of damaging evidence like a gun or a quantity of drugs.

I knew by now that in Queensland, and many other states, there was a corps of police who were known for their lack of scruples about such practices. Unfortunately these police often ended up with the majority of the important work because in a curious way, the system 'trusted' them to do the job properly. They could be relied upon to get results come what may.

A further consequence of this type of corruption is that the many honest police did not get enough practice in legitimate policing.

The practice of manufacturing evidence was so out of control that bands of police formed who were known for their ability to play 'A grade'. What this meant was that they recognised that in the real world, hardened criminals did not admit to anything. The criminals had to be 'assisted' to tell the truth. A sure way of getting a conviction through the courts was for a large team of police to conspire to invent testimony. The weight of numbers of police, all with the same story, would often guarantee a conviction. Judges and juries, not so aware of police culture, might believe one or two police would 'verbal', but they had trouble believing that a large number would engage in collective perjury.

Police have admitted to me that only rarely has their conscience been troubled, even if it was later proved the conviction was not deserved. The attitude that a defendant was 'right for it' basically meant that, even if they were not guilty of this offence, then they probably deserved the punishment for a previous crime which had escaped the attention of the courts.

If there is resistance to this secret code of behaviour, I have noticed it is more likely to come from the police women (the so called 'Dickless Traceys'). Police women, less likely to be contaminated by the Australian culture of mateship, will occasionally stand against the tide of a male-dominated force.

So I could understand the culture which would strip an innocent man of his liberty without a trace of regret. But I could not understand the culture that would cause a man to let this happen with little trace of protest.

In Brisbane I met with Aborigines and lawyers who worked on the case and quickly became convinced I was dealing with an important issue. The practice of Aborigines confessing to serious crimes they obviously did not commit was widespread. An Aborigine, in a police lockup, with a heavy white man in a grey suit standing over him, may have little perception of life beyond the moment. What they want is for the pain and fear to pass. If saying 'Yes, I did it' is what it takes to make the man in the grey suit happy, and make him stop hitting them, that is what they will do.

In Townsville there was a meeting with the Condren family. I noticed when reading the Appeal judgment that one of the judges had questioned the Aboriginality of Kelvin's mother. By doing so, he was presumably bringing doubt to Diana Eades' argument that Condren would behave to the police in the manner of an Aborigine rather than a white.

When Julia Condren opened the door I was at a loss to understand what he could have meant. Kelvin's mother, like most Aborigines, was not of pure Aboriginal blood but she was very black. If the judge felt that the presence of 'white' blood, might have somehow acted as an antidote to Aboriginality, then I cannot help thinking that the judge had not spent much time with Aborigines.

Whatever their caste, the Condrens led very 'black' lives. When we consider how often Aborigines appear in 'white' courts, it is depressing to realise how little understanding many of those who sit in judgment have of the reality of Aboriginal existence.

The prospect of a white person sitting before an Aboriginal judge and jury is too unbelievable to be of any discomfort to the white community. I don't think many blacks are called for jury service. But for Kelvin Condren and a great many others, the prospect of a black appearing before an entirely white court is very real.

Friends of the Condren family organised a meeting. There was some spirited speechmaking and noisy politicking. I stood shyly on the perimeter. Having grown up a fringe dweller to Aboriginal Australia I have a long-standing curiosity about my black neighbours. As a five-year-old in the 1950s, I can remember being given two shillings by one of the reserve blacks to buy him a bottle of methylated spirits.

The wary white grocer refused, and I rushed off to find the waiting Aborigine, and hand back the two bob. I can still see the look of complete emptiness on his face, and feel my own childhood despair as he walked away.

But I had no way then of anticipating what would happen in the intervening decades. In the room now there were any number of astute and articulate commentators on the lot of the black Australian.

Thirty years ago there were few educated Aborigines, few Aboriginal heroes. Now there are many. The despair however, was not gone from the room. But there was still the astonishing good-natured tolerance of a shocking range of white barbarity that I had noticed many times before.

In a matter-of-fact way, I was told of the many other Condrens. I was told of a young black woman who, they said, had been bashed and raped by white youths. Police, they claimed, had taken no action when she was found drunk, distraught, and wandering.

I listened, still standing at the fringe. For my part there has been a change too. I am proud of black Australia; I am grateful for my undeserved endowment of black history. I know there are others of my generation who feel the same.

But what hasn't changed is that I am still white. I could not pretend to feel and think as a black Australian.

My report would inescapably be a white man's report from a white man's perspective. White reporters who try to report from a black perspective are taking on a mission that is not only impossible, but also absurd.

We knew by now that there were two confessions to the one murder. The first confession occurred in Mt Isa, the second in Darwin.

We decided to head first for Darwin and build as much information as we could before heading back to Mt Isa.

There was a reassuring welcome in the northern capital from some of the local police. The Northern Territory Police Force was something of an outpost for respectable behaviour. There are always some problems but at least the boss, Mick Palmer, was efficient and honest; and that alone can make an enormous difference.

Palmer said he would do what he could to help. It was Palmer's policemen who arrested the killer of a Darwin woman, Gloria Pindan, and soon after extracted a second confession to a different murder, that of Kelvin Condren's girlfriend, Patricia Carlton. They were not to know that this good honest police work would bring embarrassment to some of their Queensland colleagues.

In November 1983, Darwin police discovered the body of 28-year-old Gloria Pindan slumped near a fence on a bare patch of ground a few hundred metres from the city centre. Her life had been torn from her as swiftly and callously as a thief snatching a handbag.

Within 12 hours police arrested the killer. It was impressive work and the arresting detective Dennis Hart, told me how it was done.

Observing the victim, he could tell that Pindan had been killed by someone of immense strength. Hart went walking through the local hotels looking for such a person. In time he noticed a tall strong man, who was an otherwise unremarkable member of the rowdy, alcohol-dazed crowd. When Hart moved closer, for a more forensic view, he could see specks of dried blood on the man's skin and clothing.

Andy Albury was not the type you would wish your daughter to invite home. The former soldier turned buffalo-shooter had, at one time, tried to start a local version of the Ku Klux Klan. He did nothing to hide his psychotic hatred of blacks.

Police ushered him outside the hotel. At first Albury denied the killing but when police said they would scientifically analyse and attempt to match the blood traces, the buffalo shooter, in the police vernacular, 'put his hand up'.

While there are often doubts about confessional evidence, in this case, there could be none, because police were professional enough to have a video camera on hand. The tape had been used in public court, so obtaining access was not too difficult.

It was a chilling few minutes viewing. The tape showed Albury retracing his steps of the Friday night of November 25, 1983. Albury described how he walked with Pindan past the movie theatre to the vacant allotment. He sat her by the fence and then showed how he got to his feet and began kicking her.

The big man told how he then grabbed the frail Aboriginal woman and bashed her head against a concrete Telecom box. He then reached for a broken beer bottle which he used to stab and stab again at her pelvis and vagina. When Albury got to his feet and staggered away he found his white cowboy shirt was covered in blood, so he removed it and pushed it into a nearby rubbish bin.

It was then about midnight, and Albury was hungry. The 'Kentucky Fried Chicken' shop was closed so he carried on to a pizza shop, ordered his meal and sat on the kerb eating it, while his companion of only half an hour before lay dead one block away.

Albury was unconcerned, so lacking in remorse, that when he discovered the next morning that he had lost his wallet he went to the police station to report it missing.

The videotape ends with a question from Hart about whether Albury had anything further to say and this was what the big man, standing with hands impassively pushed into his prison green overalls, had to say: 'Think I'd do it again, get enjoyment out of it, dunno why. All right when I'm out shooting, don't want to kill anyone. When I knocked off shooting, when I went on holidays in September, just had to kill something.'

The video recorder was then switched off. Later interrogations obtained more evidence about the September murder in Mt Isa. Albury said: 'I killed a gin in Mt Isa in September. I don't even feel sorry for them. I know I should be.'

The revelations caused the Darwin police to telephone their colleagues in Mt Isa, to tell them that Albury had admitted responsibility for the murder of Patricia Carlton two months earlier.

But the Mt Isa Detective Sergeant who handled the matter was not interested. They already had their man, and their own signed confession.

The death of Patricia Carlton was strikingly similar to that of Gloria Pindan. Two months earlier, on the Friday night of September 30, 1983, at another hotel, the 24-year-old Aboriginal woman, Carlton, had been seen drinking with friends.

The following morning her body was found not far from the hotel at the rear of a local pharmacy. Carlton had also been brutally killed with whatever was at hand, in this case a long piece of pipe, which had been left resting against the rear of the shop. A stone, the size of a man's fist, was then pushed into her vagina, and the pipe used to force it inside the dying woman.

Police found the body at 5.30 the next morning. The patch of ground behind the pharmacy was shaded by a small tree and was sometimes used for drinking binges by local blacks. The police story was that such a binge took place, and that Carlton's boyfriend, in a drunken jealous rage, had viciously attacked the woman.

As it turned out, there was no evidence that a drinking session had occurred there. No one had seen or heard what should have been a very noisy affair, and no empty bottles were seen lying around. Furthermore, there was plenty of evidence that Condren was elsewhere at the time. He was, in fact, in police custody.

At 5.45 on the previous afternoon, police had found Condren helplessly intoxicated in the fountain of the local Civic Centre and locked him up. The Civic Centre is about one block from the pharmacy.

Condren spent the night in the lockup. He was released on the Saturday morning. Condren's statement said he had attacked and killed Carlton before being picked up by police at the Civic Centre.

The statement was 'supported' by accounts from some of Condren's drinking friends, Stephen MacNamee, Louise Brown and another Aborigine, Fabian Butcher.

I was keen to find MacNamee and Brown and any friends of Fabian Butcher. Butcher, you will recall, was the starting point for the story. The former Sherwin stationhand was found dead in April 1984, soon after he was said to have left the 'Flora Valley' property. The person who had discovered this, Jan Mayman, was now set to join me in Darwin. I drove to the airport to collect her and deliver her to her room.

Jan is an indefatigable telephoner and she went quickly to work. Brown and MacNamee had already been located, fortunately not far from where we were staying. As it turned out, the two were, in a sense, hiding out. They were frightened of some of the Mt Isa police and scarred by the whole experience. Soon after Condren was charged, they told us, police sought statements from them revealing they had seen Condren bashing Carlton.

Two days after giving the statements, MacNamee and Brown went to the Aboriginal Legal Service office, and retracted the statements. When I asked them why, they told me the original statements were untrue.

Some Mt Isa police, they said, stood over them, threatening to hit them with a spade if they did not endorse and sign the statements.

Although still frightened, they were more troubled about the plight of their friend, Condren, now in his fifth year in prison. They agreed to be interviewed.

We drove to a park and set up the cameras. It is usually a mistake choosing outdoor locations for important interviews. The clouds shift, mowers start, dogs bark, and helicopters suddenly appear. A difficult interview for the couple became even more of a trial. But they did well, telling their story with consistency and conviction, and doing much to dispel the common judicial belief that Aborigines make terrible witnesses.

When the interview was filmed the camera reversed positions to record me repeating some of the questions I had just asked and the 'noddies', the reaction shots. I have long been scornful of the 'noddy'. It hardly seems a priority skill in a reporter's repertoire. But David Margan did not agree. In his own career as a reporter, I had to admit, David was capable of giving exemplary 'nod'.

You do not bounce your head up and down like a marionette, he told me, it is all in the eyes. If a reporter is looking off camera or on camera, achieving a look that suggests you are concentrating on the subject matter is helpful. It certainly beats the look you often see, of a reporter staring as if the camera was a cobra poised to strike.

I listened to David, tried to keep the bouncing of my head

to a minimum, and applied a meaningful stare off camera. I think I did improve a little bit, but I have to concede I have never been able to nod quite so well as David.

Before leaving Darwin we sought another witness. We wanted a professional opinion from a pathologist on the similarity of the two killings. From the Condren family we had obtained the medical report on Patricia Carlton, so we carried it with us on the way to see Dr Kevin Lee, the pathologist who examined the deceased Gloria Pindan.

Another reason I liked making programmes in Darwin is that the frontier often throws up characters who speak their mind. Kevin Lee was one.

We met him at the Casuarina Hospital. This is a newish medical centre, a multi-story concrete structure which was put up after Cyclone Tracy blew away its predecessor.

This one obviously was not going to blow away. It was about as solid as Ayers Rock, but there the similarity ends. Critics could not help pointing out its incongruity with the Territory landscape. The building was so large and intimidating that tribal Aborigines, having made their way great distances for treatment, sometimes baulked and would not go inside.

As Dr Lee showed us around, he pointed to the ramparts outside the sealed plate glass windows. Legend had it, he explained, that they were designed to keep snow at bay. The plans for the hospital were borrowed in haste from the architects who designed the Woden Hospital in much cooler Canberra, and somehow the snow ramparts managed to stay.

The tropical heat outside had soaked my shirt with sweat. In the air-conditioned corridors the clinging shirt began to chill my spine.

Dr Lee escorted us to his laboratory. The chilling persisted, this time more metaphorically. On file were the photographs taken of Gloria Pindan, after she was beaten to death. When life vanishes so swiftly and unexpectedly there is a look that somehow lingers, of surprise and disbelief in the cruelty of man.

Dr Lee explained the injuries and compared them with the injuries sustained by Patricia Carlton. Both women had been killed with whatever was at hand; both had their panties torn from them; both were attacked about the vagina. There were further similarities which prompted Kevin Lee to the reasonable view that they could have been victims of the same murderer.

He also suggested the injuries were not like those commonly seen in Aboriginal communities, which suggested the murderer might be more likely white than black.

On March 29 we left Darwin for Mt Isa. Jan Mayman would stay on, to continue the northern research before returning to Perth.

At the Darwin airport I telephoned Police Commissioner Palmer, thanking him for his help. At Mt Isa I expected no help from the constabulary and did not seek it.

We did our own leg work. At the local St Vincent de Paul hostel we found a receipt for Albury's stay in Mt Isa on the very day Patricia Carlton was killed.

We learned he had been at the Greyhound bus terminal, a stone's throw from the hotel, at half past seven that night. We know he boarded the bus with a case of beer and left Mt Isa at 8 p.m. He had later joked with Darwin police about having 'half an hour to kill'.

By now I had just about lost the objectivity I usually try to cling to. Albury confessed to the murder of Patricia Carlton. He was in Mt Isa at the time of the murder. He killed another black woman in a virtually identical manner. Beyond this there was a range of reasons to doubt the evidence mounted against the person convicted of the murder, Kelvin Condren.

I was taught to be wary of too readily believing the media knows better than the law. One of the occupational hazards you have to deal with in investigative journalism is the procession of entreaties from the convicted, protesting their innocence.

It is very easy for the media to be duped and used. I can think of at least one example where profound journalistic endeavour went towards overturning a court ruling, after which the person convicted began to look even more guilty.

It is important in journalism to test the evidence and test it again. If a long-held theory is suddenly overturned then this should be seen as a relief rather than a disaster. It is better to know you are wrong before you go to air than afterwards.

I telephoned a lawyer who assisted with the prosecution of Condren. I asked him how he could reconcile the fact that another man, a known psychotic, had not just confessed to the murder but had detailed knowledge of the incident.

With regard to the confession, he explained that Albury had since recanted, and all in all had proved to be a supremely unreliable witness.

This I could understand. But how could he explain Albury's detailed description of the murder, which included an accurate diagram of the murder scene, and the knowledge a rock had been thrust into the victim's vagina?

He told me Albury probably observed this from a hiding place behind a fence and got the idea to later copy the murder. Sometimes I wonder about lawyers.

He also told me that Condren could have accepted a plea of manslaughter whereby he would have probably served only a few years instead of a life sentence. I happened to know the reason Condren refused to accept a verdict of guilty of manslaughter was the rather compelling one of believing in his own innocence.

So instead of accepting a token sentence for falsely proclaiming guilt, a man must serve a life sentence for honestly protesting his innocence. Sometimes I wonder about the law.

But even so, I knew the courts had heard all this before.

The evidence had already been before a Voir Dire, a Committal Hearing, a Trial and an Appeal, and Condren was still in gaol.

As one Appeal Judge put it, 'without the confessional evidence he would not have been convicted'. It would take new evidence to overturn the large and burdensome rock of Condren's confession.

It must have been a divine hand that provided us, on March 31 with the force of evidence that would help shift the rock. It was now two days into the Mt Isa shoot and we needed some pictures of the murder scene. We drove to the carpark behind the shops and hotel where Carlton spent her last hours.

I was a little anxious about pulling out the camera. There was no reason to feel welcome, and always the chance that if we sought permission to film, even from a public carpark, there could be complications and obstructions.

But when we appeared at the scene we were sighted immediately by the pharmacist who happened to be standing at the back of his store talking to his brother. The most prudent step might have been to retire but something caused me to pull open the door of the car and approach the two men.

I might be fooling myself, but there was something almost mystical about that moment. I am a shy person, and I think under normal circumstances, I would have suggested we drive on.

The question of whether to telephone a prospective interviewee and make an appointment or whether to just bowl up is an important one. There is no common answer, different circumstances call for different tactics. Reporters who 'doorstop' people will most often do so because they know they would be refused if they attempted to make an appointment.

This hit and run, or rather crash and burn approach, is not the one I would generally make. I prefer to telephone first. If the first approach is refused, some persistence might be required and there is a good chance success will follow.

However, if you confront someone and make a bad impression, they are unlikely to give you a second chance.

Considering all this it is hard to explain my actions in that carpark on that day. I knew that a blind encounter was dangerous because it could lead to an instant irreversible decision not to cooperate. In this case we could easily have been told that our camera was not welcome, so the opportunity to film an important scene might have been lost.

But something told me to get out of the car. I walked up to the two men and told them what we were doing. The pharmacist, John Price, remembered the murder and said to me something like, 'But she could not have been killed when they said she was killed, because I left the shop between 5.30 and 5.45 that afternoon and saw no sign of a body'.

I asked if he would be interviewed and he agreed. Within minutes the interview was in the can and David Margan and I were beginning to smile.

John Price's evidence was crucial. If Carlton was killed after 5.45 then Condren could not possibly have been the murderer.

Evidence from the police themselves put Condren in their custody from 5.45. Even if Price left earlier at 5.30, it was still impossible to believe Condren could have committed the murder.

The Aborigines would have needed to arrive after 5.30, get into a heavy drinking session and then a fight. Condren would have attacked and killed Carlton and then found his way to the Civic Centre, one block away. There he would have continued drinking until reaching the state of helpless intoxication which attracted the attention of police. And all this in 15 minutes.

John Price's evidence was also important because he was respectable, believable and very white. There were plenty of Aborigines who could also give evidence that Carlton was alive after 5.45, and that Condren was not with her anyway, but there was doubt that they would be believed.

The very best feature of journalism is discovering new information. But in television journalism you need pictures too. I wanted pictures which showed that helpless state of intoxication the Aborigines call, 'choking down drunk'.

I wanted the pictures because it is important to show other Australians what life is like for Aboriginal Australians. It was also important to show what kind of physical state Condren was in at the time.

And here was another of the many ethical dilemmas you face in this work. To get these pictures we had to join the creek blacks, to get inside their camp and the drinking session.

I have a basic rule in film-making that you never simply paste what we call 'wallpaper' over your narrative. 'Wallpaper' is nondescript vision, like shots from the footpath of people walking down the street.

Such shots should never be used. The vision should complement the story, like a section of an orchestra harmonises with a symphony. The pictures should never be visual musak.

When the suggestion arises that the passing parade be filmed, this should be seen as a creative challenge to come up with something better. If you want some establishing shots of street scenes it is better to set something up. Film one of the locals sitting on a park bench with the daily newspaper opened in the foreground so that the passing parade moves in soft focus in the background; or follow the milkman on his morning round; and so on.

In this case the pictures we wanted were not to be found in the street but down in the dry river bed. Getting among the creek blacks meant we would intrude, and we would probably be unwelcome. Like everyone else, Aborigines prefer not to show their worst side. We went down to the creek with one of the representatives of the black communtiy and tried to explain what we wanted.

Appealing to logic among a gathering of drunks, black or

white, is pretty much a lost cause. After some near useless talking we began filming. Our cameraman, Les Seymour, got the close ups of the hopelessness that producer David Margan and myself asked for.

We were intruding, it is true. We were also unwelcome, but we were getting close to a useful truth. In the end I think it is better to get the close-ups openly rather than skulk in the distance behind the protective screen of a telephoto lens.

On April 2 we left Mt Isa, and in doing so had to break another rule. Film crews do so much flying our chances of taking an unlucky flight are higher than most. Although the chance of misfortune is still slight, another basic rule is to avoid the charter of light planes when commercial passenger flights are available.

But to get to Townsville quickly meant we had to take a light plane. We could not afford delay because an important appointment was waiting.

The Queensland Government had relaxed its rules about media interviews with prisoners, and allowed us rare access to Kelvin Condren. I can understand the rule about barring prisoners from media exposure. I can see the danger in allowing prisoners to gain further profit and notoriety from crime. But as with most things you hope there is room for discretion.

Prisons Minister Russell Cooper gave us the room. It was important to understand why Condren, knowing he was innocent, would apply his own signature to a life sentence.

I had to ask him that question, and it was decent of Cooper to give me the chance.

We made our way through the crashing, clanging iron barriers of Townsville Gaol. Queues of listless prisoners were distracted from their boredom by the unusual spectacle of longer hair and polished shoes, coloured shirts and searching eyes.

Kelvin, like all the other inmates, had learned to adjust his gaze to eliminate focus. He sat on a bench with a guitar and a prayer book. One compensation of five years imprisonment was that it had given him religion and music.

We talked. When I asked him why he signed the confession he said it was because he was pressured. He told me that there was no one there to help him and tell him what to do. He was scared and just wanted to get out of the place.

I believed Kelvin. But what about Fabian Butcher's evidence that Kelvin had admitted having murdered Patricia Carlton?

He said Butcher lied, after being threatened by police, and had then run away from Mt Isa in disgrace.

I began to wonder whether Butcher's suicide was because he could not bring himself to return to Mt Isa where he knew he would be shunned by the other Aborigines. Butcher's inability to resist being forced into the role of Judas may have been a death sentence in itself.

The full canvas of this story was beginning to look as bleak and as sad as a ten-year drought.

On the way back to the Townsville airport my objectivity was not so much lost as abandoned. It flew from the back window of the car like a loose garment and became entangled in a cane field, where it might be still.

Condren was not guilty. I know the court said he was guilty and I know the law should know better than me, but I still thought the law, in this case, was wrong.

Back in Sydney we assembled the story. The facts were carefully arranged. The videotape danced back and forth, choreographing action and drama in a way that is supposed to keep the audience attentive. (*Page One* preferred videotape to film.)

There was a bit of an argument over the use of Andy Albury's taped confession. At one point the killer described, graphically and gruesomely, how he gouged his victim's eye from its socket and flicked it away into the grass. I felt this segment need not be included, so left it out despite some protest.

Although it was not loudly stated, I think there was a bit of disappointment too. The problem was that I had not 'named names'. The story might have been seen as more successful if the focus of attention had been directed at a white policeman rather than a black prisoner.

If all the facts are assembled to show Condren could not have done what his signed statement said he did, and if indeed he was pressured to sign a false confession, serious questions are raised about the police conduct in the case.

I raised the questions but did not answer them. I cannot reconcile the contradiction. It would not surprise me that a group of men could, possibly believing honestly that Condren was guilty, fabricate a case against him.

I know the culture in that police force well enough to be aware that they could have thought they were doing him a favour. The lockup and the gaol system has been used as a drying-out tank before. By stripping away Kelvin Condren's liberty they may have thought they were merely imposing an enforced sobriety.

This is despicable behaviour and it did and does go on in many of our police forces. To some degree it was encouraged. But I did not know enough about this case to be certain what had happened.

Besides, I have never been a captive of the media culture that believes big time journalism is all about 'naming names'. To me the pursuit of scalps is more like small-minded journalism.

But I did hope that someone would investigate properly why Condren confessed to a murder he could not have committed, and I said so at the end of the report.

To date, as far as I know, it has not happened. One man who might have been interested in reviewing the Condren case was, at the time, looking into the subject of police corruption. As it

'TWO CONFESSIONS' 235

happened, Tony Fitzgerald QC had defended Condren at his failed appeal.

The case was heard just before Fitzgerald was given his celebrated appointment. I have sometimes wondered whether his experience on the Condren case caused him to be not quite the 'babe in the woods' about the way police behaved, that many presumed him to be.

Anyway, it was clear from the body language around the office that they knew this report was not going to turn into another Royal Commission. But whatever the disappointment, it was not shared by David Margan and myself.

We were proud of the report. We knew we had uncovered new evidence which could force a retrial and perhaps bring about Condren's release.

Important though it was, the programme sat on the shelf for some time. It went to air two months after our return from Queensland.

When it was screened on June 9, 1988, it made little impact. Now I was disappointed. I could not help feeling that, had the programme been run on *Four Corners*, there would be a widespread clamour for Condren's release.

The problem, perhaps, was that not only were commercial stations unused to getting angry about Aboriginal injustice, but commercial audiences were not conditioned to caring.

Then again, perhaps the real problem was that we had made a lousy report. It is true that I was having trouble finding my feet in commercial television and understanding the new value system.

But in time the story was picked up. Murray Hogarth of the *Australian* newspaper took an interest in the Condren case and made mention of the new evidence. The Queensland Crown Law Office was obliged to review the matter; but in what seemed a particularly mean judgment, someone decided the new evidence was not worth pursuing. They did not bother to interview John Price.

But there are lawyers and there are lawyers. I had plenty of reason to be grateful for the considerable endeavour of a team of Brisbane lawyers now entrenched in the Fitzgerald Inquiry. And now my gratitude was on overtime as one of them agreed to find some rare time for the Condren matter.

Bob Mulholland is a lanky and likeable Queens Counsel. He manages to meld a lofty legal intellect with a common man's sense of fair play. Mulholland took the Condren case to the High Court in Canberra.

The High Court recommended that the fresh evidence be tested by the Queensland Court of Criminal Appeal. When this court looked at the new evidence there was a two-to-one ruling for a new trial. The third judge went further and recommended Condren's immediate release.

The Crown Law Department looked at the case and decided, at last, not to try the case again. A little over two years had passed since we broadcast the report revealing the new evidence.

As it happened, I was back in Mt Isa, and back with the ABC when the news reached me. I mentioned earlier how one story tends to lead to another, and this was the impetus that helped complete the circle.

When I was filming the Condren story, a sad-faced Aborigine had searched me out to tell me of the death of his brother. He said the brother had been killed when a local doctor, who had been drinking with police, knocked him over in the street while driving home.

The white doctor did not stop and render assistance. When he was picked up later, the doctor refused to give a breath analysis. The Aborigine died.

The doctor was charged but won his case on appeal. I was reporting this story two years on when we learned of Condren's own success in court. The dark ages had not passed; Mississippi was still burning.

Soon afterwards another circle was completed. When I

returned from the second assignment in Mt Isa, I spent a week waiting outside a court before I was finally interrogated about my experiences with Dr Geoffrey Edelsten. (see Chapter 4)

Edelsten had been charged with conspiracy to assault a former patient of his practice. On Friday July 27, 1990, I was home watching the news and learned Edelsten had been convicted. That afternoon the news came through that the last legal formalities were complete, and Kelvin was to be released.

I did not gloat about having helped to put Edelsten in gaol. Journalism is not about punishment. We are lucky we do not have the responsibility of passing sentence and determinining appropriate punishment. But I was very pleased about Condren's release. Journalism is about justice.

I telephoned Kelvin at his mother's house. My family was standing nearby. They saw a tear on my cheek. It is not often that journalists can feel a tangible, worthwhile result of their work.

By now *Page One*, or *Public Eye* as it later became, was just a rather sad memory. When the programme was axed in August 1989, I left Channel Ten, and soon after won a new job back at the ABC.

My experience in commercial television was an unhappy one. This still disappoints me, because I know the commercial media is not the Evil Empire. I know the people who work in private and public broadcasting are the same human beings. The problem is that the commercial media are scared about delivering bad news. There is an understandable desire to soothe the public, to convince them all is well, to be careful about threatening their prejudice and ignorance, and upsetting the status quo. It is hard to convince the public they are right to buy Coca-Cola or Corn Flakes, but wrong about something else.

The worst thing about commercial television is that you are taught to work for yourself and not for the community. You are sometimes even quietly taught to despise the public — but journalists and television people are members of the public too.

I believe that 'star' journalists in commercial television have a responsibility to use their influence to maintain their standards. They have a responsibility, easily forgotten when they are paid so well and adored so widely, to try to make worthwhile journalism as popular as they manage to make themselves popular. It is a tough job and they have a lot of my respect. It was a bit too tough for me.

But now I have returned to the public service, with a new respect for my employer, and a continuing affection for the people we serve.

9

DIRTY SECRETS

In my eight-year-old daughter's room there is a small painted tin, on which is hand-printed the following sign, DO NOT OPEN — PRIVATE.

The culture of secrecy has captured Laura as comprehensively as it captures so many other Australians. We protect our secrets with extraordinary determination, out of fear, common sense, laziness and, as in my daughter's case, innocence.

Knowing when to prise open the tin is one of the more important skills a journalist has to learn. There are times when privacy should be respected, there are other times when the secrets are harmless and many more times when the greatest danger emerges from our failure to prise open the tin.

The secret, well known to politicians and law officials, that Chief Stipendiary Magistrate Murray Farquhar had interfered with a court case back in 1977, was stupid and dangerous. It poisoned confidence in the judicial process within the system itself for years.

The secret that the Queensland Police Commissioner, Terry Lewis, was a dedicated criminal was also stupid and dangerous. Lewis was allowed, for more than a decade, to turn that expensive police force over to the criminal community. The real powers behind law enforcement were a few spivvy brothel keepers and drug dealers from the Brisbane Valley. The secret that kept them all in power turned them into paragons of respectability. It allowed, in time, a metamorphosis which seemed to convert these public enemies into public friends.

So when it comes to secrets, I am, all in all, against them. And as a resolute enemy of concealment, I can have no hesitation in exposing some of the internal workings of my own profession.

When it comes to the craft of storytelling I am happy to reveal all that I have learned. There is justifiable anger when a rival steals your research but there is no reason to conceal the formula that discovered the information in the first place.

All journalists profit from the worthwhile labour of their fellows. *Four Corners* has certainly taught me that. I owe my colleagues at the ABC an enormous debt for all the encouragement and the genuine pleasure that has been derived from our mutual successes.

I have known workplaces where meanness is the predominant, pervasive energy source. The only way workers feel they can improve their own status is by ensuring the reputation of others does not climb too high.

When you walk through the door at *Four Corners* you understand the standard that has been set. You understand what has to be achieved. You know that every honest support will be given to ensure you do your very best.

To all my predecessors who set the standard and created this remarkable work culture: to Bob Raymond, Allan Ashbolt, Mike Willesee, Peter Luck, John Penlington, Caroline Jones, John Temple and many others, there is acknowledgement and further gratitude.

Four Corners has won a reputation in the last 30 years for challenging, important, 'investigative' journalism. With the word 'investigative' I do have a small quarrel. It seems to me that investigation is, or should be, an integral part of all journalism. The alternative is simply the recycling of press releases. So 'investigative journalism' is in itself a tautology, but one, I suspect, we are stuck with forevermore.

I have no quarrel, however, with the choice of subject we have so assiduously investigated in the past 30 years: public corruption. As it happens I have never found it a particularly appealing topic. Corruption is a tawdry and uninspiring business, and I would love to think it trivial enough to be left to one side. But I have never been able to take such a comfortable view.

If the dirty secrets are not revealed, corruption is bonded into the social framework like a corpse folded into the concrete foundations of a Woolloomooloo highrise. In time we don't even realise it is there.

This is a major problem with the corruption which has infested NSW. It is so much a part of the landscape that it is often difficult to recognise. We seasonally adjust our collective conscience so that the issue becomes unrecognisable.

I would also like to be able to say that corruption is a passé subject. On occasions I have almost been persuaded that a little corruption is a good thing. It oils the wheels of industry and as the story goes, persistent exposure only contributes to costly and time-wasting stoppages.

But there are serious problems still. Just ask the few, like Frank Costigan, Donald Stewart, Ian Temby and Tony Fitzgerald, who have been given the job of sticking their heads down the sewer.

I believe there is such intense mutual blackmail among some elements of our police forces that very heavyweight criminals, inside and outside the forces, remain protected. Even when something as serious as the murder, or attempted murder, of a high-profile policeman occurs, we can't get to the bottom of the problem.

Drug law enforcement remains such a rat's nest that some police, despite all the corruption revelations, continue to side with the rats.

I have seen nothing to convince me that corruption is passé. My only hope is that I can take a rest from it and let other colleagues take over. But I have been saying that for years.

When we report, it is helpful to give perspective and dimension to important issues like corruption. It should not, above all, be reported as someone else's problem. The media has a habit of parading little villains before the populace and pretending society's ills are some other bugger's fault. The exposure of the culture that encourages the corruption is what helps the public accept responsibility.

The world is a complicated place. Information is the currency that helps us stumble through the complications without going completely mad. The higher the quality of the information the more the pain is minimised.

Working out the truth is an exasperating business; but it is helped a little by knowing that you will probably never have a **certain** understanding of any particular truth. As Masters' law has it, the truth varies according to the amount of information accumulated.

So what is true today may be less true tomorrow — and so on. In my 25 years in journalism I have never fully understood what the truth is. When you recognise that, you find yourself with an inbuilt motivation to keep searching.

Although we are searchers and it is easy for us to be seen as crusaders, as men and women with a mission, we have to remember that we are storytellers, not missionaries. From the very beginning, the missionaries cling to a faith that their story is correct. Only a very silly journalist would do the same. We hear many different versions of a story. The truth is in there somewhere, but it is never absolute.

There is commendable skill in paring down a story to a degree that helps its comprehension. But there is no credit in trivialising the story so that only one luminous corner is understood. The habit of telling a story through one eloquent spokesperson, works some of the time, but it is mostly inadequate.

The best storytellers capture the whole story, or as much of it as they have the time and energy to grasp. They then use their own skills to distil and polish so that the complications are accommodated and understood.

The best journalists, like the best politicians and the best plumbers, are people who care about their jobs. If we have a sense of working for the wider community and not just ourselves, then the cheques and balances in our work are more likely to fall into place.

I am a practitioner more than a philosopher. Colleagues with greater intelligence and a more theoretical bent may regard these reflections as inadequate or naive. But they are my own, and they have at least the virtue of being rooted firmly in experience.

I am 42 now, I have been in this business long enough to have heard people refer to me as a veteran journalist. I still think of myself, however, as more of an innocent bystander.

APPENDIX I

CHRIS MASTERS: A TELEVISION CAREER

1977–1979 ABC CURRENT AFFAIRS, QUEENSLAND

Reporter, *Focus*, ABC Rockhampton.
Contributor to *This Day Tonight* and *Nationwide*, Brisbane.

1979–1982 ABC RURAL, SYDNEY

Reporter, 'Horse Talk'
(A short documentary on the Australian Light Horse in Palestine and Gallipoli during World War I.)

Reporter/Producer *A Big Country*

'Outward Bound' with Ron Iddon.
(A wilderness trek in Far North Queensland with a group of adult urban dwellers.)

'Targets' with Paul Williams.
(A look at Australasian Training Aids combat training range in an Albury backyard where the world's armies are taught to shoot straight.)

'Tommy' with John Dutton.
(A profile of the former strapper of Phar Lap and trainer of Reckless.)

'Clowning About' with Geoff Barlow.
(Victoria's mobile library visits a one-teacher school in rural Victoria.)

'Paying Back' with Peter Lipscomb.
(A profile of George Stewart, a Western Australian showman/boxer turned writer.)

'Musicians in Uniform' with Ron Iddon.
(On tour in NSW with the Second Military District Band.)

'Luck of the Chinaman'
(Going bush with two Northern Territory miners to the old Chinese gold diggings at Pine Creek as they 'prospect for contentment'.)

Reporter/Producer *The Blainey View* with Professor Geoffrey Blainey.

Contributor to:

'Footprints'
(The triumph of the nomads — Australian prehistory.)

'When Muscles Were King'
(A history of work and leisure.)

'The Great Depression'
(The years 1929-1935 — when one in three wage earners were without a job.)

'Invasion'
(The causes of the Pacific War.)

'Whirlwind of Change'
(A history of mining in Australia.)

Reporter *Countrywide*

'Power Cuts'
(The effect of electricity strikes on rural industry.)

'Growth Centre'
(A review of the Albury/Wodonga growth centre ten years down the track.)

'Drought'
(Coming to terms with land use in a semi-arid country.)

'Nardoola'
(Scandal and mismanagement at an Aboriginal Development Corporation property in Northern NSW.)

'Wing and a Prayer'
(Taking to the skies with a flight of vintage Tiger Moths and their pilots who talk about the early days of aerial spraying.)

'Fairy Penguins'
(East of Eden, NSW, with the last mainland fairy penguin colony and the local human fishing community as they both struggle to survive.)

1983–1987 ABC CURRENT AFFAIRS, SYDNEY

Reporter *Four Corners*

'The Big League' with Peter Manning.
(Corruption in the NSW Rugby League and the NSW judiciary.)

'Crime Debate' with Michael Berry.
(Studio debate about crime and the need for a new National Crime Authority.)

'Black Sickness, Black Cure'.
(Aboriginal sickness and Aboriginal healing in northern Australia.)

'After the Apocalypse' with Peter Manning.
(The aftermath of war in Vietnam and Kampuchea.)

'The Poisoned Army' with Peter Manning.
(In the shadow of the Agent Orange Royal Commission as evidence is taken in Australia, the United States and Vietnam.)

'S.P.' with Allan Hall.
(A look at the culture of one of Australia's most tolerated illegal industries, Starting Price bookmaking.)

'Search Without Rescue' with Gordon Bic.
(An air sea rescue bungle in Bass Straight that exposed deficiencies in search and rescue procedure.)

'What the Doctor Ordered'.
(An investigation of fraud and overservicing in the medical profession.)

'Costigan's Commission' with Peter Manning.
(A review of the Costigan Royal Commission as it wound to a close.)

'Branded'
(Dr Geoffrey Edelsten and his entrepreneurial approach to medicine, including his controversial tattoo removal business.)

'Banned Aid' with Allan Hall.
(Behind enemy lines in Tigray where aid is officially denied by the Government of Ethiopia.)

'Top End High Rollers' with Dascha Ross.
(Scandal in the communities of government and gambling in the Northern Territory.)

'Communication Gap' with Shaun Hoyt.
(Australia at odds with Indonesia and Malaysia over what should and should not be reported.)

'French Connections' with Bruce Belsham.
(Investigation into the sinking of the Greenpeace flagship *Rainbow Warrior* which revealed French Government involvement.)

'Atomic Bodyline' with Phillip Whitehead.
(Co-production with Britain's Channel Four on the Maralinga Royal Commission.)

'The Heroin Culture' with Deb Whitmont.
(Middle class heroin use — a report on heroin finding the vein of mainstream Australia.)

'The Family Business' with Andrew Clark.
(A retrospective on the murder of Donald Mackay and Australia's 'mafia' connections.)

'Unsafe Deposit' with Sue Spencer.
(Electronic banking fraud in Australia and the robberies that go on behind the counter.)

'Alliance Francaise' with Martin Butler.
(Tensions with our French colonial neighbour in the South Pacific including an interview with Prime Minister Jacques Chirac.)

'The Moonlight State' with Shaun Hoyt and Deb Whitmont.
(Police corruption in the Brisbane Valley and beyond.)

'The Dead Heart' with Paul Williams.
(The mystery of the disappearance of two teenage stationhands in the Kimberley region of West Australia.)

'Gallipoli — The Fatal Shore' with Harvey Broadbent and Sue Spencer.
(An extended bicentennial documentary on Australia's best known military campaign.)

1988–1989 CHANNEL 10, SYDNEY

Reporter *Page One/Public Eye*

'Tunnel Rats' with Bruce Dover.
(Australia's role in the underground war in Vietnam.)

'Two Confessions' with David Margan and Jan Mayman.
(Investigation into the wrongful conviction of Mt Isa Aborigine, Kelvin Condren who was given a life sentence for a murder he could not have committed.)

'Cyclone Smith' with Bruce Dover.
(In the wake of John Smith, the Australian cook who led an uprising of Solomon Islanders against Australian resort operators.)

APPENDIX I 247

'Vietnam Aftershock' with Bruce Dover.
(Vietnam, losing the peace — a report on widespread poverty in the North and South of Vietnam.)

'Aboriginal Olympics' with Toni Whitmont.
(The Yuendemu Games bringing together tribal Aborigines in Central Australia.)

'Suppression City' with John Budd and Jayne Anderson.
(South Australian police corruption in the city of churches and the problems of drug law enforcement.)

'Hazel' with Phil Williams.
(On tour with the Sydney Symphony Orchestra to the United States with Australia's first lady, Hazel Hawke.)

'Guilt Money' with John Budd.
(A report on Aboriginal funding and the performance of the Aboriginal Development Corporation.)

'Hayden' with Bruce Dover.
(A profile of Bill Hayden as he moves from suburban Ipswich to his new post of Australian Governor General.)

'Mr Big Enough' with John Budd.
(Mark Christopher, a confessed heroin trafficker who told his story before he ended his life.)

'Capital Offence' with John Budd and Jayne Anderson.
(The Australian Federal Police investigation of the murder of Assistant Commissioner Colin Winchester.)

'Voice of the People' with Andrew Fowler.
(Chinese students in Australia speak of their anger and sadness following the Tianamin Square massacre.)

'Peoples Liberation Army' with Andrew Fowler and John Budd.
(A report on the army responsible for the massacre and interviews with Australian witnesses.)

'Guarding the Guards' with Andrew Fowler.
(A profile of retiring National Crime Authority Chairman, Justice Donald Stewart.)

'Fitzgerald's Law' with David Margan.
(The impact of the Fitzgerald Inquiry on the Moonlight State.)

1990–1991 ABC CURRENT AFFAIRS, SYDNEY

Four Corners/Channel 10 co-production
'Dirty Secrets' with John Budd.
(The James Hardie company's record of asbestos poisoning and their policy of settling compensation claims in private.)

Relief Compere *7.30 Report* NSW

'Secret State' with Jayne Anderson.
(Allegations of corruption and potential blackmail within the South Australian vice community and police.)

'Cancer Ward'
(The approach of Christmas at a children's cancer ward in Sydney.)

Reporter ABC *Hindsight*

'Greek Tragedy' with Shaun Hoyt.
(A report on the second Gallipoli, the ANZACs and the Greek campaign of World War Two.)

'Billy Tea and Goulash' with Don Featherstone.
(Multiculturalism in the outback — the largely happy balance of Europe and the bush as seen through thirty years of history in Mt. Isa.)

'White Asians' with Jonathan Holmes.
(A history of often violent racist contact between Australia and our most powerful neighbour, Japan.)

1991–1992 ABC-TV

Reporter 'Weapons of War', *The Gulf Report*.

Reporter *Four Corners*

'R.I.P — Retirement Income Perils' with Andrew Haughton and Sally Wiadrowski.
(The wisdom and the danger of investing in one of our largest growth industries — retirement.)

'Cloak and Dagger' with Shaun Hoyt and Pierre Vicary.
(New light cast on Australia's longest running court case and one of the graver miscarriages of justice — the Croatian Six affair.)

'The Callous Country' with Murray McLaughlin.
(The impact of economic rationalism on Cringila and other suburbs of South Wollongong that have become overwhelmed by the corrosion of unemployment.)